CITIES AND SEA–COASTS
AND ISLANDS

Arthur Symons
from a portrait by Augustus E. John

CITIES AND SEA-COASTS AND ISLANDS

BY
ARTHUR SYMONS

THE MARLBORO PRESS / NORTHWESTERN

EVANSTON, ILLINOIS

The Marlboro Press/Northwestern
Northwestern University Press
Evanston, Illinois 60208-4210

First published 1918 by Brentano's, New York. The Marlboro Press/
Northwestern edition published 1998. All rights reserved.

Printed in the United States of America

ISBN 0-8101-6054-4

Library of Congress Cataloging-in-Publication Data

Symons, Arthur, 1865–1945.
    Cities and sea-coasts and islands / by Arthur Symons.
       p. cm. — (Marlboro travel)
    Essays.
    Originally published: New York : Brentano's, 1919.
    ISBN 0-8101-6054-4 (alk. paper)
    I. Europe—Description and travel. 2. Symons, Arthur,
1865–1945—Journeys—Europe. I. Title. II. Series.
D921.S94 1998
914.04'51—dc21
                                    98-2621
                                        CIP

TO
AUGUSTUS JOHN

Contents.

Contents.

I.
Spain.

Seville.

I.

SEVILLE, more than any city I have ever seen, is the city of pleasure. It is not languid with pleasure, like Venice, nor flushed with hurrying after pleasure, like Budapest; but it has the constant brightness, blitheness, and animation of a city in which pleasure is the chief end of existence, and an end easily attained, by simple means within every one's reach. It has sunshine, flowers, an expressive river, orange groves, palm trees, broad walks leading straight into the country, beautiful, ancient buildings in its midst, shining white houses, patios and flat roofs and vast windows, everything that calls one into the open air, and brings light and air to one, and thus gives men the main part of their chances of natural felicity. And it has the theatres, cafés, shops, of a real city, it is not provincial, as Valencia is; it is concentrated, and yet filled to the brim; it has completely mastered its own resources. Life is everywhere; there are no melancholy gaps, vacant spaces, in which a ruinous old age has its own way desolately, as in most really picturesque cities; as in Venice, for instance, which it resembles in so many points. It has room for itself, and it is not too large for itself. And in living gaily, and in the present, it is carrying on a tradition: it is the city of Don Juan, the city of Figaro.

I am coming, more and more, to measure the charm of cities, at all events their desirability for living in, by the standard of their parks, public

Cities and Sea-Coasts and Islands.

gardens, and free spaces where one can be pleasantly unoccupied in the open air. I want the town, not the country, but I want the town to give me the illusion of the country, as well as its own characteristic qualities. Rome itself, without its villas, even Rome, would not be Rome; and Seville, which is so vividly a town, and with so many of a town's good qualities, has the most felicitous parks, gardens, and promenades (with that one great exception) that I have ever found in a city. Gardens follow the river-side, park after park, and every afternoon Seville walks and drives and sits along that broad road leading so straight into the open country, really a Paseo de las Delicias, a road of trees and sunlight. Turn to the right or to the left, and you are in a quiet shadow, under lanes of orange trees and alleys of acacias. There are palms and there is water, and there are little quaint seats everywhere; paths wind in and out, roses are growing in mid-winter, they are picking the oranges as they ripen from green to gold, and carrying them in the panniers of donkeys, and pouring them in bright showers on the ground, and doing them up into boxes. Great merchant vessels lie against the river-side, unloading their cargoes; and across the park, on the other side of a wall, drums are beating, bugles blowing, and the green meadow-grass is blue and red with soldiers. In the park, girls pass wrapped in their shawls, with roses in their hair, grave and laughing; an old gardener, in his worn coat with red facings, passes slowly, leaning on his stick. You

4

can sit here for hours, in a warm quiet, and with a few dry leaves drifting about your feet, to remind you that it is winter.

Seville is not a winter city, and during those months it seems to wait, remembering and expectant, in an acquiescence in which only a short and not uneasy sleep divides summer from spring. To the northern stranger, its days of sunshine and blue sky seem to make winter hardly more than a name. Sun and air, on these perfect winter afternoons, have that rare quality which produces what I should like to call a kind of active languor. The sharpening of a breath, and it would become chill; the deepening of the sunshine, and it would become oppressive. And just this difficult equilibrium, as it seems, of the forces of summer and winter, adds a zest to one's contentment, a kind of thankfulness which one does not find it needful to feel in the time of summer. How delightful to sit, perfectly warm, under a tree whose leaves are scattered about the ground, yellow with winter; to watch the bare branches, among these always green palms and orange trees, remembering winter in the North.

But to enjoy sympathetically all that Seville, even in winter, can be to its own people, it is not enough to go to the parks and the Paseo; one must go, on a fine Sunday afternoon, to the railway line which stretches onwards from the Barqueta, along the river-side, but in the opposite direction. The line is black with people, at one hour going, at another hour returning, an unending stream which broadens

5

and scatters on both sides, along the brown herbage by the river, and over the green spaces on the landward side. At intervals there is a little venta, there are bowling-alleys, swings, barrel-organs, concertinas, the sound of castanets, people dancing, the clapping of hands, the cries of the vendors of water, shell-fish, and chestnuts, donkeys passing with whole families on their backs, families camping and picnicking on the grass, and everywhere chairs, chairs on the grass, two sitting on each chair, in a circle about the dancers, as they dance in couples, alternately; chairs and tables and glasses of manzanilla about the ventas; and always the slow movement of people passing, quietly happy, in a sort of grave enjoyment, which one sees in their faces when they dance. Here is the true *pueblo*, the working-people, *cigarreras*, gipsies, all Triana and the Macarena; and could people amuse themselves more simply or more quietly, with a more enjoyable decorum? As they turn homewards, in another long black line, the sun is setting; a melancholy splendour burns down slowly upon the thin trees across the water, staining the water with faint reflections, and touching the dreary, colourless shrubs along the river-side with delicate autumn colours, as sunset ends the day of the people.

II.

There are seven hundred streets in Seville, and there is hardly a street which has not some personal

6

character of its own, or which does not add one more line to the elaborate arabesque of the city. One of my favourite aspects, for it is an aspect from which Seville looks most Eastern, is at just that point of the Paseo de Catalina de Rivera where it is joined by the Calle San Fernando. One sees the battlemented outer wall of the Alcazar, with its low, square towers, the Giralda, the brown turrets of two or three churches, and then nothing but white walls and brown roofs, with a few bare branches rising here and there delicately against the sky, between the sharp, irregular lines of the houses, all outlined in bright white. One can fancy a whole Kremlin or Hradcin clustered inside that low, white, battlemented wall; outside which the dreary Paseo, and the dim green of the Prado San Sebastian, seem to be already the country.

And it is from this point too, as one turns homeward from the river-side, that evening seems to come on most delicately: those sunsets of blue and rose and gold, as the sun goes down across the Guadalquivir, and that rosy flush which encircles all Seville after the sun has gone down, as if the city lay in the hollow of a great shell, tinged with rose at the edges. It is at just this hour that Triana looks its best, heaped somewhat irregularly on the other bank, in a long, white and pink line, above the brown slime; and from the Triana bridge, always crowded with lean, beaten horses, dragging too heavy loads, and lines of white donkeys with panniers, nodding their jingling heads, as they wander along by themselves, one sees the whole river, and the Moorish Tower of Gold, and the crowded masts, changing colour as the light changes moment by moment.

The streets of Seville are narrow, for shade in the summer and warmth in the winter, and many of them, like the central Calle Sierpes, with its shops, and clubs, and cafés, a street of windows, are closed to wheels. Every house has its balconies, and the older ones their barred windows on the ground floor; and every house has its patio, that divine invention of the Moors, meant, certainly, for a summer city, and meant, as one sees it in Morocco, for houses without windows, in which all the light comes from the open roof above an inner court. The Spaniards have both patios and windows, for summer and winter, in their wise, characteristic passion for light. All the doors, leading to the patio, are of open iron-work, no two doors alike, in their surprisingly varied, and often exquisite, arabesques of pattern. This throwing open of one's house to the street, yet with an iron door, always closed, setting a boundary to the feet if not to the eyes, seems to me again characteristic of these natural, not self-conscious people, who seem often so careless of their own dignity and liberty, and are so well able to preserve them.

Seville lights up for a feast-day as a face lights up with a smile. The night before the great feast of the Immaculate Conception, I went into the streets to find the whole place transformed, glittering.

8

Seville.

Crimson or white and blue cloths were thrown over balconies, rows of lamps and candles burned above them, and between the lights eager faces leaned over, looking down at the eager faces looking up at them. The public squares were brilliant with light, and the whole place became suddenly filled with people, passing to and fro in the Sierpes, and along the streets of shops, which I hardly recognised, so brilliantly lighted were all the windows. The transformation seemed to have been done in a minute, and here was the true Seville, idle, eager, brilliant, moving gaily, making the most of the world on the Church's terms of felicity for the other world.

And yet this, if the true Seville, is not all Seville, and I found another, silent, almost deserted city, which fascinated me almost more than this living and moving one, whenever I wandered about at night, in streets that sank to sleep so early, and seemed so mysteriously quiescent, under the bright sky and the stars. Night passed rarely without my coming out of some narrow street upon the vast Plaza del Triunfo, which holds the Cathedral, its Pagan counterpart, the Giralda, the Alcazar, and the Lonja. The tall tower of the Giralda was always the first thing I saw, rising up, like the embodied forces of the delicate powers of the world, by the side of the Christian Cathedral. Seen from the proper distance, it is like a filigree casket that one could lift in the hand, as Santa Justa and Santa Rufina lift it, in Murillo's picture; looking up from

9

close underneath it, it is like a great wall hiding the stars. And the Moors have done needlework on a wall as solid as a Roman wall; far finer work than that bastard splendour of the Alcazar, with its flickering lights, and illuminations like illuminations on parchment.

Looking back at the Giralda and the Cathedral from the gateway of the Patio de las Banderas, one sees perhaps the finest sight in Spain. The Giralda stands motionless, and a little aloof; but by its side the vast, embattled magnificence of the Cathedral seems to change in every aspect, full of multiform life, ordered to a wonderfully expressive variety, throwing out new shoots in every direction, like a tree which grows into a forest in some tropical country, or like a city grouping itself about a citadel. It is full of the romantic spirit, the oriental touch freeing it from any of the too heavy solemnity of the Middle Ages, and suiting it to a Southern sky. Above all, it has infinitely varied movement: yes, as it seems to lean slightly from the perpendicular, all this vivid mass might be actually about to move, to sail away like a great ship, with all its masts and spread sails and corded rigging.

III.

Much of what is most characteristic in the men of Seville may be studied in the cafés, which are filled every evening with crowds of unoccupied persons, who in every other country would be literally of the working class, but who here seem to have endless leisure. They are rough-looking, obviously poor, they talk, drink coffee, buy newspapers and lottery tickets, and they are all smoking. They fill rows of tables with little companies of friends; they are roughly good-humoured, affectionately friendly with one another; and their conversation echoes under the low ceiling with a deafening buzz. The typical Andalusian, as one sees him here, is a type quite new to me, and a type singularly individual. He is clean-shaved, he wears a felt hat with a broad flat brim, generally drab or light grey, clothes often of the same colour, and generally a very short coat, ending where a waistcoat ends, and very tight trousers; over all is a voluminous black cloak lined at the edges with crimson velvet. He is generally of medium height, and he has very distinct features, somewhat large, especially the nose; a face in which every line has emphasis, a straight, thin, narrow face, a face without curves. The general expression is one of inflexibility, the eyes fixed, the mouth tight; and this fixity of expression is accentuated by the arrangement of the hair, cut very short, and shaved around the temples, so as to make a sharp line above the ear, and a point in the middle of the forehead. The complexion is dull olive, and in old age it becomes a formidable mass of wrinkles; by which, indeed, many of these old men with their clean-shaved cheeks, bright eyes, and short jackets, are alone to be distinguished from their sons or grandsons. There is much calm strength in the Andalusian face, a dignity which is half defiant, and which leaves room for humour, coming slowly up through the eyes, the mouth still more slowly lengthening into a smile; room also for honest friendliness, for a very inquiring interest in things, and very decided personal preferences about them. Often the face runs all to humour, and the man resembles a comic actor. But always there is the same earnestness in whatever mood, the same self-absorption; and, talkative as these people are, they can sit side by side, silent, as if in brooding meditation, with more naturalness than the people of any other race.

The Andalusian is seen at his finest in the bull-fighter, the idol of Seville, whom one sees at every moment, walking in the streets, sitting in his club, driving in his motor car, or behind his jingling team of horses, dressed in the tight majo costume, with his pig-tail drawn up and dissimulated on the top of his head, his frilled shirt with great diamond studs, his collar clasped by gold or diamond fastenings, diamond rings glittering on his well-shaped fingers. I once sat opposite one of the most famous toreros at a *table-d'hôte* dinner, and, as I contrasted him with the heavy, middle-class people who sat around, I was more than ever impressed by the distinction, the physical good-breeding, something almost of an intellectual clearness and shapeliness, which come from a perfect bodily equipoise, a hand and eye trained to faultless precision.

Seville.

The women of Seville are not often beautiful, but one of the most beautiful women I have ever seen was a woman of Seville whom I watched for an hour in the Café America. She had all that was typical of the Spaniard, and more; expression, the equivalent of a soul, eyes which were not merely fine, but variable as opals, with twenty several delights in a minute. She was small, very white, with just that delicate hint of modelling in the cheeks which goes so well with pallor; she had two yellow roses in her black hair, at the side of the topmost coil, and a yellow shawl about her throat. One wished that she might always be happy.

More often the women are comfortable, witty, bright and dark, *guapa*, rather than beautiful; almost always with superb hair, hair which is like the mane or tail of an Arab horse, and always with tiny feet, on which they walk after a special, careful way of their own, setting down the whole foot at each step, level from heel to toe, and not rising on it. In Seville, more than anywhere else, one sees the Spanish woman already mature in the child, and nothing impressed me more than these brilliant, fascinating little people, at once natural and conscious, with all the gestures of grown women, their way of walking, their shawls, and, in their faces, all that is finest in the Sevillana, a charm, seductiveness, a sort of caressing atmosphere, and not merely bright, hard eyes, clean-cut faces, animation, which are to be seen everywhere in Spain. They have

13

Cities and Sea-Coasts and Islands.

indeed that slightly preoccupied air which Spanish children affect, and which deepens, in some of the women, into a kind of tragic melancholy. Pass through the Macarena quarter in the evening, and you will see not the least characteristic type of the women of Seville: strange, sulky, fatal creatures, standing in doorways, with flowers in the hair, and mysterious, angry eyes; Flamencas, with long, ugly, tragic, unforgettable faces, seeming to remember an ancestral unhappiness.

There is a quality which gives a certain finish to Spanish women, and which is unique in them. It is a sort of smiling irony, which seems to penetrate the whole nature: the attitude of one who is aware of things, not unsatisfied with them, decided in her own point of view, intelligent enough to be tolerant of the point of view of others, without coquetry or self-consciousness; in fact, a small, complete nature, in which nothing is left vague or uneasy. It is a disposition such as this which goes to make life happy, and it is enough to have watched the gay, smiling, contented old women to realise that life is happy to most women in Spain. Look in all these faces, and you will see that they express something very definite, and that they express everything, while Northern faces have so much in them that is suggestion, or, as it seems to the Spaniard, mere indefiniteness. The Southern nature, for its material felicity, has retained the Pagan, classic ideals; the Northern has accepted the unquiet, dreaming soul of the Middle Ages.

14

Seville.

But in Spanish women, along with much childishness and much simplicity, there is often all the subtlety of the flesh, that kind of secondary spiritual subtlety which comes from exquisitely responsive senses. This kind of delicacy in women often stands in the place of many virtues, of knowledge, of intellect; and, in its way, it supplies what is lacking in them, giving them as much refinement as knowledge or the virtues would have done, and itself forming a very profound kind of intelligence. I recognise it in the mournful pallor, and that long, immobile gaze, which seems to touch one's flesh, like a slow caress; that cold ardour, which is the utmost refinement of fire. And these white people carry themselves like idols. Singularly different is that other Spanish kind of animality, where life burns in the lips, and darkens the cheeks as if with the sun, and bubbles in the eyes, the whole body warm with a somewhat general, somewhat over-ready heat. It is enough to have heard the laughter of these vivid creatures. It is the most delicious laughter in the world; it breaks out like a song from a bird; it is sudden, gay, irresponsible, the laughter of a moment, and yet coming straight from the deep unconsciousness of life. The Spanish woman is a child, but a mature Spanish child, knowing much; and in the average woman of Seville, in her gaiety, humour, passion, there is more than usual of the childlike quality. Their faces are full of sun and shadow, often with a rich colour between Eastern and Western, and with the languor

15

Cities and Sea-Coasts and Islands.

and keenness of both races; with something in-
toxicating in the quality of their charm, like the
scent of spring in their orange groves. They have
the magnetism of vivid animal life, with a sharp
appeal to the sensations, as of a beauty too full of
the sap of life to be merely passive. Their bodies
are so full of energy that they have invented for
themselves a new kind of dance, which should tire
them into repose; they live so actively to their
finger-tips that their fingers have made their own
share in the dance, in the purely Spanish accompaniment of the castanets. A dance is indicated
in a mere shuffle of the feet, a snapping of the fingers,
a clapping of hands, a bend of the body, whenever
a woman of Seville stands or walks, at the door
of her house, pausing in the street, or walking,
wrapped in many shawls, in the parks; and the
dance is as closely a part of the women of Seville
as their shawls, the flowers in their hair, or the
supplementary fingers of the fan.

IV.

A significant quality of the Andalusians is the
profound seriousness which they retain, even when
they abandon themselves to the most violent
emotions. It is the true sensuality, the only way
of getting the utmost out of one's sensations, as
gaiety, or a facile voluptuousness, never can. The
Spanish nature is sombre and humorous, ready to
be startled into vivid life by any strong appeal:

love, hate, cruelty, the dance, the bull-fight, whatever is elemental, or touches the elemental passions.
Seeing Seville as I did, in winter, I could not see
the people under their strongest, most characteristic
intoxication, the bull-fight; but I had the oppor-
tunity, whenever I went into the street, and saw a
horse dragging a burden, of seeing how natural
to them is that cruelty which is a large part of the
attraction of bull-fighting. And their delight in
violent sensations, sensations which seem to others
not quite natural, partly perverse, partly cruel, as
in the typical emotion of the bull-fight, is seen at
Seville in the *cuerpo de baile infantil* which
dances at the Café Suizo. These children of ten
or eleven, who dance till midnight, learned in all
the contortions of the gipsy dances, which they
dance with a queer kind of innocence, all the more
thorough in its partly unconscious method, and
who run about in front, sitting on men's knees in
their tawdry finery, smiling out of their little painted
faces with an excited weariness; is there not a
cruelty to them, also, in the surely perverse sentiment which requires their aid in one's own amusement? I shall never forget one particular dance
of two children, one of the most expressive gipsy
dances, danced in trailing dresses, inside which, as
inside some fantastic, close prison or cage, they
hopped and leaped and writhed, like puppets or
living tops, to the stupefying rattle of castanets;
parodying the acts of physical desire, the coquetry
of the animal, with an innocent knowingness, as if it

were the most amusing, the most exciting of games. One of them was a little, sallow, thin creature, with narrow eyes and an immense mouth, drawn almost painfully into a too-eager smile; a grimacing, Chinese mask of a child, almost in tears with nervous excitement, quivering all over with the energy of the dance. I went to see them, indeed, frequently, as I should have gone to see the bull-fights, and with the same mental reservation. They reminded me of the horses.

All Spanish dancing, and especially the dancing of the gipsies, in which it is seen in its most characteristic development, has a sexual origin, and expresses, as Eastern dancing does, but less crudely, the pantomime of physical love. In the typical gipsy dance, as I saw it danced by a beautiful Gitana at Seville, there is something of mere gaminerie and something of the devil; the automatic tramp-tramp of the children and the lascivious pantomime of a very learned art of love. Thus it has all the excitement of something spontaneous and studied, of vice and a kind of naughty innocence, of the thoughtless gaiety of youth as well as the knowing humour of experience. For it is a dance full of humour, fuller of humour than of passion; passion indeed it mimics on the purely animal side, and with a sort of coldness even in its frenzy. It is capable of infinite variations; it is a drama, but a drama improvised on a given theme; and it might go on indefinitely, for it is conditioned only by the pantomime, which we know to have wide

18

limits. A motion more or less, and it becomes obscene or innocent; it is always on a doubtful verge, and thus gains its extraordinary fascination. I held my breath as I watched the gipsy in the Seville dancing-hall; I felt myself swaying unconsciously to the rhythm of her body, of her beckoning hands, of the glittering smile that came and went in her eyes. I seemed to be drawn into a shining whirlpool, in which I turned, turned, hearing the buzz of the water settling over my head. The guitar buzzed, buzzed, in a prancing rhythm, the gipsy coiled about the floor, in her trailing dress, never so much as showing her ankles, with a rapidity concentrated upon itself; her hands beckoned, reached out, clutched delicately, lived to their finger-tips; her body straightened, bent, the knees bent and straightened, the heels beat on the floor, carrying her backwards and round; the toes pointed, paused, pointed, and the body drooped or rose into immobility, a smiling, significant pause of the whole body. Then the motion became again more vivid, more restrained, as if teased by some unseen limits, as if turning upon itself in the vain desire of escape, as if caught in its own toils; more feverish, more fatal, the humour turning painful, with the pain of achieved desire; more earnest, more eager, with the languor in which desire dies triumphant.

A less elaborate, less perverse kind of dancing is to be seen in the cafés, in little pantomimic ballets, imitated from French models, but done

Cities and Sea-Coasts and Islands.

with a Spanish simplicity of emphasis. There is, in such things, a frank, devil-may-care indecency, part of a boisterous hilarity, which has all the air of an accidental improvisation, as indeed it often is; and this hilarity is tossed to and fro from stage to audience and from audience to stage, as if a crowd of lively people had become a little merry at the corner of a street. The Spanish (look at their comic papers) are so explicit! It is not cold or calculated, like that other, more significant, kind of dancing; it is done with youth and delighted energy, and as among friends, and by people to whom a certain explicit kind of coarseness is natural.

V.

Seville is not a religious city, as Valencia is; but it has woven the ceremonies of religion into its life, into its amusements, with a minuteness of adaptation certainly unparalleled. Nowhere as in Spain does one so realise the sacred drama of the Mass. The costumes, the processions, the dim lighting, the spectacular arrangement of the churches and ceremonies, the religious attitude of the people, kneeling on the bare stones, the penitent aspect of their black dresses and mantillas, intermingled with the bright peasant colours which seem to bring the poor people so intimately into association with the mysteries of religion: all this has its part in giving the Church its dramatic pre-eminence. And in Seville the ceremonies of the Church are carried

20

out with more detail, more spectacular appeal, than anywhere else in Spain, that is to say, more than anywhere in the world. All Europe flocks to see the celebrations of Holy Week, which must have come down unchanged from the Middle Ages; a piece of immense mediæval childishness, which still suits the humour of Seville perfectly. And it is not only in Holy Week that one may see the most characteristic of all these ceremonies, the sacred dances in the Cathedral, but also at the great feast of the Immaculate Conception, which is peculiarly a Sevillan feast.

On that day, the 8th December, I attended Mass in the Cathedral. The gold and silver plate had been laid out by the side of the altar, crimson drapings covered the walls, the priests wore their *terno celeste*, blue and gold vestments; the Seises, who were to dance later on, were there in their blue and white costume of the time of Philip III.; the acolytes wore gilt mitres, and carried silver-topped staves and blue canopies. There was a procession through the church, the Archbishop and the Alcaldia walking in state, to the sound of sad voices and hautboys, and amidst clouds of rolling white incense, and between rows of women dressed in black, with black mantillas over their heads. The Mass itself, with its elaborate ritual, was sung to the very Spanish music of Eslava: and the Dean's sermon, with its flowery eloquence, flowers out of the Apocalypse and out of the fields of *la Tierra de Maria Santísima*,

Cities and Sea-Coasts and Islands.

was not less typically Spanish. At five o'clock I returned to the Cathedral to see the dance of the Seises. There was but little light except about the altar, which blazed with candles; suddenly a curtain was drawn aside, and the sixteen boys, in their blue and white costume, holding plumed hats in their hands, came forward and knelt before the altar. The priests, who had been chanting, came up from the choir, the boys rose, and formed in two eights, facing each other, in front of the altar, and the priests knelt in a semicircle around them. Then an unseen orchestra began to play, and the boys put on their hats, and began to sing the *coplas* in honour of the Virgin:

> *O mi, O mi amada*
> *Immaculada!*

as they sang, to a dance-measure. After they had sung the *coplas* they began to dance, still singing. It was a kind of solemn minuet, the feet never taken from the ground, a minuet of delicate stepping and intricate movement, in which a central square would form, divide, a whole line passing through the opposite line, the outer ends then repeating one another's movements while the others formed and divided again in the middle. The first movement was very slow, the second faster, ending with a pirouette; then came two movements without singing, but with the accompaniment of castanets, the first movement again very slow, the second a quick rattle of the castanets, like the rolling of kettle-drums, but done without raising the hands above the level of the elbows. Then the whole thing was repeated from the beginning, the boys flourished off their hats, dropped on their knees before the altar, and went quickly out. One or two verses were chanted, the Archbishop gave his benediction, and the ceremony was over.

And, yes, I found it perfectly dignified, perfectly religious, without a suspicion of levity or indecorum. This consecration of the dance, this turning of a possible vice into a means of devotion, this bringing of the people's art, the people's passion, which in Seville is dancing, into the church, finding it a place there, is precisely one of those acts of divine worldly wisdom which the Church has so often practised in her conquest of the world. And it is a quite logical development of that very elaborate pantomime, using the word in all seriousness, which the ceremonies of the Church really are, since all have their symbolical meaning, which they express by their gestures. Already we find in them every art but one: poetry, the very substance of the liturgy, oratory, music, both of voices and instruments, sculpture, painting, all the decorative arts, costume, perfume, every art lending its service; and now at last dancing finds its natural place there, in the one city of the world where its presence is most perfectly in keeping.

Winter, 1898.

The Painters of Seville.

SPANISH art, before Velasquez discovered the world, is an art made for churches and convents, to the glory of God, never to the glory of earth. "The chief end of art," says Pacheco, the master of Velasquez, in his treatise on the art of painting, "is to persuade men to piety, and to raise them to God." In other countries, men have painted the Virgin and the Saints, for patrons, and because the subject was set them; sometimes piously, and in the spirit of the Church; but more often after some "profane" fashion of their own, as an excuse for the august or mournful or simple human presence of beauty. But in Spain pictures painted for churches are pictures painted by those to whom God is more than beauty, and life more than one of its accidents. The visible world is not a divine plaything to them. It is the abode of human life, and human life is a short way leading to the grave. They are full of the sense of corruption, actual physical rotting away in the grave, as we see it in two famous pictures of Valdés Leal. And they have also a profound pity for human misery, that pity for the poor which is still one of the characteristics of the Spaniard; their pictures are full of halt and maimed beggars, rendered with all the truth of a sympathy which finds their distortion a natural part of the world, a part to be succoured, not to be turned away from. But Heaven, the Saints, the Virgin, are equally real to them; and Murillo will paint the Trinity, without mystery and without

24

The Painters of Seville.

dignity, with only a sense of the human closeness of that abstract idea to the human mind. Thus we have, for the most part, no landscapes, rarely an indication, even in a background, of external nature loved and copied, and brought into the picture for its own sake, as a beautiful thing. Seriousness, and absorption in human life, a mystical absorption in the divine life, these qualities are the qualities which determine the whole course of Spanish painting.

Emotion, in the Spaniard, is based on a deep substratum of brooding seriousness; some kind of instinctive pessimism being always, even in those untouched by religion, the shadow upon life. In Velasquez it is the intolerable indifference of nature, of natural fate, weighing upon those unhappy kings and princes whom he has painted, from their solemn childhood to their mature unhappiness. In Murillo it is a tragic intensity of ascetic emotion, the darkness out of which his sunlight breaks. In Zurbaran darkness swallows daylight, and his kneeling monk, contemplating the emptiness of life in the extravagant mirror of a skull, in the midst of a great void of night, shows us to what point this religious gloom can extend. Ribera lacerates the flesh of his martyrs, and tears open their bodies before us, with almost the passion of Goya's cannibal eating a woman. In Goya we see both extremes, the whole gamut from wild gaiety to sombre horror of the Spanish temperament. The world for him is a stage full of puppets, coloured almost more naturally than nature, playing at all the games of humanity

25

Cities and Sea-Coasts and Islands.

with a profound, cruel, and fantastic unconsciousness. Rarely indeed do we find a painter to whom
the idea of beauty has been supreme, or who has
loved colour for its own sake, or who has passionately apprehended ornament. The moment the
sense of beauty is not concentrated upon reality,
or upon vision which becomes reality, it loses precision, passing easily into sentimentality, affectation,
one form or another of extravagance.

This overpoweringly serious sense of reality,
human or divine, to which everything else is
sacrificed, brings with it, to Spanish painters, many
dangers which they have not escaped, and gives
them at their best their singular triumphs. Their
broad painting, with so little lingering over detail,
except at times anatomical detail, their refusal to
pause by the way over the seductions and delicate
unrealities of beauty, point the way to the great
final manner of Velasquez. Velasquez, we say, *is*
life; but life was what every Spanish painter aimed
at, and some surprised, again and again, with fine
effect. All these painters of Martyrdoms, and
Assumptions, and Biblical legends, painted with a
vivid sense of the reality of these things: their
pictures tell stories, a quality which it is the present
unwise, limited fashion to deprecate; that is to say,
they are always conscious of human emotion ex-
pressing itself actively in gesture — Spanish gesture
of course, which is very different from ours. Doubtless there is no aim so difficult of attainment, so
dangerous in intention, as this aim at fixing life,

26

The Painters of Seville.

movement, and passionate movement, in a picture. Doubtless, also, for the perfect realisation of this aim, we have to wait for Velasquez, who sees the danger, and avoids it, as no one had yet perfectly succeeded in avoiding it, by an art wholly untraditional, wholly of his invention.

At Seville, where Velasquez was born, and did his early, perfunctory, religious painting, there is not a single example of his work, with the very doubtful exception of the small picture of the Virgin giving her mantle to Saint Ildefonso, which hangs in the private part of the Archbishop's Palace. But Velasquez, who was of Spanish and Portuguese origin, and who worked almost entirely for the Court, is not properly a Sevillan painter. The painters properly of Seville, those who were born there, or at no great distance, and did the main part of their work there, from Juan Sanchez de Castro in the fifteenth century, to Murillo and his immediate successors at the end of the seventeenth, can be seen very thoroughly, and can only be thoroughly seen, in the Museo and the churches of Seville. Out of Seville Murillo is an enigma, Alejo Fernandez is unknown. And in tracing the course of painting in Seville, we are not far from tracing the course of Spanish painting, so few are the painters, except the little group at Valencia, who were born out of Andalusia.

Painting in Seville begins with pure decoration, in the three fourteenth-century frescoes of the Virgin; the *Antigua* in the chapel named after

27

it in the Cathedral; *Nuestra Señora del Corral,* in San Ildefonso; and *S. Maria de Rocamador,* in San Lorenzo. All three come from a wise and happy childhood of art, when painters were content with beautiful patterns, the solid splendour of gold, a Byzantine convention in faces, these long oval faces, with their almost Japanese outlines of cheek and eyebrows. S. Maria de Rocamador is larger than life-size, she wears a blue robe and a mantle of dull purple, spotted with golden stars and acorns, and bordered with gold braid; an arched or bent coronet is on her head, against the glowing halo; she holds the child in her arms, and two little angels kneel on each side of her head. The background is all of gold, the Gothic gold, woven into a conventional pattern. It is a piece of pure convention, in which colour and pattern are felt delicately, as so much decoration.

With the fifteenth century life comes playfully into this artificial paradise; and the first signed picture in Seville, the *Saint Christopher* of Juan Sanchez de Castro in San Julian, is a vast, humorous thing, reaching nearly to the ceiling, more than three times life-size, a child's dream of a picture. It is painted in all seriousness, and, so far as one can judge through bad repainting and subsequent rotting away of the plaster, painted with no little power. The Saint fills almost the whole of the picture; he carries the child Christ on his shoulder, leaning on a pine tree, and the hermit comes out on shore with his lantern, in front of a little chapel,

28

The Painters of Seville.

and looks into the darkness. The hermit reaches just above Saint Christopher's knee, and two pilgrims, with staves and cloaks and pilgrim bottles, are travelling along his girdle, as he wades in the deep water, which just covers his ankles. His face is naïve and homely, with a certain pensiveness in the huge eyes; and the child seems to hold in his hand the glove of the world, on which rises already the symbol of his cross. The whole picture, with its humour and yet solemnity, its childish sense of the natural wonder of a miracle, is a quite sincere attempt to render a scene supposed to have really happened, just as it might have happened. It may be contrasted with the other huge *Saint Christopher* in Seville, the fresco of Matteo Alessio in the Cathedral, where an Italian painter has done no more than paint an unconvincing picture of a miracle in which, it is evident, he had no more than the scene-painter's interest.

Between Sanchez de Castro and his pupil, Juan Nuñez, there is a wide interval; for Nuñez, in the wooden panel in the Cathedral, a Pietà, is completely but very archaically Flemish, with quite another, more formal, more awkward, kind of childishness in design and colour. But he leads, quite naturally, to Alejo Fernandez, and in Alejo Fernandez we have almost a great painter, and a painter in whom Spanish painting in Seville first becomes conscious of itself, and capable of saying what it has to say. In some of his pictures an archaic stiffness has not yet freed itself from the golden bonds of that early

29

Cities and Sea-Coasts and Islands.

Gothic work of which his work so often reminds us; but Flemish models showed him the way which he was seeking for himself; and, under that Northern influence, always so salutary for the Spanish temperament, he makes at last a new thing, profoundly his own.

In the delicious *Virgin of the Rose* in the church of Santa Ana in Triana, we see those early Virgins of the fourteenth century growing human, but in the same embowering decoration of gold and stars. She sits with the child under a golden canopy in a robe of elaborate pattern, an almost Chinese pattern of leaves and stems, in pale gold on brown, and she holds a white rose in her hand. She holds out the rose to the child, who looks with serious, childish interest into the open pages of a brightly illuminated book. Two angels lean, a little awkwardly, on each arm of her chair; but with a certain charm in their naïve, pointed faces, in their bright gold curls falling over. Higher up two strange figures, probably cherubim, stand, arrested in flight, against the upper folds of the canopy. At the back there is a glimpse of rocky and wooded country in pale blue. A smaller picture in the same church shows another Virgin and Child with the same bright gold canopy, with little flying angels holding a coronet above the halo; and here, too, in the pathetic eyes of the Virgin, in the child's gesture, there is the same humanity, coming not too sharply through a traditional form. In two other small pictures, the *Adoration of the Magi* and

30

The Painters of Seville.

Saint Rufina and Saint Justina, we have this delicate, just a little fettered, sense of beauty; in the Virgin, meek, and with flowing golden hair; in the almost sly, Sevillan smile of the Patron Saint of the Giralda. There is always the same delight in colour and ornament: the bright swords and cloaks of the Magi, their golden goblets, the elaborate patterns of gold on brown in robes and cloaks; and it is precisely this quality which we find so rarely in Spanish painters, never, indeed, quite thoroughly, except in the pictures of this one painter.

In the church of St. Julian there is an altar-piece in eight divisions (of which one is a copy), telling many incidents in the life of the Virgin; and in this series of pictures we see Alejo Fernandez under a somewhat different aspect, as a painter for whom the visible world exists, not only as beauty, but as drama. Natural feeling, a vivid and tender simplicity, a curious personal kind of sentiment, distinguish these pictures, in which St. Joseph, for the most part no very active spectator in the events of the divine drama, is for once accepted as a natural, prominent actor in them. In one, the Virgin and St. Joseph kneel on either side of the newly-born child, with a serene, homely unity of devotion. In the Adoration of the Magi, Joseph leans over his wife's shoulder, his finger-tips set together, watching curiously. At the Circumcision, both hold the child before the priest. As Jesus goes up the steps of the Temple, to reason with the doctors, Joseph sits reflectively beside Mary. And at the end, after

31

Cities and Sea-Coasts and Islands.

all is over, it is into Joseph's arms that Mary flings
herself, her face distorted with sorrow; and it is
mainly with solicitude for her that his face is sorrowful. Both grow old together, older in every picture,
the hair whitening, the wrinkles forming in the face
of Joseph; and in every picture there is a simple,
earnest attempt to tell the real story, with thought-
fully and tenderly felt details. Whatever may still
be at times conventional in the painting, as in the
long oval face of the Virgin, there is no convention
in the arrangement of the scene, the way of telling
a story.

In the large Adoration of the Magi, and in the
three still larger pictures of the Birth and Purifica-
tion of the Virgin and the Reconciliation of St.
Joachim and St. Anne, of which the first is now in
the Sagrario de los Calices, and the three others in
almost impenetrable darkness in the Sacrista Alta
of the Cathedral, we see united in the same composition the half artificial beauty of the Virgin of
the Rose and the dramatic sense and human simplicity of the altar-piece in San Julian. Here there
is the same solid gold and elaborate raiment and
jewelled magnificence: in the robes of the Magi,
for instance, and the elaborately arranged hair of
Melchior with its golden hair-pins; but nowhere
else has life come so directly into the picture. Jan
Van Eyck might almost have painted the sombre
and suffering face of Melchior under the golden
hair-pins; but it is Alejo Fernandez, now entirely
master of his method, who has brought a new beauty

32

The Painters of Seville.

into the face of the Virgin, as she kneels, in the very act of life, in one of the pictures done in her honour. Two serving-maids, in another of the series, have in them the whole warmth and brightness of Seville, and might have been painted from models of to-day. And there are grave, bearded faces, the face of Joseph, who stands beside Mary as the angel descends out of heaven, in which life has no less of the exact impress of life. Seeing these pictures as I did, point by point at the end of a candle and a bunch of tow, without the possibility of seeing them as a whole, I can only guess at how much I have lost, in compositions so finely imagined, so truthful and full of tender human feeling, and at the same time so gravely splendid in colour and decoration.

Here, for all the influence of Flemish art and of the art of the unknown Spanish masters of the fourteenth century, we have an art essentially Spanish, going indeed beyond the usual Spanish limits in its delicate care for beauty. The Dutchman Kempeneer, known in Spain as Pedro Campaña, whose painting is almost contemporary with that of Alejo Fernandez, belongs to quite another world of form and sentiment, and in his attempt, as we are told, to imitate Michel Angelo, he becomes at times almost more Spanish than the Spaniards. His very vigorous, extravagant Descent from the Cross, in the Sacrista Mayor of the Cathedral, with its crude colour and powerful sense of action, was greatly admired and extravagantly praised by Murillo. At other times Campaña shows us all his inequalities

33

Cities and Sea-Coasts and Islands.

at a glance, as in the altar-piece in many compartments of the Capilla del Mariscal, where the meek
and serious heads of the donors, painted with
admirable Flemish realism in the lower compartments, contrast with the exclamatory, spectacular
movement of the central scenes.   I am quite unable
to understand the enthusiasm which still exists in
Spain for this painter, as I am unable to understand
the enthusiasm which exists for his more interesting
contemporary, Luis de Vargas.   Just as I am told
that Campaña is the Spanish Michel Angelo, so
Luis de Vargas, I am told, is the Spanish Raphael.
Luis de Vargas had been a pupil of Perino del Vaga,
perhaps of Raphael himself, and he brought back
with him from Italy many secrets of painting and
much of the manner of the men who came after
Raphael.   Much of his work has perished; the
famous frescoes have been washed off from the walls
of the Giralda, leaving only a few faintly coloured
traces of bishops' mitres and the outlines of kneeling
figures.   I was unfortunate in not being able to
see his masterpiece, the Temporal Generation of
Christ (known as *La Gamba*), and the pictures
of the Altar del Nascimiento, so carefully had they
been covered during the restoration of the Cathedral.
The portrait of Fernando de Contreras, in the
Sagrario de los Calices, is a serious study after
nature, faithful to all the details of half-shaved
cheeks and the like, hard, unsympathetic, not
without character.   But the large Pietà in Santa
Maria la Blanca seemed to show me a thoroughly

34

The Painters of Seville.

skilful, but an insincere painter, whom Italy had spoilt, as just then it was spoiling all Spanish art. Pacheco, in his *Arte de la Pintura*, tells us that Luis de Vargas was "a rare example of Christian painters," that he confessed and partook of the sacraments often, devoted a certain space of every day to religious meditation, "and, with the profound consideration of his death, composed his life;" after his death, a hair shirt and scourge were found, *asperisimos cilicios y disciplinas*. His pictures preach, says Pacheco; and indeed in this picture I am perfectly willing to believe in his religious sincerity, but I cannot believe in his artistic sincerity. The painting is flat and smooth, the composition elegant, with a curious mingling of Raphaelesque sweetness with extreme realism, as in the careful anatomy of the dead Christ, ghastly in death, showing the stains of blood, the falling open of the mouth, the darkening of the flesh of the feet. Here, the piety of the feeling, the aim at telling a story, at rendering a scene with dramatic emphasis, have produced only unreality; it is academic, not emotional; we see only an effect that has been aimed at, and indeed skilfully realised, not a story that has been told for its own sake, as it might have happened.

The influence here is Raphael; in *el divino* Morales, a painter in whom religion seems to darken into fanaticism, we see a more personal originality evolving itself from a very eclectic training. In his early pictures, none of which are to be seen in Seville, but of which the Prado has a charming

35

Cities and Sea-Coasts and Islands.

Virgin and Child and a Presentation in the Temple, there is a certain *naïveté*, a pale Italian elegance. Later on, as he becomes himself, the colouring darkens, the composition hardens, the emphasis of expression becomes painful, the anatomical minuteness of this lean, brown flesh is like that of the early Flemish painters, or like that of German woodcarvers; might indeed almost be carved out of brown wood. In such pictures as the triptych in the Cathedral, or as the Pietà in the Bellas Artes at Madrid, in all his figures of the Man of Sorrows and the Mother of Sorrows, everything is sacrificed to an attempt to express superhuman emotion, and, among other qualities, the "modesty of nature" is sacrificed, so that a too intense desire of sincerity becomes, as it is so liable to do, a new, poignant kind of affectation. Intensity of sentiment in these faces is like a disease, sharpening the lineaments and discolouring the blood, and putting all the suffering languidness of fever into the eyes. They grimace with sorrow more violently than the sorrowful faces of Crivelli, or the most violent German emphasis; literally they sweat blood, they have all the physical disgrace of pain; they are no longer persons, but emblems, the emblems of the divine agony, as it appears to the pious Spaniard, whom it pleases to see the stains of blood on his crucifix.

In passing from Morales to *el clerigo* Roelas, the sharpness of the contrast is slightly broken by Pedro Villegas Marmolejo, who, in his pictures in the Cathedral and in San Pedro, works very quietly

The Painters of Seville.

under Italian influence, not without charm, though without originality. In Juan de las Roelas, who is thought to have studied at Venice, the Italian Renaissance has done all it can do for Spanish painting. Venetian in his soft warmth of colour, in the suavity of his handling, Roelas is thoroughly Spanish in his profound religious sentiment (he was a priest, and died Canon of Olivares) and in his simple and vigorous sense of human incident. There is careless brushwork in his paintings, spaces are sometimes left uncared for, the composition is at times a little awkward or a little conventional. But he has feeling, both poetical feeling and feeling for reality, all through his work, even when he is least concentrated; and at his best he anticipates Murillo, not unworthily, in what is after all only a part of his originality. In the Martyrdom of Saint Andrew, in the Museo, he is a realist; life abounds in those sturdy, deeply coloured figures, who work or watch so earnestly, with so little sense of the spectator. In the Death of S. Isidore, in the church dedicated to that Saint, the earnest, homely, expressive people who stand about the dying Saint are thoroughly Spanish people, and they are absorbed in what is happening; not, as in the Pietà of Luis de Vargas, in what we are thinking of them. And this group on earth melts imperceptibly, almost in the manner which is to be Murillo's, into a heavenly group, lifted on vague, lighted clouds: child angels, and angelic youths, singing and playing on guitars, and above,

37

Cities and Sea-Coasts and Islands.

Christ and Mary, who wait with crowns of gold
and flowers, and calm angels at their side. In
one section of an altar-piece in the University
Church, the Blessing of the Infant Christ, the same
elegant, softly coloured figures bring in the same
celestial gaiety, in these flights of singing and
playing angels with harp, viola, and guitar, out of
a golden open heaven, a cloud of delicate young
faces. And in the picture of St. Anne and the
Virgin, in the Museo, there is a singular gentleness and repose, certainly more Italian than Spanish.
The Virgin kneels at her mother's side reading
out of a book, doubtless the prophecy of her own
honour. She is crowned with a jewelled coronet,
over the flower in her hair, and wears many rings
and jewelled bracelets, and pearls sewn in the
border of her dress; St. Anne, after the fashion
of Seville, wearing many shawls, of different colours.
Angels crowd the space above them, looking out
of warm clouds, as Murillo's are to look, but with
less of his celestial atmosphere, less power of dis-
tinguishing vision, in painting, from real life. In
front of St. Anne's chair, over which hangs a
crimson curtain, is a little cabinet, the drawer open,
showing linen and lace; a dog and cat, a very
natural cat, lie together in front, with a work-
basket near them. I find myself tiring a little of
Roelas, as I see picture after picture representing
incidents in the lives of the Saints, always capably,
with natural sentiment and natural grace, but rarely
with any great intensity; here, in what is after all
38

The Painters of Seville.

his exceptional manner, and a manner which gave offence to his contemporaries, notably Pacheco, from the naïve intimacy of its detail, he paints a placid scene with a full sense of its beauty and of its beautiful opportunities.

One of the compartments of the altar-piece in the University Church, an Adoration of the Shepherds, by Francisco Varela, a pupil of Roelas, shows the influence of Roelas on a more sombre nature. It is singularly original in its effects of light and shadow: the stormy background, middle darkness and sudden light above the manger roofed with a brood of angels. There is both realism and a sense of beauty in the earnest group in the foreground, the Andalusian shepherd with a lamb on his shoulders, the inexplicable woman, half undraped and half in armour, who presents a book of music to the laughing child. Another and more famous follower of Roelas, Francisco Herrera, scarcely chooses what is best in his master to imitate, in his "furious," too vehemently Spanish way. There are two huge pictures of Herrera in the Museo, one on each side of the Martyrdom of Saint Andrew; in the earlier of the two, the St. Hermengild, vigorous as it is, the sincerity and simplicity of Roelas have already gone, the Saint is an operatic tenor, every figure poses; in the later, St. Basil, all is splash-work, extravagant contortion, and hectic light and shadow.

It was from Herrera that Velasquez took his first lessons, before he became the pupil of Francisco

39

Cities and Sea-Coasts and Islands.

Pacheco, an Italianised painter, whose series of pictures in the Museo, the Legend of S. Pedro Nolasco, has at least a certain quietude, flat, almost colourless though they are. Pacheco was a better writer than painter, and his *Arte de Pintura*, published at Seville in 1646, is full of interesting theory and detail. He is a strict traditionalist, and finds a religious basis for the colours of pictures, the position of Saints in them, and reasons of "the different kinds of nobility that accompany the art of painting, and of its universal utility." He was chosen by the Inquisition as censor of pictures, an office which he held with more impartiality than some of his theories would seem to imply. He even learnt to put a certain *naïveté* which is almost naturalness into his later pictures, perhaps from the example of his pupil, of whose *virtud, limpieza y buenas partes, y de las esperanzas de su natural y grande ingenio* he speaks with such hearty enthusiasm; finding in "his glory the crown of my later years." Pacheco's pictures in the Museo gain from their position, for by their side are the coloured lithographs of Juan de Castillo, the master of Murillo, and one of the worst painters who ever lived. Alonso Cano, architect, sculptor, and painter, who studied under Montañes and Pacheco, has been admirably defined by Lord Leighton as "an eclectic with a Spanish accent." There are many of his charming, facile pictures in Seville; and in one of them, the Purgatory in the Museo, he is for once almost wholly Spanish, as he is in

40

The Painters of Seville.

the curious, half caricature pictures of Visigothic Kings, in the Prado at Madrid. It is a panel representing souls burning in red flames; four men and two children, with others seen shadowily, lifting their hands, not without hope, out of the burning. It is a simple, dreadful realisation of a dreadful dogma; it gives, without criticism, all the cruelty of religion.

Francisco Zurbaran, in the thirty or forty pictures of his which are to be seen in Seville, sums up almost everything I have said of the typical characteristics of Spanish painting; and yet, after all, remains a passionate mediocrity, in whom I find it impossible to take any very personal interest. The Museo contains three of his largest, most notable pictures, the Virgin de las Cuevas, the Apotheosis of St. Thomas Aquinas, and the Carthusian Monks at Table; yet even in these pictures I find something hard, unsympathetic in his touch, as he tells his story so adequately, so pointedly, and with singular honesty in its emphasis. They have all his solid, uninspired care for formal outline and expression, expression counting for so much and colour for so little; though the Apotheosis has, for once, caught a little of the warmth of Roelas, of whom Zurbaran was a visitor, if not a pupil. The monks, like all his monks, seem to be reflected in a mirror suddenly placed in their cell or refectory; they have the very attitude of life, letting something of a burning inner life come through into their faces; and yet, on these canvases

Cities and Sea-Coasts and Islands.

without atmosphere, they are not alive.   Zurbaran achieves realism without attaining life.   He shows us people, copied from life, in whom we discern a brooding emotion; but he paints them without emotion.   His severe and lady-like Saints in the Hospital Civil, in their fantastic dresses, with their fixed air of meditation, are like Gothic statues painted upon canvas.   When he aims at an emotional rendering of emotion, a very Spanish kind of in-sincerity comes in, and he paints pictures like the extravagant female saint in the Sacristia Mayor, seated in a false ecstasy before a book and a skull. His Crucifixions, in which a certain intensity finds precisely the motive which it can render with all the hard, motionless truth of his natural manner, are scarcely to be called extravagant, if the horror of that death is to be painted at all.   Here the painter of monks puts into his canvas for once a kind of desperate religious ecstasy.

There is something of the spirit and manner of Zurbaran in the early realistic pictures of Murillo, in the San Leandro and San Bonaventura of the Museo, for instance.   Another early picture, an *Annunciation*, painted in the *estilo frío*, shows us a precisely Sevillan type in the almost piquant Virgin, black-haired, and with the acute hard eyes of Spanish women.   In an *Adoration of the Shepherds* in the Museo, the dark young shepherd, who has come first to the manger, looks at the divine child with a frank, unrestrained, delightfully natural curiosity, fairly open-mouthed, with the honest

42

The Painters of Seville.

peasant stare of amazement. In the *Last Supper*, in Santa Maria la Blanca, with its passionate energy of characterisation, Murillo is almost purely realistic, realising the scene, certainly, with perfect naturalness. But from the beginning, and through all his changes, his pictures live. There is not an example in Seville of what is most familiar to us in his work, the *genre* pictures, the somewhat idealised beggar-boys. But, with this scarcely important exception, we see in Seville, and we can see only in Seville, all that it is important to us to see of his work. Among the six pictures which still hang in the places for which they were painted, in the church of that Hospital de la Caridad founded by Don Miguel Mañara, the original Don Juan, as it is thought by many, are the large compositions, *La Sed*, and the *Pan y Peces*, in which Murillo shows his mastery of the drama of a large canvas, in which many human figures move and group themselves in a broad landscape. In the Museo there are twenty-three pictures, and among them the great Capuchin series; in the Baptistery of the Cathedral there is the *St. Anthony of Padua;* and elsewhere, in churches, convents, and private collections, I know not how many further pictures, sometimes, like the *Last Supper* in Santa Maria la Blanca, painfully darkened, sometimes no more than a Christ painted rapidly on a wooden crucifix for a friendly monk. But in all these pictures, so unequal, and only gradually attaining a completely personal mastery of style,

43

Cities and Sea-Coasts and Islands.

there is the very energy of life, Spanish life, burning at the points of its greatest intensity.

In Murillo the Spanish extravagance turns to sweetness, a sweetness not always to our taste, but genuine, national, and perfectly embodied in those pictures in which he has painted ecstasy as no one else has ever painted it. In the warm, mellow, not bright or glittering light of the St. Anthony of Padua, vision sweeps back the walls as if a curtain had been drawn aside before the kneeling monk, and the glory is upon him: the child, in all the radiance of divine infancy, as if leaping on clouds of golden fire, and about him a swirling circle of little angels, burning upwards to a brighter ardency, as if the highest point of their circle were lit by the nearer light of heaven. His colour, in these ecstatic pictures, is a colour one can fancy really that of joyous clouds about the gates of heaven, jewelled for the feet of Saints. And the little angels really fly, though they are otherwise perfectly human, and of the earth. The Virgin, too, has all the humanity of a young mother, as she leans out of embowering clouds, or treads on the globe of the earth, which whitens under her among drifting worlds. She is Fray Luis de Leon's

> *Virgen del sol vestida*
> *De luces eternales coronada,*
> *Que huellas con divinos piés la luna,*

and yet her gestures are full of human warmth; she lives there, certainly, as vividly, and with as

44

The Painters of Seville.

much earthly remembrance, as at any time on the earth.

The emotion of Murillo, in these pictures, is the emotion of the Spaniard as it turns passionately to religion. In such a picture as his own favourite, St. Thomas of Villanueva giving alms, he has created for us on the canvas a supreme embodiment of what is so large a part of religion in Spain, the grace and virtue of almsgiving, with the whole sympathetic contrast of Spanish life emphasised sharply in the admirable, pitying grace of the Saint, and the swarming misery of the beggars. In such others as St. Francis by the Cross and the St. Anthony of the Museo, we are carried to a further point, in which practical religion becomes mysticism, a mysticism akin to that of St. John of the Cross, in which the devout soul swoons "among the lilies." This mysticism finds its expression in these rapt canvases, in the abandonment of these nervous, feminine Saints to the sweetness of asceticism, in one to the luxury of supreme sorrow, in the other to the ecstasy of the divine childhood. It is precisely because these Saints of Murillo abandon themselves so unthinkingly, with so Spanish an abandonment, to their mystical contemplation, that they may seem to us, with our Northern sentiment of restraint, to pose a little. In desert places, among dimly lighted clouds, that rise about them in waves of visible darkness, they are dreamers who have actualised their dreams, mystics who, by force of passionate contemplation, have attained

45

the reality of their vision; and the very real forms at which they gaze are but evocations which have arisen out of those mists and taken shape before their closed or open eyes. And indeed in these pictures, in which the Virgin appears in a burst of sunlight out of the darkness, treading on the dim world and the crescent moon, or in which the Trinity flashes itself upon St. Augustine as he writes, or in which Christ comes back to the cross for the sake of St. Francis or to the cradle for St. Anthony, all is vision, vision creating vision; and the humanity in them is so real, because it is so powerfully evoked. Thought out of the void, with such another energy as that with which Rembrandt thought his visions, more real than reality, out of burning darkness, these rise out of a softer shadow, through which the light breaks flower-like, or as if it sang aloud.

To turn from Murillo to Valdés Leal is like passing from the service of the Mass in a cathedral to a representation of Mass in a theatre. He paints, indeed, effectively, but always for effect. His painting is superficial, and has the tricks of modern French painters. Shadowy figures float in the air, apparitions seen as the vulgar conceive them, as insubstantial things; showy, dressy women parade in modern clothes; worldly angels twist in elegant attitudes, the same attitude repeated in two pictures. Even the picture of St. John leading the three Maries to Calvary, which has movement, and may at first seem to have simple movement, does not bear too close a scrutiny : the figures grow conscious as one looks at them. Drama has become theatrical, and his St. Jerome in the wilderness, flinging his arms half across the canvas, with the French ladies about him, and a thunderstorm in the distance, is far indeed from the honest dramatic sense of Roelas. He is expressive, certainly, but he would express too much, and with too little conviction. In his altar-piece in the church of the Carmen at Cordova, done before he came to Seville, an immense picture in eleven compartments, architecturally arranged, giving the history of Elijah, there is a certain absorption in his subject, which gives him, indeed, opportunities for his too theatrical qualities, fire breaking out of the wheels of the chariot and the manes and tails of the horses, and out of the sword with which Elijah has slain the prophets of Baal. He did not again achieve so near an approach to spontaneity in extravagance. In his two famous pictures in the Caridad, at which Murillo is said to have held his nose, the Spanish *macabre* is carried to its utmost limits. In one a skeleton with one foot on the globe tramples on all the arts and inventions of man ; the picture is inscribed *In ictu oculi*. In the other a rotting bishop lies in his broken coffin by the side of a rotting knight, in a red and gloomy darkness ; the picture is inscribed *Finis gloriæ mundi*. Both are horribly impressive, painted brilliantly, and with an almost literally overpowering vigour. They lead the way to other, feebler, later pictures, some of which may be seen

47

Cities and Sea-Coasts and Islands.

in a side room at the Museo, where, for instance, a man in a black cloak contemplates a crowned skull which he holds in his hands, while a cardinal's red hat lies at his feet. Here Spanish painting, losing all its earnestness and simplicity, in its representation of human life or of religious ecstasy, losing direction for its vigour, losing the very qualities of painting, becomes moralising, becomes emblematical, dying in Seville a characteristic death.

Winter, 1899.

Domenico Theotocopuli: A Study at Toledo.

AN entry in the books of the church of Santo Tomé at Toledo, recently discovered, tells us that Domenico Theotocopuli died on April 7, 1614, and was buried in the church of Santo Domingo el Antiguo: *En siete del Abril 1614, falescio Dominico Greco. No hizo testamento, recibio los sacramentos, enterose en Santo Domingo el Antiguo. Dio velas.* The signature to a picture in the Escurial tells us that he came from Crete. We do not know the date of his birth; we are told that he studied at Venice under Titian; the earliest date which connects him with Toledo is 1577, when the chapter of the cathedral ordered from him the *Disrobing of Christ*, now in the sacristy. He is said to have been not only a painter, a sculptor, and an architect, but to have written on art and philosophy; he was a fierce litigant on behalf of his art and his own dignity as an artist; we are told of his petulance in speech, as in the assertion that Michel Angelo could not paint; there are legends of his pride, ostentation, and deliberate eccentricity, of his wealth, of his supposed madness; Gongora wrote a sonnet on his death, and Felix de Artiaga two sonnets on his own portrait and on the monument to Queen Margarita. The poet addresses him as *Divino Griego* and *Milagro Griego;* but the name by which he was generally known is the half-Spanish, half-Italian name, El Greco. One of the most original painters who ever lived, he was almost forgotten

49

Cities and Sea-Coasts and Islands.

until the present century; the unauthenticated story of his madness is still commonly repeated, not only by the sacristans of Toledo, and it is only quite lately that there has been any attempt to take him seriously, to consider his real position in the history of art and his real value as a painter. What follows is a personal impression of those aspects of his work and temperament which I was able to note for myself in a careful study of his pictures in Spain, and chiefly of those at Toledo and Madrid.

Theotocopuli seems to have discovered art over again for himself, and in a way which will suggest their varying ways to some of the most typical modern painters. And, indeed, I think he did discover his art over again from the beginning, setting himself to the problem of the representation of life and vision, of the real world and the spiritual world, as if no one had ever painted before. Perhaps it is rather, as the legends tell us, with an only too jealous consciousness of what had been done, and especially by Titian, whose pupil he is said to have been, and whose work his earliest pictures done in Spain are said to have resembled so closely that the one might actually have been mistaken for the other. Real originality is often deliberate originality, and though the story is scarcely true, and though it was no doubt Tintoretto and not Titian whom he studied under, I should have seen no injustice to Theotocopuli in accepting the story. What it means chiefly is, that he saw a problem before him, considered it carefully on every side,

A Study at Toledo.

and found out for himself what was his own way of solving it.

He goes back, then, frankly, to first principles: how one personally sees colour, form, the way in which one remembers expression, one's own natural way of looking at things. And he chooses, out of all the world of colour, those five which we see on his palette in his portrait of himself at Seville, white, vermilion, lake, yellow ochre, and ivory black, with, here as elsewhere, a careful limitation of himself to what he has chosen naturally out of the things open to his choice: style, that is, sternly apprehended as the man.

And he has come, we may suppose, to look on human things somewhat austerely, with a certain contempt for the facile joys and fresh carnations of life, as he has for the poses and colours of those painters of life who have seen life differently; for, even, Titian's luxurious loitering beside sumptuous flesh in pleasant gardens, and for the voluptuous joy of his colour. He wants to express another kind of world, in which life is chilled into a continual proud meditation, in which thought is more than action, and in which the flesh is but little indulged. He sees almost the spiritual body, in his search beyond the mere humanity of white and red, the world's part of coloured dresses, the attitudes of the sensual life. Emotion is somewhat dried out of him, and he intellectualises the warmth of life until it becomes at times the spectre of a thought, which has taken visible form, somewhat alarmingly.

Cities and Sea-Coasts and Islands.

And Toledo, too, has had its influence upon him, an influence scarcely to be exaggerated in the formation of his mind. Theotocopuli, it seems to me, is not to be understood apart from Toledo, the place to which a natural affinity brought him, the place which was waiting to develop just his particular originality. Toledo is one of the most individual cities in Europe. It is set on a high and bare rock, above a river broken by sounding weirs, in the midst of a sombre and rocky land. With its high, windowless walls, which keep their own secrets, its ascents and descents through narrow passage-ways between miles of twisting grey stone, it seems to be encrusted upon the rock, like a fantastic natural product; and it is at the same time a museum of all the arts which have left their mark upon Europe. Almost the best Moorish art is to be seen there, mingled with much excellent Christian art; and the mingling, in this strange place, which has kept its Arab virginity while accepting every ornament which its Christian conquerors have offered it, is for once perfectly successful. Winter and summer fall upon it, set thus naked on a high rock, with all their violence; even in spring the white streets burn like furnaces, wherever a little space is left unshaded; the air is parching, the dust rises in a fine white cloud. Walk long enough, down descending paths, until you hear the sound of rushing water, and you come out on a crumbling edge of land, going down precipitously, with its cargo of refuse, into the Tagus, or upon

A Study at Toledo.

one of the sharply turning roads which lead downwards in a series of inclined planes. On the other side of the ravine another hill rises, here abrupt grey rock, there shaded to an infinitely faint green, which covers the grey rock like a transparent garment. Every turn, which leads you to the surprise of the precipice, has its own surprise for you; there seem to be more churches than houses, and every church has its own originality, or it may be, its own series of originalities. If it had none of its churches, if it were a mere huddle of white and windowless Arab houses, like Elche, which it somewhat resembles, Toledo would still be, from its mere poise there on its desert rock, one of the most picturesque places in Spain. As it is, every stone which goes to make its strange, penetrating originality of aspect, has its history and possesses its own various beauty. To Theotocopuli, coming to this austere and chill and burning city of living rock from the languid waters of Venice, a new world was opened, the world of what is most essentially and yet exceptionally Spanish, as it can appeal, with all its strength, only to strangers. Toledo made Theotocopuli Spanish, more Spanish than the Spaniards.

And Toledo was surely not without its influence in the suggestion of that new system of colour, teaching him, as it certainly would, to appreciate colour in what is cold, grey, austere, without luxuriance or visible brightness. The colour of Toledo is marvellously sharp and dim at

53

Cities and Sea-Coasts and Islands.

once, with an incomparable richness in all the shades to which stone can lend itself under weather, and in sun and shadow; it is a colour violently repressed, a thing to be divined, waited upon, seen with intelligence. It is amply defended against indifferent eyes: it shocks, and is subtle, two defences; but there it is, the colour of Theotocopuli.

In the Museo Provincial there is a bird's-eye view of Toledo by Theotocopuli which is the most fantastic landscape I have ever seen, like a glimpse of country seen in a nightmare, and yet, somehow, very like a real Toledo. It is done with a sweeping brush, with mere indications, in these bluish white houses which rush headlong downhill and struggle wildly uphill, from the phantom Tagus below to the rushing storm-sky above. The general tone is pale earthy green, colouring the hills on which the city rests, and intersecting the streets of pale houses, and running almost without a break into the costume of the youth in the foreground, who holds a map of the city in his hands, filling a huge space of the picture. Toledo itself is grey and green, especially as night comes on over the country, and the rocks and fields colour faintly under the sunset, the severity of their beauty a little softened by a natural effect which is like an effect in painting. It is just the effect of this phantasmal landscape; and, here again, all Toledo is in the work of Theotocopuli, and his work all Toledo. Coming out from seeing his pictures in some vast, old, yellow church,

54

A Study at Toledo.

into these never quite natural or lifelike streets, where blind beggars play exquisitely on their guitars in the shadow of a doorway, and children go barefoot, with flowers in their mouths, leading pet lambs, I seem to find his models everywhere: these dark peasants with their sympathetic and bright seriousness, the women who wear his colours, the men who sit in the cafés with exactly that lean diminishing outline of face and beard, that sallow skin, and those fixed eyes.

In his portraits, as we see them for the most part in the Prado at Madrid, there is a certain subdued ecstasy, purely ascetic, and purely temperamental in its asceticism, as of a fine Toledo blade, wearing out its scabbard through the mere sharpness of inaction. There is a kind of family likeness, a likeness, too, with his own face, in these portraits of Spanish gentlemen, in the black clothes and enveloping white ruff of the period: the lean face, pointed beard, deep eyes, thin hair, olive skin, the look of melancholy pride. Seen at a little distance, the black clothes disappear into the black background; nothing is seen but the eager face starting out of the white ruff, like a decapitated head seen in a dream. Their faces are all nerves, distinguished nerves, quieted by an effort, the faces of dreamers in action; they have all the brooding Spanish soul, with its proud self-repression. And they live with an eager, remote, perfectly well-bred life, as of people who could never be taken unawares, in a vulgar or trivial moment. In their tense, intellectual aspect

55

there is all the romantic sobriety of the frugal Spanish nature.

Look for instance at the portrait of the man with a sword, his hand laid across his breast with a gesture of the same curious fixity as the eyes. Compare this portrait with the fine portrait by the pupil of Theotocopuli, Luis Tristan, through whom we are supposed to reach Velasquez. In Tristan there is more realism, a more normal flesh; there is none of that spiritual delicacy, by which the colours of the flesh are dimmed, as if refined away by the fretting and consuming spirit. In the portrait by Theotocopuli, the light falls whitely upon the man's forehead, isolating him within a visionary atmosphere, in which he lives the mysterious life of a portrait. He exists there, as if sucked out of the darkness by the pale light which illuminates his forehead, a soul and a gesture, a secret soul and a repressive gesture.

And these portraits are painted with all the economical modern mastery of means, with almost as black and hard an outline as Manet, with strong shadows and significant indications of outline, with rapid suppressions, translations of colour by colour, decomposition of tones, as in the beautiful lilacs of the white flesh. Individuality is pushed to a mannerism, but it is a mannerism which renders a very select and vivid aspect of natural truth, and with a virile and singular kind of beauty.

In the earliest pictures painted under the influence of the Venetian painters, as in the *Disrobing of*

A Study at Toledo.

Christ in the sacristy of the cathedral at Toledo, there is a perfect mastery of form and colour, as the Venetians understood them; the composition is well balanced, sober, without extravagance. In the *Assumption of the Virgin*, over the high altar of Santo Domingo el Antiguo, there is just a suggestion of the hard black and white of the later manner, but for the most part it is painted flowingly, with a vigour always conscious of tradition. A Virgin of splendid humanity reminds me of one of the finest of Alonso Cano's wooden statues. The somewhat fiercely meditative saints in the side panels are at once Spanish and Italian; Italian by their formal qualities of painting, certainly Spanish by an intensity of religious ardour which recalls and excels Zurbaran. In the *Adoration of the Shepherds* and the *Resurrection*, in the same church, we see already sharp darknesses of colour, an earthly pallor of flesh, a sort of turbulence flushing out of the night of a black background. In the latter picture there is on one side a priest, finely and soberly painted in his vestments of white and pale gold; and, on the other, almost Blake-like figures asleep in attitudes of violent repose, or rising suddenly with hands held up against the dazzling light which breaks from the rising Saviour. But it is in the *Martyrdom of S. Maurizio*, ordered by Philip II. as an altar-piece for the Escurial, and refused by him when it had been painted, that we see the complete abandonment of warm for cold colouring, the first definite search for a wholly personal manner. Is it that he has

57

Cities and Sea-Coasts and Islands.

not yet assimilated his new manner? for the picture seems to me a sort of challenge to himself and to his critics, an experiment done too consciously to be quite sincere or quite successful. There is a wild kind of beauty, harshly and deliberately unsympathetic, in this turbulent angelic host, these figures of arbitrary height, placed strangely, their anatomy so carefully outlined under clinging draperies of crude blues and yellows, their skin turned livid under some ghastly supernatural light. In another picture painted for the Escurial, and now to be seen there, the *Dream of Philip II.*, there is a hell which suggests the fierce material hells of Hieronymus van Bosch: a huge, fanged mouth wide open, the damned seen writhing in that red cavern, a lake of flame awaiting them beyond, while angels fly overhead, sainted persons in rich ecclesiastical vestments kneel below, and the king, dressed in black, kneels at the side. It is almost a vision of madness, and is as if the tormented brain of the fanatic who built those prison walls about himself, and shut himself living into a tomb-like cell, and dead into a not more tomb-like niche in a crypt, had wrought itself into the brain of the painter; who would indeed have found something not uncongenial to himself in this mountainous place of dust and grey granite, in which every line is rigid, every colour ashen, in a kind of stony immobility more terrible than any other of the images of death.

It was only three years after the painting of the *Martyrdom of S. Maurizio* that Theotocopuli painted

A Study at Toledo.

his masterpiece, the *Burial of the Conde de Orgaz,*
which was ordered by the Archbishop of Toledo
for the tomb, in the church of Santo Tomé, of
Gonzalo Ruiz de Toledo, Conde de Orgaz, who
had died in the thirteenth century. The picture
is still to be seen there, in its corner of the little
white mosque-like church, where one comes upon
it with a curious sensation of surprise, for it is at
once as real and as ghostly as a dream, and it
reminds one of nothing one has ever seen before.
The picture, as it takes hold upon one, first of all,
by a scheme of colour as startling as the harmonies
of Wagner in music, seems to have been thought
out by a brain for once wholly original, in forgetful-
ness of all that had ever been done in painting. Is
it that reality, and the embodied forms of the
imagination, have been seen thus, at a fixed angle,
instinctively and deliberately, for a picture, by an
artist to whom all life is the escaping ghost of art ?
Certainly its austerity, its spiritual realism, its
originality of composition, so simple as to be
startling, and of colour, the reticence of a passionate
abnegation; the tenderness of the outlines of the
drooping dead body, in its rich armour; the masculine seriousness in all the faces, each of which is
like one of the portraits in the Prado, and with all
their subtlety, make the picture one of the masterpieces of painting. The upper part is a celestial
company, arranged so as to drift like a canopy over
the death-scene below; and these angels are painted
in swift outline, their blue and yellow draperies

59

Cities and Sea-Coasts and Islands.

sweeping the vehement clouds. Below, where the warrior is dying, and his friends, with their distinguished Castillian faces, their black clothes which sink into the shadow, the white ruffs about their thin faces and pointed beards standing out startlingly, crowd about him, we have the real world, in all the emphasis of its contrast to the spiritual world. Every face lives its own life, there on the canvas, assisting at this death as an actual spectator, thinking of this and of other things, not as a merely useful part of a composition. And the beauty of beautiful things is nowhere neglected : the fine armour, the golden and embroidered vestments of the bishop, the transparent white linen of the surplice worn by the tall man in the foreground, the gracious charm of the young priest who stoops over the dying man. The chief indication of what is to be the extravagant later manner comes out in the painting of the hands, with their sharp, pained gesticulation, to which nature is a little sacrificed. They must exclaim, in their gesture.

Madness, it has commonly been supposed, and will still be told you by all the sacristans of Toledo ; a disease of the eye, as it is now thought ; mere insistent and defiant originality of search after what was new and powerfully expressive, as it may well have been ; something, certainly, before long set Theotocopuli *chevauchant hors du possible*, as Gautier puts it, in those amazing pictures by which he is chiefly known, the religious pictures in the Prado at Madrid, in the churches and the Hospital a fuera

60

A Study at Toledo.

at Toledo, and in some galleries and private collections outside Spain. In the immense retablo of Santa Clara, with its six large and four small panels, its gilded and painted statues, the sombre splendour of colour begins to darken, that it may be the more austere; the forms and faces, so vigorous in St. Jerome, so beautiful in St. Anne, begin to harden a little; but as yet leanness has not eaten up all, nor a devouring energy consumed away the incidents of the drama into a kind of spectral reflection of it. In the *Dead Christ in the Arms of God the Father*, in the Prado, energy has grown eager and restless, as the divine persons are seen couched upon rolling white clouds, while a burst of golden sunlight blazes upon the great white wings of God. In the *Ascension* near it, where Christ floats upwards, carrying a white banner, while the soldiers fall about his feet, throwing their arms and swords wildly into the air, the lights seem to hurdle to and fro, catching the tips of noses, the points of knees, the hollows of breast-bones, in a waste of clouds and smoke. In the *Baptism of Christ*, the anatomies grow bonier than ever, more violently distorted by shadows, as a green and blue flood pours out angels like foam about the feet of God the Father. There is a *Crucifixion* as if seen by lightning-flashes, against a sky crackling with flames, while a poisonous green light flashes upon the tormented figures below. The hollow anatomy of Christ turns livid, the little angels who flutter about the cross are shadowed by the same spectral light, which sickens

Cities and Sea-Coasts and Islands.

their wings to green; another angel, at the foot of the cross, is coloured like the gold heart and green leaves of a crocus. This angel catches the blood dripping from the feet of Christ in a handkerchief, the Magdalen kneels beside him, holding up another handkerchief to catch the blood; the other angels catch in their hands the blood dripping from the hands and side of Christ. In this picture all the extravagances of Spanish painting are outdone; but without a trace of affectation. All these emblematical details are like things seen, in a fury of vision, by one to whom sight is a disease of the imagination. In an *Assumption of the Virgin* in S. Vicente at Toledo, the whole landscape seems on fire, with flames of more than sunset, as an angel in a pale saffron robe bears up the feet of the Virgin, one gorgeous wing of ruddy brown spread out across the sky, while flame-winged angels surround her, one playing languidly upon a 'cello. And this surging tumult of colour, wild, sensitive, eloquent, seems to speak a new language, with vehement imperfection. Here, as in the *Baptism* in the Hospital a fuera, in which earnestness has become a kind of dementia, there is some of the beauty of an extravagant natural thing, of a stormy and in-coherent sunset. It is as if a painter had tried to embody such a sunset, creating fantastic figures to translate the suggestion of its outlines.

And so Theotocopuli ends, in that exaggeration of himself which has overtaken so many of those artists who have cared more for energy than for

A Study at Toledo.

beauty. His palette is still the limited, cold palette which we have seen in the hands of his portrait at Seville, but colour seems to chafe against restraint, and so leap more wildly within its limits. The influence of Tintoretto is after all unforgotten, though it is seen now in a kind of parody of itself. Lines lengthen and harden, as men seem to grow into trees, ridged and gnarled with strange accidents of growth. That spiritual body which he has sought for the reticent souls of his portraits becomes a stained, earthly thing which has known corruption. No longer, at all equably, master of himself or of his vision, he allows his skill of hand to become narrow, fanatical; and, in his last pictures, seems rather an angry prophet, denouncing humanity, than a painter, faithful to the beauty and expressiveness of natural things.

Spring, 1899.

The Poetry of Santa Teresa and San Juan de la Cruz.

I.

"Here in Spain there are many poets," said a Capuchin monk to me, as, on Christmas Day, we stood together in the convent library, looking through the barred windows at the sunset which flamed over Seville. "The people are the poets. They love beautiful things, they are moved by them; that word which you will hear constantly on their lips: *Mira!* ('Look!') is itself significant. They would say it now if they were here, looking at the sunset, and they would point out to one another the colours, the shape of that tower silhouetted against the sky; they would be full of excited delight. Is there not something in that of the poetic attitude? They have the feeling; sometimes they put it into words, and make those rhymes of which the greater part are lost, but some are at last written down, and you can read them in books."

We had been discussing the Spanish mystics, San Juan de la Cruz, Juan de Avila, Fray Luis de Leon, Santa Teresa; and I had just been turning over a facsimile of the original MS. of the *Castillo Interior* in Santa Teresa's bold, not very legible, handwriting, with its feminine blots here and there on the pages. I had been praising the great poetry of the two saints, and lamenting the rarity of really sincere, really personal, lyric poetry in Spanish; and the monk's answer, as I thought over it on

S. Teresa and S. Juan de la Cruz.

my way home that evening, seemed to me to point to the real truth of the matter. The Spanish temperament, as I have been able to see for myself during the three months I have already been in Spain, is essentially a poetical temperament. It is brooding, passionate, sensitive, at once voluptuous and solemn. Here is at least the material for poetry. But the moment a Spaniard begins to write, he has the choice of an extraordinary number of bad models, and, as in his architecture, as in so much of even his painting, he has been readier to adapt than to invent. Even Calderon, a great poet, is a perilous model; and what of Gongora or Garbilaso, of Espronceda or Zorrilla? On the one hand one finds extravagance and affectation; on the other, haste, homeliness, and lack of care. In a sense, this poetry is often enough personal, but when it is personal in sentiment it is not personal in form, as in Espronceda, who indeed wrote the poetry he was living, but wrote it in the manner of Byron. The natural human voice, speaking straight out of the heart, pure lyric poetry, that is, cannot be found in Spanish literature outside the mystics, and a final choice may indeed be limited to Santa Teresa and San Juan de la Cruz. These speak to God in Christ, the one as a mother to a child, the other as a wife to a husband. For each, the individual passion makes its own form, almost its own language, so that Crashaw's brilliant line of verse, "O 'tis not Spanish but 'tis Heaven she speaks!" is really a subtle criticism as well. And,

Cities and Sea-Coasts and Islands.

singularly unlike as is the childishly naked simplicity of Santa Teresa to the elaborate web of sweetness in which San Juan de la Cruz enfolds his rapture, each has the same supreme lyric quality: personal passion moulding individual form.

And the poetry of the people, in its lesser, its less final way, has this quality too; so that in these two great Spanish poets we see the flower at last growing directly from the root. An unknown, perfectly spontaneous poet of the people makes up his little stanza of three or four lines because he has something to say which hurts him so much to keep in that he is obliged to say it. This of itself is not enough to make poetry, but it will make poetry if so intense a desire comes to life in a nature already poetically sensitive, in a nature such as this of the Spaniards. And the Spaniard, with that something abrupt, nervous, which there is in him, is singularly well able to condense emotion into brief form, such as he has created for these popular songs, which are briefer than those of most other nations, an impassioned statement, and no more.

In the poetry of Santa Teresa we find almost the form of the popular song, and a choice of words which is for the most part no more than an instinctively fine selection of its actual language. San Juan de la Cruz, who lived habitually in an abstract world, out of which only a supreme emotion could draw him, has a more conscious choice of language, subtilising upon words that he may render all the subtlety of spiritual sensation; and he uses largely

66

S. Teresa and S. Juan de la Cruz.

a favourite literary form of that time, the five-line stanza in which, for example, the greater part of the poems of Fray Luis de Leon are written. But I am sure neither the one nor the other ever wrote a line with the intention of "making poetry," that intention which ruins Spanish verse to a deeper degree than the verse of most nations. They had something to say which could not be said in prose, a "lyrical cry" was in them which they could not repress; and heaven worked together with earth that Spanish lyrical poetry might be born and die within the lifetime of two friends.

II.

The poetry of San Juan de la Cruz is metaphysical fire, a sort of white heat in which the abstract, the almost negative, becomes ecstatically realised by the senses. Here, in a translation as literal as I can make it, line for line, and with exactly the same arrangement and repetition of rhymes, is his most famous poem, *En una Noche escura*, a poem which is the keystone of his whole philosophy:

Upon an obscure night,
  Fevered with love in love's anxiety,
(Oh, hapless-happy plight!)
  I went, none seeing me,
Forth from my house where all things quiet be.

By night, secure from sight,
  And by the secret stair, disguisedly,
(Oh, hapless-happy plight!)

Cities and Sea-Coasts and Islands.

By night, and privily,
Forth from my house where all things quiet be.

Blest night of wandering,
In secret, when by none might I be spied,
Nor I see anything;
Without a light or guide,
Save that which in my heart burnt in my side.

That light did lead me on,
More surely than the shining of noontide,
Where well I knew that one
Did for my coming bide;
Where he abode might none but he abide.

O night that didst lead thus,
O night more lovely than the dawn of light,
O night that broughtest us,
Lover to lover's sight,
Lover with loved in marriage of delight!

Upon my flowery breast,
Wholly for him, and save himself for none,
There did I give sweet rest
To my beloved one;
The fanning of the cedars breathed thereon.

When the first moving air
Blew from the tower, and waved his locks aside,
His hand, with gentle care,
Did wound me in the side,
And in my body all my senses died.

All things I then forgot,
My cheek on him who for my coming came;
All ceased, and I was not,
Leaving my cares and shame
Among the lilies, and forgetting them.

The greater part of the prose of San Juan de la

S. Teresa and S. Juan de la Cruz.

Cruz is built up out of this poem, or condensed into it: the *Noche Escura del Alma* is a line-by-line commentary upon it, and the *Subida del Monte Carmelo*, a still longer work, takes this poem for starting-point, and declares that the whole of its doctrine is to be found in these stanzas. The third and last of the three contemplative books, the *Llama de Amor Viva*, is, in a similar way, a commentary on the poem which follows:

> O flame of living love,
>   That dost eternally
> Pierce through my soul with so consuming heat,
>   Since there's no help above,
>   Make thou an end of me,
> And break the bond of this encounter sweet.
>
>   O burn that burns to heal!
>   O more than pleasant wound!
> And O soft hand, O touch most delicate,
>   That dost new life reveal,
>   That dost in grace abound,
> And, slaying, dost from death to life translate.
>
>   O lamps of fire that shined
>   With so intense a light,
> That those deep caverns where the senses live,
>   Which were obscure and blind,
>   Now with strange glories bright,
> Both heat and light to his beloved give.
>
>   With how benign intent
>   Rememberest thou my breast,
> Where thou alone abidest secretly,
>   And in thy sweet ascent,
>   With glory and good possessed,
> How delicately thou teachest love to me!

Cities and Sea-Coasts and Islands.

Thus the whole *Obras Espirituales*, 614 quarto pages in my copy of the original edition of 1618, are but a development of these two poems; the poetry, as it should be, being at the root of the philosophy.

In that strange, pedantic "figure" which stands at the beginning of the *Subida del Monte Carmelo*, the narrow way which leads to the mount is inscribed, "Nothing, nothing, nothing, nothing, nothing," and above, "and in the mount nothing"; but above that begin higher heights, inscribed with the names of the ultimate virtues, and above that the "divine silence" and the "divine wisdom," and the dwelling of the soul with God himself. With San Juan de la Cruz the obscure night is a way, the negation of all earthly things, of the earthly senses even, a means to the final union with God; and it is in this union that darkness blossoms into the glittering delights of the poems. Pierce the dark night to its centre, and you will find light, for you will find God. "And so," he tells us, "in this soul, in which now no appetite abides, nor other imaginings, nor forms of other created things; most secretly it abides in so much the more inner interior, and more straitly embraced, as it is itself the more pure, and single of all things but God." This rapture of negation becomes poetry, and poetry of the highest order, because it is part of a nature to which, if God is what Vaughan calls a "deep but dazzling darkness," he is also the supreme love, to be apprehended humanly by this

S. Teresa and S. Juan de la Cruz.

quality, for which, and in which, he put on humanity. To San Juan de la Cruz the idea of God is an idea which can be apprehended mentally only by a series of negations; the person of God can be apprehended only emotionally, and best under the figure, which he accepts from the "Song of Solomon," of earthly marriage, the marriage of the soul and Christ. At once the door is opened in the seventh heaven of metaphysics for all the flowers in which the earth decks itself for lovers; and this monk can give lessons to lovers. His great poem of forty stanzas, the *Canción entre el Alma y el Esposo*, once or twice becoming almost ludicrous in the liveliness of its natural images, as when the Spouse drinks in the "interior bodega" of the Beloved, has a peculiar fragrance, as of very strong natural perfumes, perfumes really made honestly out of flowers, though in the fieriest of alcohols. Here, and in the two mystical love-poems which I have translated, there is an abandonment to all the sensations of love, which seems to me to exceed, and on their own ground, in directness and intensity of spiritual and passionate longing, most of what has been written by the love-poets of all ages. These lines, so full of rich and strange beauty, ache with desire and with all the subtlety of desire. They analyse the sensations of the soul, as lovers do, that they may draw out their sweetness more luxuriously. In a merely human love they would be almost perverse, so learned are they in sensation. Sanctified to divine uses, they do but swing a more odorous

Cities and Sea-Coasts and Islands.

incense, in censers of more elaborately beaten gold, in the service of a perpetual Mass to the Almighty.

Of the *Canciones* there are but five; and of these I have translated another, somewhat more abstract, less coloured, than the rest.

> Well do I know the spring that doth abound,
>   Although it is the night.
>
> That everlasting spring, though hidden close,
> Well do I know whither and whence it flows,
>   Although it is the night.
>
> Beginning know I not, for none there is,
> But know that all beginning comes from this,
>   Although it is the night.
>
> I know there is not any fairer thing,
> And that the heavens and earth drink of this spring,
>   Although it is the night.
>
> I know that end within it is not found,
> Nor is there plummet that its depths can sound,
>   Although it is the night.
>
> Upon its brightness doth no shadow come:
> Well know I that all light cometh therefrom,
>   Although it is the night.
>
> I know its currents are so hard to bind,
> They water hell and heaven and human-kind,
>   Although it is the night.
>
> The current that from this deep spring doth flow,
> How mighty is its flowing, well I know,
>   Although it is the night.

72

S. Teresa and S. Juan de la Cruz.

This everlasting spring is occulted,
To give us life, within this living bread,
   Although it is the night.

Here it doth speak to man, and say to him:
Drink of this living water, although dim,
   Although it is the night.

This living spring, I have desired of old,
Within this bread of life do I behold,
   Although it is the night.

But, besides the *Canciones*, there are five *Coplas* and *Glosas*, still more abstract than this poem, but brimful of what I have called metaphysical fire, "toda ciencia transcendiendo"; the ecstasy striving to find immediate, and no longer mediate, words for its revelation. Finally, there are ten *Romances*, of which all but the last are written in quatrains linked by a single rhyme, the accommodating Spanish rhyme in "ia." They are Biblical paraphrases and statements of theological doctrine, and reverence has not permitted them to find any fine, wild liberties for themselves, like the other, more instinctive, more emotionally inspired poems. They have the archaic formality of the fourteenth-century paintings of the Madonna, stiffly embroidered with gold, and waited on by formal angels. Some personal sentiment yet remains, but the personal form is gone, and they might seem to have been really written in an earlier century.

Cities and Sea-Coasts and Islands.

III.

With Santa Teresa all is changed. Her poems are improvisations, seem to have been written by accident, and certainly with no double or treble or hundredfold meanings concealed within them, like those of San Juan de la Cruz.[1] They are impetuous, incorrect, full of joyous life, almost of hilarity. Many of them are little songs with refrains; some are composed on motives given by others, many for special occasions, such as a taking of the veil. One is a sort of paraphrase, or variant, of a poem of San Juan de la Cruz. It is interesting to compare the two, and to see how in the very first verse Santa Teresa brings in an idea entirely, and how characteristically! her own: "This divine union of love with him I love makes God my captive, and sets free my heart; but causes such grief in me to see God my prisoner, that I die because I die not." She gives herself to God, as it were, with a great leap into his arms. She has no savorous reflections, no lingering over delights; a practical swiftness, a woman's heart, and that joy which burns through all her work. "That love alone is that which gives value to all things," none knew so well as she, or realised so simply. "O pitying and loving Lord of my life! Thou hast said: 'Come unto me all ye

---

[1] He can be as minute in his explanations as to comment on the first three lines of the second stanza of *O llama de amor viva:* The *Burn* is the Holy Spirit, the *Hand* is the Father, and the *Touch* is the Son.

74

that thirst, and I will give you to drink.' How, then, can these but suffer great thirst that are now burning in living flames in the desire of these miserable things of the earth? Needs must there be much water indeed if it is not to fail and be consumed. Now know I, Lord, of thy bounty that thou shalt give it: thyself sayest it, and thou canst not fail from thy words. Yet if they, used to living in this fire, and brought up in it, feel it not, nor have reason in their unreasonableness to see how great is their necessity, what remedy, O my God? Thou hast come into the world to remedy even such great necessities; begin, Lord: in these most difficult things dost thou most show thy pity. Behold, my God, that thine enemies make much headway: have pity on those that have no pity on themselves, now that their mischance so holds them that they desire not to come to thee: come thou to them, my God. I demand it in their name, and know that when they shall hear, and return to themselves, and begin to delight in thee, these now dead shall come to life. O life, that thou givest to all! Deny me not this most sweet water that thou hast promised to those that seek it: I do seek it, Lord, and demand it, and come for it to thee: hide not thyself, Lord, from me, for thou knowest my need, and that it is the true medicine of the soul wounded by thee. O Lord, what manner of fires are there in this life! Oh, how rightly do we live in fear! Some there are that consume the soul, others that purify it, that it may live for ever, joying in thee. O living streams of the wounds of my God! How do ye flow ever with great abundance for our maintenance, and how securely shall they go through the perils of this miserable life that are sustained by this divine beverage." "O true lover!" she cries, in her prose *Exclamaciones*, "with what pity, with what softness, with what delight, with what tenderness, and with what great manifestations of love thou curest the wounds that with the arrows of that same love thou hast made!" And her verse, as in this poem, is an outpouring of love which speaks the simplest lovers' language, like a woman who cannot say "I love you!" too often.

If, Lord, thy love for me is strong
    As this which binds me unto thee,
What holds me from thee, Lord, so long,
    What holds thee, Lord, so long from me?

O soul, what then desirest thou?
    — Lord, I would see thee, who thus choose thee.
What fears can yet assail thee now?
    — All that I fear is but to lose thee.

Love's whole possession I entreat,
    Lord, make my soul thine own abode,
And I will build a nest so sweet
    It may not be too poor for God.

A soul in God hidden from sin,
    What more desires for thee remain,
    Save but to love, and love again,
And, all on flame with love within,
    Love on, and turn to love again?

S. Teresa and S. Juan de la Cruz.

Another division of her poems consists of songs for Christmas, for the Circumcision, for the Virgin as mother; and here, adapting to her use a form already existing, she practically invents a new form, in these little lyric dramas, dialogues of the shepherds, in which the same shepherds appear, with their strange names, Bras or Brasillo, Menga, with Llorente and the invariable Gil. I have translated three of them, with all the archaisms, accidents of form, omission or reversal of rhymes, of the original, and, in the refrain of the second, an assonance exactly reproducing the original assonance.

I.

Let mine eyes see thee,
　Sweet Jesus of Nazareth;
Let mine eyes see thee,
　And then see death.

Let them see that care
　Roses and jessamine;
Seeing thy face most fair,
　All blossoms are therein.
Flower of seraphin,
　Sweet Jesus of Nazareth,
Let mine eyes see thee,
　And then see death.

Nothing I require
　Where my Jesus is;
Anguish all desire,
　Saving only this;
All my help is his,
　He only succoureth.

Cities and Sea-Coasts and Islands.

Let mine eyes see thee,
    Sweet Jesus of Nazareth,
Let mine eyes see thee,
    And then see death.

II.

Shepherd, shepherd, hark that calling!
Angels they are, and the day is dawning.

What is this ding-dong,
    Or loud singing is it?
Come, Bras, now the day is here,
    The shepherdess we'll visit.
Shepherd, shepherd, hark that calling!
Angels they are, and the day is dawning.

Oh, is this the Alcade's daughter,
    Or some lady come from far?
She is the daughter of God the Father,
    And she shines like a star.
Shepherd, shepherd, hark that calling!
Angels they are, and the day is dawning.

III.

To-day a shepherd and our kin,
    O Gil, to ransom us is sent,
    And he is God Omnipotent.

For us hath he cast down the pride
    And prison walls of Satanas;
    But he is of the kin of Bras,
    Of Menga, also of Llorent.
    O is not God Omnipotent?

If he is God, how then is he
    Come hither, and here crucified?

S. Teresa and S. Juan de la Cruz.

— With his dying sin also died,
Enduring death the innocent.
Gil, how is God Omnipotent!

Why, I have seen him born, pardie,
And of a most sweet shepherdess.
— If he is God, how can he be
With such poor folk as these content?
— See'st not he is Omnipotent?

Give over idle parleying,
And let us serve him, you and I,
And since he came on earth to die,
Let us die with him too, Llorent;
For he is God Omnipotent.

These and other ecstasies over Christ in the cradle are the motherly instinct in her finding vicarious satisfaction; and though we have here an instinct for which genius finds expression in art, the whole force of the sentiment can be understood only by one who has seen a monk or nun exhibiting the conventual image of the infant Jesus to a sympathetic visitor. I have never seen a living child handled with more adoring tenderness than the monk of whom I have spoken handled the amazingly realistic "Bambino," who lay in a basket stuffed with straw, in his little frilled shirt and baby's cap with blue strings. Religion, any other controlling force, can constrain, can turn into other directions, but cannot kill an instinct; and the adoration of the divine child is the refuge of the childless, in convents and in the world.

But Santa Teresa was not only a loving woman

79

Cities and Sea-Coasts and Islands.

and a loving mother, she was that great brain and great worker whom we know; and she wrote marching songs for the soldiers of Christ in their war against the world, and songs of triumph for their victories, and songs of warning for those who were lightly undertaking so great an enterprise. In all there is the same impetuous spirit, the same close hold on reality, and one to whom religion was not contemplation but action, or action even in contemplation. In reading the poems of San Juan de la Cruz, it is not easy to remember that he too was a monastic reformer:[1] it would be impossible to read the poems of Santa Teresa without seeing the reformer, the woman of action, in the poet:

> *Caminemos para el cielo,*
> *Monjas de Carmelo!*

She sings, leading them, on that difficult way; and in that "Offering of Herself to God that she made," in the magnificent poem with the refrain "What would'st thou do with me?" we see the whole woman, "a woman for angelical height of speculation, for masculine courage of performance more than a· woman," in Crashaw's famous words. Here, in prose, are three stanzas out of the twelve:

What wouldst thou, then, good Lord, that so base a servant should do? What service hast thou given to this

---

[1] He is described on the title-page of his works as "*primer Descalzo de la Reforma de N. Señora del Carmen, Coadjutor de la Bienaventurada Virgen S. Teresa de Jesús, Fundadora de la misma Reforma.*"

S. Teresa and S. Juan de la Cruz.

sinful slave? Behold me here, sweet Love; sweet Love, behold me here; what wouldst thou do with me?

See here my heart, I lay it in thy hand, my body, my life and soul, my bowels and my love; sweet Spouse and redemption, since I offer myself to be thine, what wouldst thou do with me?

Give me death, give me life, give me health or sickness, honour or dishonour give me, give me war or perfect peace, weakness or strength to my life: to all I will answer yes; what wouldst thou do with me?

This ardent, joyous simplicity, this impassioned devotion to which every height or depth of sacrifice was an easy thing, this clear sight of God, not through the intellectual negations nor the symbolical raptures of San Juan de la Cruz, but face to face, which give Santa Teresa her unique rank among the mystics, as the one who has seen spiritual things most directly, find here their simplest expression. Here, as in those poems of the people with which I began by comparing these poems, a "flaming heart" burns outward to escape the intolerable pain of its reclusion.

Winter, 1899.

Campoamor.

Ramon de Campoamor y Campoosorio, who died at Madrid on the 12th of February 1901, was born at Navia, in the province of Asturias, on the 24th of September 1817. His career covers almost the whole century: he was the contemporary of Quintana, Espronceda, Zorrilla, yet absolutely untouched by the influences which made of Quintana a lesser Cowper, of Espronceda a lesser Byron, and of Zorrilla a lesser Longfellow. Coming into a literature in which poetry is generally taken to be but another name for rhetoric, he followed, long before Verlaine, Verlaine's advice to "take rhetoric and wring its neck." The poetry of words, of sounds, of abstractions, that poetry which is looked upon in Spain as the most really poetical kind of poetry, left him untouched; he could but apply to it the Arab proverb: "I hear the tic-tac of the mill, but I see no flour." In his *Poética* he declares boldly: "If we except the *Romancero* and the *cantares*, Spain has almost no really national lyric poetry." "There are very well-built verses, that are lads of sound body, but without a soul. Such are those of Herrera and of almost all his imitators, the grandiloquent poets." In the simple masculine verse of Jorge Manrique (whose great poem, the *Coplas por la muerte de su Padre*, is known to most English readers in its admirable translation by Longfellow) he saw an incomparable model, whose grave and passionate simplicity might well have been the basis of a national style. "Poetry," he declares,

in what seemed to his critics an amusing paradox,
"is the rhythmical representation of a thought
through the medium of an image, expressed in a
language which cannot be put in prose more naturally or with fewer words. . . . There is in poetry
no immortal expression that can be said in prose
with more simplicity or with more precision."
Prose, indeed, seemed to him not really an art at
all, and when Valera, a genuine artist in prose,
defended his own ground by asserting that "metaphysics is the one useless science and poetry the
one useless art," Campoamor replied in verse,
defining prose as "la jerga animal del ser humano"
("the jabber of the human animal"). "What
are philosophical systems," he asks, "but poems
without images?" and, protesting against the
theory of "art for art," and suggesting "art for
ideas," or "transcendental" art, as a better definition
of what was at least his own conception, he sums
up with his customary neatness: "Metaphysics
is the science of ideas, religion is the science of ideas
converted into sentiments, and art the science of
ideas converted into images. Metaphysics is the
true, religion the good, and æsthetics the beautiful."
By calling art "transcendental" he means, not
that it should be in itself either philosophical or
didactic, much less abstract, for "art is the enemy
of abstractions . . . and whatever becomes im-
personal evaporates," but that it should contain
in itself, as its foundation, a "universal human
truth," without which "it is no more than the

83

letters of tattling women." "All lyric poetry should be a little drama." "In the drama of the Creation everything was written by God in sympathetic ink. We have but to apply the reagent and hold it to the light. The best artist is the best translator of the works of God." "It has been my constant endeavour," he tells us, "to approach art through ideas, and to express them in ordinary language, thus revolutionising the substance and form of poetry, the substance with the *Doloras* and the form with the *Pequeños Poemas*." Beginning at first with fables, he abandoned the form of the fable, because it seemed to him that the fable could only take root in countries in which the doctrine of the transmigration of souls was still believed. "The *Dolora*, a drama taken direct from life, without the metaphors and symbols of indirect poetry, seemed to me a form more European, more natural, and more human than that of the oriental fable." But the *Dolora* was to retain thus much of the fable, that by means of its drama it was to "solve some universal problem," the solution growing out of the actual structure of the story. Thus, in poetry, subject is all-important, subject including "the argument and the action." "In every pebble of the brook there is part of an Escurial: the difficulty and the merit are in building it." "Novelty of subject, regularity of plan, the method with which that plan is carried out": these, together with the fundamental idea, which is to be of universal application, "transcendental," as he calls it, are

84

the requisites of a work of art; it is on these grounds
that a work of art is to be judged. "Every work
of art should be able to reply affirmatively to these
four questions:

The subject: can it be narrated?
The plan: can it be painted?
The design: has it a purpose?
The style: is it the man?"

Campoamor was no classical scholar, and it is
but hesitatingly that he suggests, on the authority
of "a French critic, who had it from Aristotle,"
that the theory of the Greeks in poetry was in many
points similar to his. If we turn to Matthew
Arnold's preface to his *Poems*, we shall find all
that is fundamental in Campoamor's argument
stated finally, and in the form of an appeal to
classical models. "The radical difference between
their poetical theory" (the Greeks', that is) "and
ours consists, it appears to me, in this: that with
them the poetical character of the action in itself,
and the conduct of it, were the first consideration;
with us attention is fixed mainly on the value of the
separate thoughts and images which occur in the
treatment of an action." And, further on in that
admirable preface, Matthew Arnold assures "the
individual writer" that he "may certainly learn
of the ancients, better than anywhere else, three
things which it is vitally important for him to
know: the all-importance of the choice of a subject,
the necessity of accurate construction, and the
subordinate character of expression." Is not this

Cities and Sea-Coasts and Islands.

precisely the aim of Campoamor? and is it not as a natural corollary to this severe theory of poetical construction that he tells us: "Style is not a question of figures of speech, but of electric fluid"; "rhythm alone should separate the language of verse from that of prose"; yet that language should always have an inner beauty, "the mysterious magic of music, so that it should say, not what the writer intends, but what the reader desires"? And so we come, not unnaturally, to his ideal in writing: "To write poems whose ideas and whose words had been, or seemed to have been, thought or written by every one."

Upon these theories, it might well seem to us, a writer is left at all events free, and with a very reasonable kind of liberty, to make the most of himself. Only, after all, the question remains: What was Campoamor's conception of subject and development; how far was his precision a poetical precision; did he, in harmonising the language of prose and of verse, raise the one or lower the other?

The twelve volumes of Campoamor's collected poems contain *El Drama Universal*, a sort of epic in eight "days" and forty-seven scenes, written in heroic quatrains, and worthy, a Spanish critic assures us, of "an Ariosto of the soul"; *Colon*, a narrative poem in sixteen cantos, written in *ottava rima; El Licenciado Torralba*, a legendary poem in eight cantos, written in iambic verse of varying length; three series of *Pequeños Poemas*, each containing from ten to twelve narrative poems written in a similar form of verse; two series of *Doloras*, short lyrical poems, of which I have already quoted his own definition; a volume of *Humoradas*, containing some hundreds of epigrams; and two volumes of early work, brought together under the name of *Poesías y Fábulas*. Besides these, he wrote some plays, the admirable volume called *Poética Polémicas Literárias* and a contribution to metaphysics called *Lo Absoluto*. Of his long poems, only one is what Rossetti called "amusing," only *El Licenciado Torralba* has that vital energy which keeps a poem alive. With this exception we need consider only the three collections in which a single thing, a consistent "criticism of life," is attempted under different, but closely allied forms: the *Humoradas*, which are epigrams; the *Doloras*, which he defines as "dramatised *Humoradas*"; and the *Pequeños Poemas*, which he defines as "amplified *Doloras*."

Applied by a great poetical intellect, Campoamor's theories might have resulted in the most masterly of modern poems; but his intellect was ingenious rather than imaginative; his vivid human curiosity was concerned with life more after the manner of the novelist than of the poet; his dramas are often anecdotes; his insight is not so much wisdom as worldly wisdom. He "saw life steadily," but he saw it in little patches, commenting on facts with a smiling scepticism which has in it something of the positive spirit of the eighteenth century. Believing, as he tells us, that "what is most natural

87

Cities and Sea-Coasts and Islands.

in the world is the supernatural," he was apt to see the spiritual side of things, as the Spanish painters have mostly seen it, in a palpable detachment from the soil, garlanded in clouds. Concerned all his life with the moods and casuistries of love, he writes of women, not of woman, and ends, after all, in a reservation of judgment. Poetry, to him, was a kind of psychology, and that is why every lyric shaped itself naturally into what he called a drama. His whole interest was in life and the problems of life, in people and their doings, and in the reasons for what they do. Others, he tells us, may admire poetry which is descriptive, the delineation of external things, or rhetorical, a sonorous meditation over abstract things; all that he himself cares for are "those reverberations that light up the windings of the human heart and the horizons that lie on the other side of material life." Only, some imaginative energy being lacking, all this comes, for the most part, to be a kind of novelette in verse, in the *Pequeños Poemas*, a versified allegory in the *Doloras*, or an epigram in the *Humoradas*.

Can verse in which there is no ecstasy be poetry? There is no ecstasy in the verse of Campoamor; at the most a talking about ecstasy, as in some of the *Pequeños Poemas*, in which stories of passion are told with exquisite neatness, precision, sympathetic warmth; but the passion never cries out, never finds its own voice. Once only in his work do I find something like that cry, and it is in *El Licenciado Torralba*, the story of a kind of Faust,

Campoamor.

who, desiring love without unrest, makes for himself
an artificial woman ("la mujer más mujer de las
mujeres"), *Muliercula*, to whom he gives

> *El ánimo del bello paganismo,*
> *Que, siendo menos que alma, es más que vida.*

Torralba is arrested by the Inquisition as a necro-
mancer and Muliercula is burnt at the stake. I
have translated the description of her death:

> Midmost, as if the flame of the burning were
> A bed of love to her,
> *Muliercula*, with calm, unfrightened face,
> Not without beauty stood,
> And her meek attitude
> Had something of the tiger's natural grace.
> She suffers, yet, no less,
> Dying for him she loves, broods there,
> Within the burning air,
> Quiet as a bird within a wilderness.
> The wild beast's innocency all awake
> Enwraps her, and as she burns,
> The intermittent flaming of the stake
> To the poor fond foolish thing now turns
> Into a rapture, dying for his sake;
> And then, because the instinct in her sees
> This only to be had,
> Nothingness and its peace,
> For her last, surest end, utterly glad,
> With absolute heart and whole,
> That body without a soul,
> As if the bright flame brings
> Roses to be its bed,
> Dies, and so enters, dead
> Into the august majesty of things!

There, in that fantastic conception of "la belleza

natural perfecta" of woman, as the thinker, above all others, has desired to find her, I seem to discover the one passionate exception to Campoamor's never quite real men and women, the novelist's lay-figures of passion, about whom we are told so many interesting anecdotes. A witty story-teller, a sympathetic cynic, a transcendental positivist, he found the ways of the world the most amusing spectacle in nature, and for the most part his poems are little reflections of life seen as he saw it, with sharp, tolerant, worldly eyes. At his best, certainly most characteristic, when he is briefest, as in the *Humoradas*, he has returned, in these polished fragments, to the lapidary style of Latin poetry, reminding us at times of another Spaniard, Martial. Idea, clearness, symmetry, point, give to this kind of verse something of the hardness and glitter of a weapon, even when the intention is not satirical. With Campoamor the blade is tossed into the air and caught again, harmlessly, with all the address of an accomplished juggler. He plays with satire as he plays with sentiment, and, when he is most serious, will disguise the feeling with some ironical afterthought. Here are some of the *Humoradas*, in Spanish and English. I have translated them, as will be seen, quite literally, and I have tried to choose them from as many moods as I could:

> *Al mover tu abanico con gracejo.*
> *Quitas el polvo al corazón más viejo.*

> You wave your fan with such a graceful art,
> You brush the dust off from the oldest heart.

Campoamor.

Las niñas de las madres que amé tanto
Me besan ya como se besan á un santo.

The children of the mothers I loved, ah see,
They kiss me as though they kissed a saint in me!

Jamás mujer alguna
Ha salido del todo de la cuna.

No woman yet, since they were made all,
Has ever got quite outside of the cradle.

Prohibes tu amor con tus desdenes.
Sin frutos prohibidos no hay Edenes.

Let your consent with your disdain be hidden:
No Paradise whose fruit is not forbidden.

No le gusta el placer sin violencia,
Y por eso ya cree la desgraciada
Que ni es pasión, ni es nada,
El amor que no turba la conciencia.

She tastes not pleasure without strife,
And therefore, hapless one, she feels
That love's not good enough for life
Which hales not conscience by the heels.

Si es fácil una hermosa,
Voy y la dejo;
Si es difícil la cosa,
También me alejo,
Niñas, cuidad
De amar siempre con fácil
Dificultad.

If too easy she should be,
I, beholding, quit her;
If the thing's too hard for me,
Trying proves too bitter.
Girls, now see,
Best it is to love with easy
Difficulty.

Cities and Sea-Coasts and Islands.

Niegas que fuiste mi mejor amiga?
Bien, bien; lo callaré: nobleza obliga.

That you were my best friend, do you deny?
Well, well; noblesse oblige; then so will I.

Te he visto no sé donde, ni sé cuando.
Ah! sí; ya lo recuerdo, fué sonando.

Have I not seen you? Yes, but where and when?
Ah, I remember: I was dreaming then.

Te es infiel! y la quieres? No me extraña;
Yo adoro á la esperanza, aunque me engaña

She's faithless, and you love her? As you will:
Hope I adore, and hope is faithless still.

Vas cambiando de amor todos los años,
Mas no cambias jamás de desengaños.

You change your love each year; yet Love's commandment
Is, that you never change your disenchantment.

Por él la simetría es la belleza,
Aunque corté á las cosas la cabeza.

Beauty for him was symmetry, albeit
He sometimes cut the heads off things, to see it.

I will add three short pieces from the *Doloras:*

Shamed though I be, and weep for shame, 'tis true,
I loved not good what evil I love in you.

They part; years pass; they do not see
    Each other: after six or seven:
"Good Heaven! and is it really he?"
    "And is it really she? good Heaven!"

Campoamor.

THE SOUL FOR SALE

One day to Satan, Julio, flushed with wine:
  "Wilt buy my soul?"   "Of little worth is it."
"I do but ask one kiss, and it is thine."
  "Old sinner, hast thou parted with thy wit?"
"Wilt buy it?" "No." "But wherefore?" "It is mine."

In such work as this there is much of what the Spaniards call "salt": it stings healthily, it is sane, temperate, above all, ingenious; and the question as to whether or not it is poetry resolves itself into a question as to whether or not the verse of Martial, indeed Latin epigrammatic verse in general, is poetry. To the modern mind, brought up on romantic models, only Catullus is quite certainly or quite obviously a poet in his epigrams; and his appeal to us is as personal as the appeal of Villon. He does not generalise, he does not smile while he stabs; the passion of love or hate burns in him like a flame, setting the verse on fire. Martial writes for men of the world; he writes in order to comment on things; his form has the finish of a thing made to fulfil a purpose. Campoamor also writes out of a fruitful experience, not transfiguring life where he reflects it. If what he writes is not poetry, in our modern conception of the word, it has at least the beauty of adjustment to an end, of perfect fitness; and it reflects a temperament, not a great poetical temperament, but one to which human affairs were infinitely interesting, and their expression in art the one business of life.

1901.

93

A Spanish Poet : Núñez de Arce.

POETRY in Spain, when I wrote that article, was represented by two admired and popular poets, Ramón de Campoamor and Gaspar Núñez de Arce. The popularity of Campoamor may be inferred from the fact that cheap editions of his works, and cheap selections from them, are to be found everywhere in Spain; but in the case of Núñez de Arce it is possible to speak with greater precision. In the preface to a poem published in 1866 he states that no Spanish work has been reprinted, in this century, so many times in so short a space of time, as the collection of his poems; and that between 1879 and 1885 a hundred and three editions, varying in number from 500 to 2000, have appeared in Spain, and nearly a hundred more in America. It may be interesting to consider for a moment the position of so popular a poet, the reason of his popularity, and the degree to which he deserves that popularity.

Núñez de Arce is one of those many poets who expect to get credit for the excellent nature of their intentions, who do for the most part get credit for it, and who are genuinely surprised if it is pointed out that in poetry intention counts for nothing, apart from achievement. In the preface to *El Vértigo* he tells us that all the poems he has hitherto published are "tentatives in which I exercise my forces and assay my aptitude for the various kinds

94

of contemporary poetry." Thus, *La Última Lamentación de Lord Byron* is an attempt to obtain the epical tone in relation to a subject of our own times; the *Idilio* is an attempt to write domestic poetry; *La Selva Oscura* is an attempt to express thought under a symbolical form; *La Visión de Fray Martin* is an attempt to unite, "under a grave and severe form, the fantastic and the supernatural with the real and the transcendent." In the *Gritos del Combate* he develops a whole theory of the mission of art, in order to justify a book of political poems; and in a lecture on contemporary poetry, reprinted in the same volume, apologises for occupying himself with æsthetic questions at a time when grave social problems are troubling the minds of men.

This preoccupation with politics, morals, and other problems more suited to prose than poetry, is characteristic of Spain, where it has always been so rare for a man of letters to be merely a man of letters, and where poets have so often been political leaders as well. Núñez de Arce was appointed governor of the province of Barcelona at the time of the revolution of 1868; he has held other public posts at intervals during his life; and it is evident that he looks at least as seriously upon what he conceives to have been his services to his country, as upon the poems which he has written with such well-defined intentions of "fulfilling those sacred duties, and carrying on that moralising mission," which he attributes to poetry. Nowhere, not even

95

Cities and Sea-Coasts and Islands.

in England, are these "serious" views received with more favour than in Spain; and a poet with a mission, and with distinctly explained ambitions, has an audience always awaiting him.

Nor has he only an audience : the critics are on his side. Núñez de Arce is a typical instance of precisely the kind of writer who is certain of an indulgent treatment at the hands of the critics. There is so little to blame; yes, so little either to blame or to praise. Here is a poet who takes himself seriously, who produces good, careful, thoughtful work, here impressive by its rhetoric, there by its simplicity, always refined, always earnest in its declamation, without vulgarity, or extravagance, or artificiality, so often the faults of Spanish poetry; he can write vigorous narrative, of more than one kind, as in *Raimundo Lulio* and *La Pesca;* he can be romantic without being absurd, as in *La Visión de Fray Martin;* he can write verse which is technically correct, dignified, accomplished : is there not some excuse for mistaking so apparently admirable a result for poetry? And yet what avail all the negative virtues, and all the taste in the world, in the absence of the poetic impulse, poetic energy, the soul and body at once of poetry? It is like discussing the degree to which a man who is certainly not alive is dead. Núñez de Arce has no intense inner life, crying out for expression; his emotion is never personal, but generalised; he has no vision, only an outlook. There is no singing note in his voice; every line is

Núñez de Arce.

intellectually realised, line follows line as duly as in an argument; but the exquisite shock or the more exquisite peace of poetry is in none of them. To be thoughtful is after all so slight a merit in a poet, unless the thought is of some rare or subtle kind, a thoughtfulness of the instincts rather than of the reason. Let the quality of his thought be tested by a glance at his epithets. In *La Última Lamentación de Lord Byron* he invokes Greece: "Greece, immortal Greece! Loving mother of heroes and geniuses! Calm fount of rich inspiration! Fruitful spouse of Art! Eternal light of the mind!" Where, in these epithets, is that "continual slight novelty" which poetical style requires if it is to be poetry?

And even his patriotic feeling, strong and sincere as it is, is not of a fine poetical quality; it is not to be compared with the patriotic feeling of Quintana, a poet whom he honours. Quintana, celebrating the defeat of Trafalgar, could say: "Para el pueblo magnanimo no hay suerte." But Núñez de Arce, narrowly political, can but see "sad Spain, our mother Spain, bleeding to death in the mud of the street," because a Senate is Republican or not Republican. He discusses, he does not sing; and for discussion poetry has no place. And his discussion is a declamatory discussion, as in the poem called *París*, where a Bourgeois and a Demagogue of 1871 toss to and fro the arguments for and against Anarchy, and are both solemnly rebuked by the poet at the end of the poem. His verse is full of an

97

Cities and Sea-Coasts and Islands.

uninspired discontent, the discontent of an orator, not the passionate or ecstatic discontent of the poet:

Hijo del siglo, in vano me resiste a su impiedad,

he tells us, with a sort of melancholy pride in representing, as it seems to him, so faithfully, a century whose materialising tendencies he so sincerely deplores. *La Duda* (*Doubt*) is one of his most popular poems, read with applause on the occasion of the "Juegos Florales" of the Catalan poets in 1868. "In this age of sarcasm and doubt, there is but one muse," he tells us; "the blind, implacable, brutal muse of analysis, that, armed with the arid scalpel, at every step precipitates us into the abyss, or brings us to the shores of annihilation." And it is always of this muse that he is uneasily conscious, unwilling to follow, and unable to turn aside. It has been part of his aim to write, not merely poetry, but modern poetry. But he comes to the task a moralist, a disbeliever in his own age, whose influence he feels as a weight rather than as an inspiration; and he brings no new form, he adds no flexibility to an old form. Himself no new force, he has had the misfortune to be born in a country lacking in original forces. For a Spanish poet of to-day there is no environment, no helpful tradition. He looks back on a literature in which there is not a single great or even remarkable poet since Calderon. He has been brought up on Espronceda, Quintana, Zorrilla; which is as if an English poet of our days had no choice of models but a lesser Byron, a lesser Cowper, and a lesser

Núñez de Arce.

Longfellow. He looks around him, and discovers no guiding light in other countries. In his *Discourse on Contemporary Poetry*, delivered in 1887, Núñez de Arce gives his opinion of English, French, Italian, and Russian poets, with a significant preference for English poets, and among them for Tennyson, and a not less significant horror at what seems to him the shamelessness and impiety of poetry in France. But he is not content with even English poetry. "Swinburne," he tells us, "sometimes sings as Nero and Caligula would have sung if they had been poets;" and he groups together *Atalanta in Calydon* and *Anactoria* as poems in which "impure passion, Pagan sensuality, erotic extravagance, acquire monstrous proportions, bellowing like wild beasts hungering for living flesh." Of Browning he has little to say, except "que no siento por él admiración alguna." Richepin he looks upon as one of the typical poets of France, and he repeats the usual vague phrases about the Decadent School, without naming a single writer, and with a perfectly ingenuous lack of comprehension. The conclusion he brings back from his survey is that "humanity has lost its wings, and walks along unknown ways, not knowing whither it is going." And his final expression of hope in a regeneration of poetry, and of the world through poetry, is but a phrase of the rhetoric of despair.

To all this there is but one answer, and the answer is briefly given in a single line of Sidney:

Fool, said my muse to me, look in thine heart and write.

99

Moorish Secrets in Spain.

THE Moors, when they were driven out of Spain, left behind them, as if for some stealthy purpose, many of their secrets. Wherever you walk, in the south of Spain, you will come upon mosques, palaces, towers, gateways, which they built to perpetuate themselves in a strange land, and you will find in ruined fragments upon hills and windowless white houses under palm trees both actual remains and persistent followings of their cool, secluded way of building, meant for even fiercer skies and an even more reticent indoor life. Often, as in the Giralda by the side of the Gothic cathedral at Seville and in the mosque into which a Christian church has been built at Cordova, you can see at one glance the conflict or the contrast of two religions, of two theories of the universe. The mosque has no solemnity, no mystery; it is a place of closed-in silence, shut in even from the sky, in a paradise of abstract art. I think of the plumage of tropical birds, the waving of palms, a darting fugue on the clavichord, to figure to myself the particular, after all unique, kind of fascination which the masterpieces of Arab architecture convey to one. Nothing so brilliant was ever imagined by a Gothic carver, so full of light, so airy, so serpentine in swiftness. A mosque, it seems to one as one walks among its pillars, is not a church at all, but rather a city, the arcades and alcoves of a city of fiery people, in whom strength runs all to delicacy. The Arabs did not build high, they

built wide; and they sent their imagination out
like arrows, hither and thither, in a flight at once
random and mathematical. How singular a contrast, is there not, with Gothic building, whose
broad base is set for a steady heavenward ascension,
yet whose caprices, in every entertainment to which
line lends itself, are all so material and of the earth!
And so it seems to me that the architecture of the
mosque is after all a more immaterial worship of
the idea of God than any Christian architecture.
Here there is invention of pattern, into which no
natural object is ever allowed to intrude, the true
art for art's sake, pure idea, mathematics, invention
in the abstract; for it is the work of an imagination
intoxicated with itself, finding beginning and end
in its own formally beautiful working out, without
relation to nature or humanity. Christianity has
never accepted this idea, indeed could not; it has
always distrusted pure beauty, when that beauty
has not been visibly chained to a moral. Hence it
has built its Bibles in stone, the Gothic cathedrals.
But Islam, for which God has never put on humanity,
worships an immaterial God in beautiful pattern,
which it applies equally to its daily, its choicer
daily uses. Is not this more truly the worship of
the invisible and the unimaginable, of what is highest
in the idea of God, than the Christian worship which
we see under the same roof, with its divine images
tortured with sorrow, ungracious with suffering,
which do but drag down the mind from pure contemplation, from the eternal idea to its human

manifestation in time? That, at all events, is one
of the secrets of the Moors.

And they have left other secrets. You cannot
walk through a little town in the south of Spain
without hearing a strange sound, between crying
and chanting, which wanders out to you from
behind barred windows and from among the tinkling bells of the mules. The Malagueña, they call
this kind of singing; but it has no more to do with
Malaga than the mosque at Cordova has to do
with the soil on which it stands. It is as Eastern
as the music of tom-toms and gongs, and, like
Eastern music, it is music before rhythm, music
which comes down to us untouched by the invention
of the modern scale, from an antiquity out of which
plain-chant is a first step towards modern harmony.
And this Moorish music is, like Moorish architecture, an arabesque. It avoids definite form just
as the lines in stone avoid definite form, it has the
same endlessness, motion without beginning or
end, turning upon itself in a kind of infinitely varied
monotony. The fioriture of the voice are like
those coils which often spring from a central point
of ornament, to twist outward, as in a particular
piece of very delicate work in the first mihrab in
the mosque at Cordova. In both, ensemble is
everything, and everything is pattern. There is
the same avoidance of emphasis, the same continuance on one level; no special part starts out for
separate notice, as in Gothic architecture or Western
music. But the passion of this music is like no

102

other passion; fierce, immoderate, sustained, it is like the crying of a wild beast in suffering, and it thrills one precisely because it seems to be so far from humanity, so inexplicable, so deeply rooted in the animal of which we are but one species.

Moorish music is inarticulate, and so it brings a wild relief which no articulate music could ever bring. It is the voice of uncivilised people who have the desires and sorrows common to every living being, and an unconsciousness of their meaning which is, after all, what we come back to after having searched through many meanings. It is sad, not because of personal sorrow, but because of all the sorrow there is, and always has been, in the world. The eyes of Spanish women have something of the same fierce melancholy, and with as little personal meaning. It is a music which has not yet lost companionship with the voice of the wind, the voice of the sea, the voices of the forest. It has never accepted order and become art; it remains chaotic, elemental, a part of nature trying to speak.

The monotony of this music (a few repeated notes only of the guitar accompanying it when there is any accompaniment to the voice) gives it much of its singular effect on the nerves. It speaks directly to the spine, sending an unaccountable shiver through one; without racking the heart or the brain, after the manner of most pathos, even in sound. The words, it is true, are generally sombre, a desperate outcry; but the words of the three or four lines which go to make up a song

103

Cities and Sea-Coasts and Islands.

are repeated over and over, in varying order, lingering out an incalculable time, so that the bare meaning is changed into something of a pattern, like the outlines of a flower in Moorish architecture. Yes, abstract as their architecture, their music has none of the direct, superficially human appeal which pathetic Western music has. These songs are largely improvisations, and a singer will weave almost any web of music about almost any fragment of verse: whether the words wail because Spain has lost Cuba or because a lover has lost his beloved, it is all the same; it all comes from the same deep, fiery place in the soil.

Singing and dancing in Spain are as the right hand and the left; and the same airs, throbbing on a guitar, guide the most characteristic kind of dancing. Here the meaning is more explicit; like the pantomime of all Eastern dancing, like the shapeless jog-trot of the Soudanese, which you can see at Earl's Court, like the undisguised mimicry of the women in the Rue du Caire at the last Paris Exhibition, it is wholly sexual. But in the dancing, inherited from the Moors, which the gipsies have perfected in Spain, there is far more subtlety, delicacy, and real art than in the franker posturing of Egypt and Arabia. It is the most elaborate dancing in the world, and, like the music, it has an abstract quality which saves it from ever, for a moment, becoming vulgar. As I have watched a Gitana dancing in Seville, I have thought of the sacred dances which in most religions have given

Moorish Secrets in Spain.

a perfectly solemn and collected symbolism to the creative forces of the world. Hieratic, not perverse, centred upon the central fact of existence; moving gravely, without frivolity, in a sense without passion, so deeply is the passion rooted in the nature of things; the dance coils round upon itself as the trails of music and the trails in stone coil round upon themselves. It is another secret of the Moors, and must remain as mysterious to us as those other secrets, until we have come a little closer than we have yet come to the immaterial wisdom of the East.

Autumn, 1899.

Valencia.

PAST the deserts, orange groves, and watered gardens, winding up and down between low jagged hills and the sea, which, against the red soil about Cabañal and the harbour, is often blood-red, suddenly, turning inland, we are in Valencia. It was dark when I reached it, and I have never seen, except point by point in its midst, this city of tall towers and blue domes. I have followed all its windings, and on every side it dwindles out to dusty and cheerless boulevards, a half-dry river-bed, gardens with palms and all manner of slim, feathery trees, thirsty for lack of rain, and grey with dust. It is a maze of tall and narrow streets, in which houses of irregular height and size, and colour and style, follow one another with a uniform profusion of balconies, all with their shutters or their *persianas;* here and there four or five streets debouch into an oddly shaped square, for the most part a mere space between street and street, and for the most part with a church at one of its corners. There are whole streets of shops, every shop with its little oval signboard, painted with the image of a saint; every shop open to the street, and hung outside with sashes, and plaids, and lengths of cloth and velvet, and shawls, and blankets, and every kind of long, bright stuff. And, stagnant amidst the constant flowing of busy life, to and fro in these vivid, narrow streets, a beggar stands at every crossing; men with a horrible absence of hands, men without legs, men doubled up, and

Valencia.

twisted into strange shapes, hopping like frogs, blind men, men sitting against the wall with cloaks drawn over their faces, old men tottering with age, women carrying sick children, or with children running beside them with little tin plates in their hands.

Valencia is both old and new, and much in it seems to be at once old and new. The people are busy, thriving, but they work with their hands, not with machinery, and they work almost in the open air, in shops laid open like Eastern bazaars, in great doorways, where whole families assemble with their chairs, or sitting on balconies, in the Spanish fashion, with their backs to the street. The women pass, bare-headed, in their bright clothes, on their tiny feet, carrying pitchers to the fountain, and pitchers of beautiful ancient form, like two-handed amphoræ. They pass, dressed in black, with their black mantillas and their fans, on their way to the churches, to which they are always going, and from which they are always coming. And in the men's handkerchiefs, twisted into a turban, with a hanging tail; in many of the faces, in which brown blackens to so dark a shade; in fingers and finger-nails, stained like a negro's, I see the Moors, still unconquered in Spain.

And the colour! I have never seen so much colour in any streets before, except indeed in the streets of Moscow, where it hurts. Here it is bright, moving, not insistent, and clothing gay life. I like to walk in the market-place on a sunny

107

morning, among those white stalls, set up with coverings like sails, at which brown women sit in their comfortable chairs, laughing, calling to one another, fanning the fruit to keep off the cloud of flies and mosquitos. There is a ceaseless noise, passing, sound of voices; bright dresses, shawls, aprons throng the pavement and the roadway; every one, as people do in Spain, is hurrying leisurely; they are at once serious and good-humoured, as Spanish people are. And this coloured crowd is moving under the shadow of the Lonja, with its delicate fifteenth-century Gothic (still, as naturally as ever, the Exchange), and before the barbaric rococo of the church of Los Santos Juanes, in the one spacious square of Valencia, where, in the days of the Cid, tournaments were held, and men have been burned alive.

This living on of the Middle Ages, in a busy town, into the present, came home to me with singular force one Thursday morning as I went to the Cathedral Square to see the Tribunal of the Waters. Outside the Apostles' Door an iron railing had been set up on the broad pavement, and, within the railing, an old-fashioned sofa, semicircular in form, had been placed; and at half-past eleven six old men, peasants, took their seats, bare-headed, in their peasants' blouses. Then two peasants came forward, entered the enclosure, and each stated his case briefly. The case was heard, discussed, and decided in five minutes. The six old men sat there leaning forward on their sticks, listening attentively, for the most part saying nothing, tacitly accepting the judgment of their president, a keen-faced, unhesitating man, who sat with his head bent, and his eyes raised scrutinisingly, never moving from the face of the man before him. His decision has the force of law, and this tribunal, which, since the time of the Moors, has sat here every Thursday at half-past eleven to decide all questions relating to the watering of the lands, is a remnant of mediæval democracy, peasants judging peasants, which is not the least surprising of popular survivals.

Another morning I seemed to myself more than ever in the Middle Ages, as I attended a Latin discussion in the cathedral, when D. Tariny Rafael Torres propounded the thesis that three things are needed for a perfect repentance: *oris confessio, cordis contritio, atque operis satisfactio*, and the Sres. Martinez and Fuset disputed the thesis. Against the entrance to the choir, over which hung a lighted lamp, a carpet had been laid, on which was placed a row of crimson-covered arm-chairs and a table covered with crimson cloth. Opposite, immediately against the door of the principal entrance, a movable pulpit had been set up, also hung with crimson, and standing on a high wooden frame, to which steps led at the back. On both sides were benches for the audience. Six church dignitaries, in their crimson and ermine robes, sat on the seats at the table, one or two others at the side, and the disputants on an ancient leather-covered settle on

the right of the pulpit. The orator was led in with
ceremony. He spoke, seated, for exactly an hour.
After he had spoken, the younger of the two disputants, a man with the face of an intellectual
fighter, rose with his first *contra*. He spoke rapidly,
almost disdainfully, with a suppressed smile, as
he proposed his difficult questions. I left after
nearly two hours, while the older of the two
disputants was proposing his objections. I found
Latin surprisingly like Spanish, when pronounced
with a Spanish accent, the Spanish lisp and gutturals:
nunquam, for instance, sounding like the Spanish
nunca, *etiam* like *ethiam*. And the audience, that,
too, reminded me of what those audiences must
have been that flocked to hear the Schoolmen. On
and around the benches, in a dense mass on each
side, were priests and students, a certain number
of men who had probably once been students, and
then boys, old men, women, beggars — people who
certainly could not understand a word that was
said, but gazing, and apparently listening, with
rapt attention, as if to a strange religious service,
quite out of the usual course, which it was partly
curious and partly pious to attend. One old
woman, not far from me, knelt.

The churches of Valencia, so numerous, and
filled during all the hours of service with so constant
a devotion, are of but moderate value architecturally,
apart from the curiosity of their structure, in such
churches as San Andrés and San Nicolás, where
the original form of the mosques, out of which

they have been built, still persists, almost unaltered. Many churches, once Gothic, have been spoiled out of recognition; plaster and whitewash and gold paint have been at work on almost every interior; and the few good pictures which might be seen, the Ribaltas, Juanes, an interesting Goya, are put into dark corners, where it is impossible to see them properly. The Cathedral itself, built on the site of a mosque, and seen at its best in the bell-tower and cimborio, which rise very effectively against different aspects of the sky, has suffered restoration, and its principal entrance is now tawdry with meaningless ornament. The one satisfying piece of Gothic here is in none of the churches, but in the Lonja, with its pillars spiring to the roof and branching out into stone palm trees, with a really broad effect of delicacy. Renaissance architecture is but just seen in the audiencia; and, in the palace on which I am looking out as I write, a terrible example of eighteenth-century barocco, a very masterpiece of the art of heaping up the unnecessary. The river of Valencia, the Turia, which, strictly speaking, scarcely exists, is to me almost the most fascinating thing here, framing in the picture I make for myself of this intricate place, with an effect that pleases me. The river banks, with their stone quays, are wide enough for the Seine, and the Turia is a thread of water lost in the sand. The dry river-bed is a mass of brown sand, like the seashore; trees grow on each side and grass about the trees; the horse-market

Cities and Sea-Coasts and Islands.

is held here in the morning, carts pass to and fro, cattle lie there on heaped straw, soldiers gallop over it on their horses, black sheep wander along it in a fantastic dark crowd, the dust rising whitely from under their little hoofs. And there are moments when the thin stream, flowing in and out among the sand, touches all these colours with an exquisite light, drawing into itself the green of the trees, and shining daintily amidst the dust. In such moments one seems to see Africa, the desert and the oasis.

Under a stormy sky the river-bed has a wild and savage aspect, its brown sand reddening under the dark clouds, droves of black cattle roaming over it, the wind stirring in the leaves of the trees; and one night I saw across it one of the most original sunsets I had ever seen; a sunset in brown. Standing on the bridge next beyond the Moorish "Bridge of the Law" and looking towards the Gate of Serranos, with its fourteenth-century battlements, every line distinct against a rim of pale green sky, I saw the clouds heaped above them in great loose masses of brown, nothing but shades of brown, and every shade of brown. It was as if the light smouldered, as if an inner flame scorched the white clouds, as flame scorches paper, until it shrivels into an angry, crackling brown. Under these loose masses of brown cloud the battlemented gate, the tall houses, a square and narrow tower which rose beyond them, darkened to exactly the same colour in shadow; and all but the upper part
112

vanished away into complete darkness, which extended outwards over the trees on the quay and over a part of the dry river-bed, coming suddenly to an end just before the water began. The thin stream was coloured a deep purple, where the reflection of the clouds fell right upon it; and higher up, where a foot-bridge crossed the river, reversed shadows walked in greenish water, step for step with the passers on the bridge. It was long before the light faded out of the clouds, which sank to a paler and paler yellow; and I stood there thrilled with admiration of those violent and daring harmonies, which seemed to carry Nature beyond her usual scheme of colour, in what I could not help almost hearing as the surge of a Wagnerian orchestra.

Winter, 1898.

Tarragona.

SEEN from the sea, Tarragona is a cluster of grey houses, full of windows, on a hill rising steeply from the shore; and the grey houses climb to a yellow point, the Cathedral. At the foot of the hill the black line of railway crosses a strip of ruinous land, from which the abrupt rock goes up to the Paseo de Santa Clara; and, leaning there over the railings, one looks down on that strip of ruinous land, whitened harshly by the great open square of the prison, whenever one looks seawards.

And, indeed, all Tarragona is expressed in those two words, ruins and the sea. Whichever way one follows it, it ends in half-hewn rock, and in a new aspect of the sea, and it is built out of the ruins of a Roman colony. The Roman walls themselves, of which such considerable fragments remain, rise on the foundations of a Cyclopean wall, built of vast unhewn masses of stone; the Cathedral stands on the site of a Moorish mosque; a public square, lined with houses, the Plaza de Fuente, still keeps the form of the Roman circus. Most of the houses in the old town are made out of the ruins of Roman houses, modern windows break out in solid Roman walls, left to end where ruin left them to end; there are Roman fountains in the squares, Roman tombstones are built into the walls of the Archbishop's palace, fragments of triumphal arches are set into the walls about Roman gateways; the "Tower of Charles V." comes up from the tiled roof of the Arsenal, and "Pilate's Tower," once part of the Palace of Augustus, is a prison. And out of all these ruins of great things there has come, for the most part, only something itself dilapidated, to which the ruins lend no splendour. They exist, but half themselves, as if unwillingly made a part of the stagnant life about them, unwillingly closing in the coloured movement of markets, the rapid, short steps of Spanish soldiers. They have seen narrow streets come up in their midst, twisting between them, winding up and down steps, and around corners, and jutting out into irregular squares and odd triangles; doorways, windows, busy iron balconies, flat roofs, the whole idly active Spanish life open to the street, or disappearing behind green *persianas;* and they see the Spaniards still quarrying about them, restless, and leaving their impoverished, fragmentary city still unfinished.

Yet Tarragona has its one marvel, the Cathedral, as the Cathedral has itself its marvel, the cloisters. Its façade, coloured the brown of the earth, and warmed with a tinge of almost ruddy gold, fills the whole space of sky at the end of the steep street by which one approaches it, whose narrow lines indeed cut into the great rose-window, and the arched Gothic portal, in which the Virgin and Child stand in the midst of prophets and apostles, carved simply and devoutly by the thirteenth-century sculptor, who has set over them a Last Judgment in relief, crowded with small, indistinguishable dead, while the great saints — each saint distinct with his written history beside him — rise visibly from their coffins,

and two flying angels blow long trumpets above
their heads. Walking round it, by ways which
lose and find it again, we see the long, irregular,
late Romanesque structure, like house added to
house, with its low octagonal turret, exactly the
deep, rich colour of plum pudding. Inside, the
church, with less of that properly Spanish mystery
which we find in the Cathedral at Barcelona, for
example, has an ample dignity, and at night, before
the altar candles are lit, becomes splendid in shadow.
In its detail, in the gradual accumulation of structure
and ornament, the statues of the retablo, the windows,
doorways, columns, it is in itself an almost complete
historical museum of Spanish art in stone. But it
is, after all, in the cloisters that one cares chiefly to
linger. To walk there, looking between the slim
white columns, with their history of the Bible or
of the world carved minutely and with mediæval
humour on the capitals; looking past them into
that inner court where a garden of trees and shrubs
blossoms with many greens — the green of palm, of
cypress, of oleander; in that coolness under the
sunshine visible upon the foliage, is to surrender
oneself to an enchanted peace. Here Tarragona at
least still sleeps perfectly, in that permanent dream
of the Middle Ages.

Ruins and the sea, I have said, make up most of
Tarragona; and the sea here has some particular
charm of its own, new to me, after all I have seen
of the sea. A wide rambla, planted with trees,
where, in the afternoon, every one walks, leads to

116

that iron railing at the cliff's edge from which, but for the pedestal of a modern statue, one could look right through the new town to the open country and the vine-covered hills of the Priorato. To the right is the harbour, with its long curving mole; to the left, a little neck of land runs out into the sea, making a kind of tiny bay; in front, the unlimited sea. At night the gaslight mole becomes a horseshoe with golden nails, the little neck of land might be the first glimpse of a desert island. Something in the point from which one looks down on it, the sense of being almost theatrically perched on the edge of a great balcony, helps, no doubt, to make one look on this view of the sea as a great spectacle, arranged against a magnificent moving background of clouds. Certainly I never saw the clouds dispose themselves with so conscious an air of being scenery, a background, as about that vast plain of blue sea, pillaring a kind of fleecy dome over it. And the strip of black ruinous land made its own line of footlights, dark-coloured for contrast with that watery, and variable, and gentle brilliance.

It is certain that the expressive quality of Tarragona comes out, not only in the union, but in the emphatic contrast, of sea and ruins. And that particular harsh spot on the shore, the great prison, "El Milagro," has its own singular value in the composition. One looks down, from those railings, on the whole inner court, open to the sky, and painted sky-blue, where a line of prisoners sits in the sun, wearing broad-brimmed straw hats, rope-making,

117

Cities and Sea-Coasts and Islands.

and the others stroll about, drink out of earthen pitchers, or sit on great stones, all over the court, or with their backs against the doors of the prison-chapel. They have hung up their coats on nails in the wall, and they lounge there in their shirt-sleeves, and white sandal-shoes, exactly as they would lounge in their own doorways. Outside the high white walls, soldiers, with fixed bayonets, stand on guard; and at night, after the prison is silent behind its grated windows, one hears their long cry of *Alerta* echoing other voices from up the hill. And that centre of lives that have come to grief, all that pent-up violence, is set there between the city and the sea, for idle people to look down upon all day; and all day long, beggars, or children, or casual passers, stand leaning over those railings, staring down into the prison-yard. As many people, I think, look at the prison as at the sea; some of them cannot see the sea for the prison, and their eyes stop there on the way. And for every one who looks at the sea there is the prison thrusting itself between one's sight and the sea, more desolate than any ruin, a wicked spot which one cannot wipe off from the earth.

Winter, 1898.

Cordova.

SEEN from the further end of the Moorish bridge by the Calahorra, where the road starts to Seville, Cordova is a long brown line between the red river and the purple hills, an irregular, ruinous line, following the windings of the river, and rising to the yellow battlements and great middle bulk of the cathedral. It goes up sheer from the river-side, above a broken wall, and in a huddle of mean houses, with so lamentably picturesque an air that no one would expect to find, inside that rough exterior, such neat, clean, shining streets, kept, even in the poorest quarters, with so admirable a care, and so bright with flowers and foliage, in patios and on upper balconies. From the bridge one sees the Moorish mills, rising yellow out of the yellow water, and, all day long, there is a slow procession along it of mules and donkeys, with their red saddles, carrying their burdens, and sometimes men heavily draped in great blanket-cloaks. Cross the city, and come out on the Paseo de la Victoria, open to the Sierra Morena, and you are in an immense village-green with red and white houses on one side, and black wooded hills on every other side; the trees, when I saw it for the first time at the beginning of winter, already shivering, and the watchers sitting on their chairs with their cloaks across their faces.

All Cordova seems to exist for its one treasure, the mosque, and to exist for it in a kind of remembrance; it is white, sad, delicately romantic, set in the midst of a strange, luxuriant country, under the

Cities and Sea-Coasts and Islands.

hills, and beside the broad Guadalquivir, which, seen at sunset from the Ribera, flows with so fantastic a violence down its shallow weirs, between the mills and beneath the arches of the Moors. The streets are narrow and roughly paved, and they turn on themselves like a maze, around blank walls, past houses with barred windows and open doors, through which one sees a flowery patio, and by little irregular squares, in which the grass is sometimes growing between the stones, and outside the doors of great shapeless churches, mounting and descending steeply, from the river-bank to the lanes and meadows beyond the city walls. Turn and turn long enough through the white solitude of these narrow streets, and you come on the dim arcades and tall houses of the market-place, and on alleys of shops and bazaars, bright with coloured things, crimson umbrellas, such as every one carries here, cloaks lined with crimson velvet, soft brown leather, shining silver-work. The market is like a fair; worthless, picturesque lumber is heaped all over the ground, and upon stalls, and in dark shops like caves: steel and iron and leather goods, vivid crockery-ware, roughly burnt into queer, startling patterns, old clothes, cheap bright handkerchiefs and scarves. Passing out through the market-place, one comes upon sleepier streets, dwindling into the suburbs; grass grows down the whole length of the street, and the men and women sit in the middle of the road in their chairs, the children, more solemnly, in their little chairs. Vehicles pass seldom, and only through certain streets, where a board tells them it is possible to pass; but mules and donkeys are always to be seen, in long tinkling lines, nodding their wise little heads, as they go on their own way by themselves. At night Cordova sleeps early; a few central streets are still busy with people, but the rest are all deserted, the houses look empty, there is an almost oppressive silence. Only, here and there, as one passes heedlessly along a quiet street, one comes suddenly upon a cloaked figure, with a broad-brimmed hat, leaning against the bars of a window, and one may catch, through the bars, a glimpse of a vivid face, dark hair, and a rose (an artificial rose) in the hair. Not in any part of Spain have I seen the traditional Spanish love-making, the cloak and hat at the barred window, so frankly and so delightfully on view. It brings a touch of genuine romance, which it is almost difficult for those who know comic opera better than the countries in which life is still, in its way, a serious travesty, to take quite seriously. Lovers' faces, on each side of the bars of a window, at night, in a narrow street of white houses: that, after all, and not even the miraculous mosque, may perhaps be the most vivid recollection that one brings away with one from Cordova.

Winter, 1898.

Montserrat.

LIKE one not yet awakened from a dream I seemed to myself while I was still in Montserrat; and now, having left it, I seem to have awakened from the dream. One of those few exquisite, impossible places which exist, properly, only in our recollection of them, Montserrat is still that place of refuge which our dreams are; and is it not itself a dream of the Middle Ages, Monsalvat, the castle of the Holy Graal, which men have believed to be not in the world, and to contain something not of the world, seeing it poised so near heaven, among so nearly inaccessible rocks, in the lonely hollow of a great plain? Solidly based on the fifteen miles which encircle it, the mountain goes up suddenly, in terrace after terrace, with a sort of ardent vigour, close-pressed columns of rock springing step by step higher into the air, pausing for a moment where the Monastery stands on its narrow ledge, 2900 feet high, and then going on for another thousand feet, ending in great naked fingers of rock which point to the sky. The tall, bare buildings of the monastery are built of yellow stone, and, seen from a distance, seem to become almost a part of the mountain itself, in which the grey stone is ruddy-hearted, like the colour of the soil at its feet. And as the monastery seems to become almost a part of the mountain, so the rock itself takes the aspect of a castle, a palace; especially at night, when one seems to look up at actual towers overtopping the tall buildings. And from this narrow ledge between

122

heaven and earth, a mere foothold on a great rock, one looks up only at sheer peaks, and down only into veiled chasms, or over mountainous walls to a great plain, ridged as if the naked ribs of the earth were laid bare, the red and grey soil spotted dark with trees, here and there whitened with houses, furrowed by a yellow river, the white line of roads barely visible, man's presence only marked by here and there a little travelling smoke, disappearing into the earth, insect-like, or, insect-like, crawling black on its surface.

With all its vastness, abruptness, and fantastic energy, Montserrat is never savage; it is always forming naturally into beautiful, unexpected shapes, miracles of form, by a sort of natural genius in it for formal expression. And this form is never violent, is always subtly rounded, even when it is bare grey rocks; and often breaks out deliciously into verdure, which is the ornament on form. There is something in it, indeed, at times, of the highest kind of grotesque, pointing fingers, rocks which have grown almost human; but in all this there is nothing trivial, for here the grotesque becomes for once a new, powerful kind of beauty. From the height of S. Jeronimo, the highest point of the mountain, a whole army of beckoning and threatening rocks comes up about one, climbing gigantically, among sheer precipices, tumultuously, in that place of great echoes. But they have the beauty of wild things, of those animals which are only half uncouth until man has tamed them, and shut them up in the awkwardness of prisoners. And they are solemnised too, by the visible height to which they have climbed into the serene air, out of a plain that rolls away, curve on curve, grey and ruddy, to the snow of the Pyrenees, and the broad, glittering, milkwhite line of the Mediterranean.

But the beauty of Montserrat lies in no detail, can be explained by no analysis: it is the beauty of a conscious soul, exquisite, heroic, sacred, ancient, in the midst of the immemorable peace, dignity, and endurance of high mountains. Without the monastery, the pilgrims, the worship of the Virgin, the chanting of the monks and of the *Escolania* (that school of ecclesiastical music which has existed here since the twelfth century), Montserrat would be a strange, beautiful thing indeed, a piece of true picturesque, but no more, not the unique thing that it is. Quite out of the world, singularly alone, one is in the presence of a great devotion; and in the pilgrims who come here, humble people with the grave and friendly gaiety of the Spaniard I found the only perfectly sympathetic company I have ever found about me in travelling. Life is reduced to its extreme simplicity: the white-washed cell, the attendance on oneself, the day marked only by one's wanderings over the mountain, or by the hours of worship. I went one morning to the "visitation of the Virgin," when the dark image is unveiled for the kisses of the pilgrims; and I saw in the sacristy the innumerable votive offerings hanging on the walls, moulded limbs, naïve (indeed hideous)

124

pictures representing the dangers from which the Virgin had saved her faithful, little jackets of children who had been cured from sickness, great plaits of hair which women had cut off and hung there, in thankfulness for the saving of a husband. And I went every evening to the singing of the *Salves* at the *Ave Maria*, ending the daylight with that admirable chanting, in those deep, abstract voices of the monks, and with that sense of divine things, that repose, which always deepened or heightened in me, as I came out through the cloisters into the court of the plane trees, and looked up at the vast, obscure, mysteriously impending heights, gulfing downwards into unseen depths, with a kind of grateful wonder, as if all one's dreams had come true.

And this sense of natural felicity, moved to astonishment, to the absoluteness of delight in being where one is, grew upon me during those three days of my visit, forming a new kind of sentiment, which I had never felt before, and which modified itself gently during the hours of the day, from the blitheness of the morning climb, through the contented acceptance of the afternoon sunshine, to that placid but solemn ending. For once, I was perfectly happy, and with that element of strangeness in my happiness without which I cannot conceive happiness.

I have always held that it is unwise to ask of any perfect thing duration as well as existence. Supreme happiness, if it could be continued indefinitely, would in time, without losing its essence, lose its supremacy, which exists only by contrast. When I have seen a face, a landscape, an aspect of the sky, pass for a moment into a sort of crisis, in which it attained the perfect expression of itself, I have always turned away rapidly, closing my eyelids on the picture, which I dread to see fade or blur before me. I would obtain from things, as from people, only their best; and I hold it to be not only wisdom towards oneself, but a point of honour towards them. Therefore, intending as I did to make a long stay in Montserrat, and having provided myself, in case of difficulty, with a letter to the Abbot, I left, without regret, at the end of the traditional three days, certain that I could get nothing more poignant in its happiness than what those three days had given me, and that by leaving at the moment of perfection I was preserving for myself an incomparable memory, which would always rise for me, out of the plain of ordinary days, like the mountain itself, Monsalvat, where I had perhaps seen the Holy Graal.

Winter, 1898.

Cadiz.

In the spring of 1899 I spent five days at Cadiz. I was waiting for a summons to cross over to Tangier, a summons which, as it happened, never came, or was never obeyed. But that expectation gave me, all the time I was there, a peculiar sensation, a restlessness, an unsettled feeling, as of one pausing by the way. I was alone, unoccupied, I had one of those dark, windowless rooms at my hotel, opening inwards, which Spaniards seem to find quite natural, but which it is not easy for a stranger to feel comfortable in. I walked about the streets all day, and along the Muelle looking down on the harbour, and along the Alameda and the Parque Genoves looking down on the sea, and along the rough, unpaved Recinto del Sur, against which the sea is always tossing. If I walked long enough in any direction I came out upon a great white wall and the sea. I felt as if I were on a narrow island, waiting for a ship to deliver me.

All Cadiz is tall and white, built high, because there is only a neck of land to build on, and the breath of the sea is in every street. Walking, even in the centre of the town, one is conscious of the neighbourhood of another, an uncertain and shifting, element. The people who passed me seemed as conscious as I of this restless friend or enemy at their doors. Some of them had but just landed from the ships in the harbour, others were just going out to sea in them. Every day there were different people in the streets; I had not time to

Cities and Sea-Coasts and Islands.

get accustomed to seeing them before they were gone. No one seemed to be expected to stay there long. I felt almost ashamed, as day followed day, and I was still there; I felt as if people were wondering why I, too, did not go on.

Every town, I suppose, in every country, has its Sunday evening walk, along a certain route; and the Sunday evening walk at Cadiz is downward from the Plaza de la Constitución, through the Calle del Duque de Tetuan and a series of narrow, twisting streets to the Plaza de Isabel II., or to the Cathedral, or to the slanting, queerly shaped market-place, where the sea-wind, which you have been leaving behind as you go farther from the bay, meets you again, blowing up from the open sea. This walk through streets reminded me of the winding promenade of the Venetians, from the Piazza di San Marco along the Merceria to the Rialto. Cadiz, too, like Venice, an "all-but-island," comes naturally to adopt the same way of pacing to and fro within its narrow limits. Many of the people go on walking until ten; some drop off into theatres or cafés. A circus, when I was there, had taken one of the theatres; I stood by the entrance to the ring among the jockeys, and heard them talking English; the sight of the horses put all thought of the sea out of my mind.

On Sunday afternoon every one walked in the park; the women wore their best clothes; and I watched them pass and re-pass, with a feeling which I was not used to feel in Spain. There was some-

128

thing modern, fashionable, Parisian, in these toilettes, an aim at Parisian taste — a little extravagantly followed, it must be admitted. And these women had a look (what shall I say ?) more French than the women I had seen anywhere else in Spain. They had, indeed, the perfect Spanish calmness, but with it a slight self-consciousness, almost coquetry, with less of the sleepy animal. Is it merely fancy, or the unconscious prejudice of a Latin tradition, which makes me think that the Gaditanæ are really, in some sense, "improbæ," more than other Andalusian women? Perhaps it is only that they are less absorbed in themselves, more attentive to those who look at them, winningly aware of their sex, as their eyes show. They are taller, slighter, and fairer than the women of Seville, their faces are more neatly finished, the nose more delicately curved, the eyelids very arched, the eyes wide open and very active. Here not only the women of the upper and lower classes, but of the middle classes as well, have more than the usual Spanish piquancy in their smooth oval faces. Is there something in the sea itself, or is it only the natural hazards of that mixture of races which a position by the sea brings about? Certainly the women of Cadiz are not like other Spanish women.

There is nothing to see in Cadiz, only the white houses, and the ships in the harbour, and the water surging and swinging against the walls. At night I used to wander on the desolate stretch of ground behind the Cathedral, pushing my way against the

Cities and Sea-Coasts and Islands.

wind until I leaned over the wall, and could watch the grey waves heaving up and down with the long roll of the Atlantic. They were white at the edge, where they pushed hard at the wall, and sank back, and pushed hard at it again. A chill wind blew across them, with a dreary and melancholy sound. I listened anxiously; for once the sea gave me no pleasure. I wanted to be on the other side of it, under the African sun, with the friend from whom I was waiting to hear. I was impatient at being still in Europe.

Spring, 1899.

A Bull Fight at Valencia.

I HAVE always held that cruelty has a deep root in human nature, and is not that exceptional thing which, for the most part, we are pleased to suppose it. I believe it has an unadmitted, abominable attraction for almost every one; for many of us, under scrupulous disguises; more simply for others, and especially for people of certain races; but the same principle is there, under whatever manifestation, and, if one takes one's stand on nature, claiming that whatever is deeply rooted there has its own right to exist, what of the natural rights of cruelty? The problem is troubling me at the moment, for I was at a Spanish bull fight yesterday, the first I had ever seen; and I saw many things there of a nature to make one reflect a little on first principles.

The Plaza de Toros at Valencia is the largest in Spain. It holds 17,000 people, nearly 3000 more than those of Barcelona, Seville, and Madrid. Yesterday it was two-thirds full, and, looking from my seat in the second row of boxes, that is, from the highest point of the house, I saw an immense blue circle filling the space between the brown sand of the arena and the pale blue sky overhead. The *Sol*, the side of the sun, the cheaper side, was opposite to me, and the shimmer of blue came from the *gradas*, where the blue blouses of the workmen left the darker clothes of their neighbours and the occasional coloured dress of a woman hardly distinguishable as more than a slight variation

131

in a single tone of colour. Below me was the President's box, and half way round to the right the band, which, punctually at three, began to play a march as a door in the arena, immediately opposite to me, was thrown open, and the procession came in — the espadas and banderilleros in their pink and gold, with their bright cloaks, walking, the picadores, pike in hand, on their horses, the chulos following. There were to be eight bulls, four in *plaza partida*, that is, with a barrier dividing the arena into two halves, and four in *lidia ordinaria*, with the whole of the arena. As soon as the men were in their places a trumpet was blown, two doors in the arena were thrown open, and two bulls, each with a rosette on his neck, galloped in. The two fights went on simultaneously, in the traditional three acts — the *Suerte de Picar*, when the picadores, on horseback and holding long wooden pikes with a short head, meet the bull; the *Suerte de Banderillera*, when the banderilleros plant their coloured darts in his neck; and the *Suerte de Matar*, when the espada, with his sword and his red cloth, gives the death-blow. Each fight lasted about half an hour, and was divided into its three acts by the sound of trumpets.

The first act might be called the Massacre of the Horses. There is no pretence of fighting, and the picador rarely attempts to save his horse, although nothing would be easier; on the contrary, the horse is deliberately offered to the bull, with the very considerable chance, of course, that the

A Bull Fight at Valencia.

picador himself may be wounded through his pads, or as he rolls over with his horse. The horses are old and lean, one eye is often bandaged, and if, as they often do, they press back in terror against the barrier, or become unmanageable, a red-coated chulo comes forward and takes the bridle, and another follows with a stick, and the horse is led up to the bull and placed sideways to receive the charge. The bull, who has not the slightest desire to attack the horse, is finally teased into irritation by the red coats and by the pink cloaks, which are tossed and flaunted before him; he paws the ground, puts down his head, and charges. The pike pricks him, and his horns plunge into the horse's belly, or are caught on the loose wooden saddle, or, as happened once yesterday, scrape the picador's leg. The cloaks are flourished again, and the bull follows them. Then the horse, if he is still on his feet, is again turned to the bull. There is a great red hole in him, and the blood drips; but he is dragged and beaten forward. The bull plunges at him a second time, and this time he rolls over with his rider, who scrambles out from under him, his yellow clothes stained with red. Then one chulo takes the bridle and beats the horse on the head, and another chulo drags him by the tail, and, if he can, he staggers to his feet. He is literally falling to pieces, he has not ten minutes to live; but the saddle is thrown on him again and the picador helped into the saddle. He makes a few steps, the picador drives his heels into him, and then jumps

Cities and Sea-Coasts and Islands.

off as he falls for the last time and lies kicking on the ground, a torn and battered and sopping mass. Then a chulo goes up to him, hits him on the head to see if he can be made to get up again, and, finding it useless, takes out a long, gimlet-like dagger, and drives it in behind his ear. Then, keeping an eye on the bull, the chulo scrapes up the blood clotted among the sand into a basket, and strews fresh sand about. Meanwhile another horse is being butchered, and the bull's horns have turned crimson, and his neck, where the pike has stuck into him, begins to redden in a thin line down each side.

The trumpet sounds again, and if one of the horses is still living he is led back to the stables, to be used a second time. Now comes what is really skill in the performance, the planting of the banderilleras. The bull has tasted blood, he is still untired, and but slightly wounded. Little shouts of delight went through the house, and I could not but join in the applause, as Velasco nodded to the bull and waved the banderilleras close to his eyes, between his very horns, and planted them full-face before he leapt sideways. And Velasco's play with the cloak: the whole house rose to its feet, in fear and admiration, once as he wiped the ground with it, only its own length from the bull, again and again and again, and then, wrapping it suddenly about him with its white side outwards, turned his back on the bull, and stood still.

The trumpet sounds again, and the espada takes

his sword and his muleta, and goes out for the last scene. This, which ought to be, is not always the real climax. The bull is often by this time tired, has had enough of the sport, leaps at the barrier, trying to get out. He is tired of running after red rags, and he brushes them aside contemptuously; he can scarcely be got to show animation enough to be decently killed. But one bull that I saw yesterday was splendidly savage, and fought almost to the last, running about the arena with the sword between his shoulders, and that great red line broadening down each side of his neck on the black — like a deep layer of red paint, one tricks oneself into thinking. He carried two swords in his neck, and still fought; when at last he, too, got weary, and he went and knelt down before the door by which he had entered, and would fight no more. But they went up to him from outside the barrier, and drew the swords out of him; and he got to his feet again, and stood to be killed.

As the espada bows and renders up his sword the doors of the arena are thrown open, and there is a sound of bells. Teams of mules, decked with red and yellow bows and rosettes all over their heads and their collars, are driven in, a rope is fastened to the heads of the dead horses and to the horns of the dead bulls, and they are dragged out at full speed, one after the other, each tracing a long, curving line in the sand. Then the trumpets are blown, and the next fight begins.

I sat there, in my box, from three until half-past

Cities and Sea-Coasts and Islands.

five, when the eighth bull was killed in the half-darkness. Two men had been slightly wounded and ten horses killed — a total which, for eight bulls, as *El Taurino* said next day, *dice bien poco en favor de los mismos.* An odour, probably of bad tobacco, which my imagination insisted on accepting as the scent of blood, came up into my nostrils, where it remained all that night. Out of the open sky a bird flew now and again, darted hurriedly to and fro, and escaped into the free air. Women were sitting around me, with their children on their knees. When a horse had been badly gored, a lady sitting next to me put up her opera-glasses to see it better. There was no bravado in it. It was simple interest.

There were moments when that blue circle, as I turned my head away from the arena, seemed to swim before my eyes. But I quickly turned back to the arena again; I hated, sickened, and looked; and I could not have gone out until the last bull had been killed. The bulls were by no means a good *ganado;* I could have wished them more spirited. The odds are so infinitely in favour of the bull-fighter; he can always count on the pause which the bull makes between one rush and another, and on the infallible diversion of the red rag. It is a game of agility, presence of mind, sureness of foot and hand; dangerous enough, certainly, but not more dangerous than the daily exercises of an equilibrist. But there is always that odd chance, like the gambler's winning number, which may

136

A Bull Fight at Valencia.

turn up — the chance of a false step, a miscalculation, and the bull's horns in a man's body. The small probability of such a thing, and yet the possibility of it; these, combined, are two of the motives which bring people to the bull-fight.

Yet I cannot help thinking, suppress the *Suerte de Picar*, and you suppress the bull-fight. This is the one abomination and the abominable attraction. I have described it with as much detail as I dare, and even now I feel that I have hardly rendered the whole horror of it. Coming away from the Plaza, I saw every horse I passed in the street, as I had seen those horses, with gaping and dripping sides, rearing back against the barrier, and dragged and beaten up to the horns of the bull. Well, that red plunge of horns into the living flesh, that living body ripped and lifted and rolled to the ground, that monstrous visible agony dragging itself about the sand; and, along with this, the rider rolling off, indeed, on the safe side, but, for the moment, indistinguishable from his living barrier, and with only that barrier between him and the horns — it is this that one holds one's breath to see, and it is to hold one's breath that one goes to the bull-fight.

The cruelty of human nature — what is it? and how is it that it has struck root so deep? I realise it more clearly, and understand it less than ever, since I have come from that *novillada* at Valencia.

Winter, 1898.

137

Alicante.

I REACHED Alicante during this last stormy night, seeing something of the country we were passing through by lightning flashes; and when I went out this morning the roads were heaped with the mud of a night's rain. The sun shone, and bright drops of rain fell, drying as they fell, under that almost tropical heat; and as I found myself, suddenly, a dozen steps from the door of my hotel, standing under a palm tree on a beach where barefooted sailors were dragging up the boats, with the whole shining sea before me, green and silver and pale grey to the abrupt edge of the horizon, where blue-black clouds rose like a glittering wall, I could have fancied myself scarcely in Europe. I lingered there for some time, making the most of that sensation of friendly isolation which the sudden, unexpected presence of the sea always brings to me, and then began to walk slowly along the Paseo, under the double row of palm trees, watching the ships rocking in the harbour; one of them, no larger than a fishing vessel, a Cornish boat, the *Little Mystery* of Fowey. I walked under the palms the whole length of the harbour, and stopped when I came to the great mole and the further beach, on which the waves were coming in. No waves have the same way of coming in on any two shores. These were stealthy, sudden, rising unexpectedly out of a smooth surface, as a snake rises out of the grass, and then gliding forward with a rushing subsidence. I walked out on the mole, and sat down at the very end, where an old fisherman was paddling in his boat after crabs; and then for the first time I saw Alicante.

I saw, across the blue, swaying water of the harbour, an immense, bare, brown rock, lined with fortifications, crowned with a castle, and at its foot a compact mass of flat, white houses, which trailed off to the left into apparently a single line along the water, white and blue and mauve and pink, on the other side of that double row of palm trees, and with a surprising effect of elegance. Near the centre, one or two blue domes, towers topped with blue, square grey towers, rose from among the low roofs; two high banks of rock continued the central mass to the right, with gaps between, after which a low curve of bare rock ended the bay. Behind, a low range of hills, rising and falling in peaks and broken curves, bare for the clouds to paint their colours on, shut off this bright edge of seashore from the world.

I have been lounging about the harbour all day, merely drinking in sunshine and sea air, and as yet I know nothing of Alicante. But to-night, walking about these muddy streets in which the mud is like that on a deep country road, and watching the people who pass to and fro at that hour of five, when, in Spain, everybody is in the street, I figure Alicante to myself as a rough, violent little place, still barbarous. And, looking down from the high Plaza de Ramiro, those singular, neat little cabins on the seashore, bathing-cabins, I suppose, let for the season, and at other times lived in by the people of the place, might be huts on a savage beach, as they stand there under the palm trees. And the clouds are growing stormier over the sea, stained with bright, watery colours, green and rose, towards the sunset; darkness is coming on; a steamer glides out across the water, straight into the stormy clouds, through which a soft, pink lightning flushes at intervals.

I am beginning to know Alicante. All this morning I have been wandering through the bye-streets, seeing the whole life of the place as I pass, in doorways and at windows, and in houses thrown wide open to the street. I might almost be seeing hill-tribes squatting in their caves. The streets, rising from about the harbour, beyond the one or two regular, level streets with shops, are planted as irregularly as the streets of Le Puy or of St. Ives. Often steps lead from one level to another; and houses are of different heights, thrown together at random, a one-storied house by the side of a three-storied house; and they rise or dwindle upwards and downwards until they seem to merge imperceptibly into the hill itself. As in the East, women are to be seen all day long going to the well with their pitchers, which they carry on their hips, with one arm thrown round them. And these women, the women who sit at their doors, sewing, or making lace, or knitting, or reading, or talking, have in their faces a ruddy darkness which I have as yet rarely seen in Spain, the colour of the pure

Moor, every shade of colour, from a dead olive to a black-brown lit as by an inner fire. Sometimes the black blood shows in flat nose and thick lips, sometimes in bushy eyebrows meeting; sometimes the outline of features is almost Mongolian. And there is not a link in the chain which joins the Moor and the Spaniard, not a gradation in the whole series of types, which is not to be seen here, in these heterogeneous streets.

To-night, just before Vespers, I went into the church of Santa Maria, which fills one side of a little square, high up, from which, as from a lofty platform, one can see the sea, over and between the houses. It was quite dark as I entered, and, feeling my way, I came through a side chapel to an iron gate, which stood open, through which I saw some one in a far corner with a lighted candle in his hand, and, near to me, a long dark figure moving mechanically, which I did not at first distinguish as a man pulling a bell-rope. I stumbled forward and looked about me. At first it seemed to me that I had found my way into a crypt, with side crypts all round. Gradually I perceived a Gothic vaulting and the arches of side chapels, which succeeded one another without division down the whole length of the church. A tiny light twinkled here and there from a suspended lamp. I saw a kneeling figure in black; the sacristan passed on the other side of the arches with his candle, which he blew out, and the church returned to its silent darkness.

Cities and Sea-Coasts and Islands.

This morning the sea has been magnificently joyous. I have been spending hours on the two branches of the mole which closes in the harbour, watching its bright extravagances; and now, as afternoon advances, the fishing boats are coming home, like great white birds, one after the other, with wings lifted. The first has already passed me, entered the harbour. Never was there a harbour so delicate, so elegant, with its ample space, its whiteness, the exquisite lines which the bare masts and yard-arms make against the palm trees, which one sees through swaying cordage and between half-reefed sails. Ships here are what they should be, the humanising part of the sea's beauty; and they are still as much as ever a part of the sea as they are lifted on these moving tides, inside the harbour, and along the quay. At night I am watching them again, under a sunset blackening the West with darkness, and devouring the darkness with flame. The whole harbour burns, and the masts rise into the fiery sky, out of the purple water, and across violet mountains.

And so day follows day in a happy monotony. I spent yesterday at Elche, a little rocky town of palms, thirteen miles off, which is really Africa in Spain. High up a bare, crumbling bank, rising from the yellow river, where lines of stooping women are pounding clothes, one sees, looking from the bridge, a crowd of squat, white square houses, set one beside and above another, like the dwellings of savage people, blank walls with a few barred holes for windows; above, a blue-domed church that might be a mosque. Palms overtop the walls, rise in the midst of the houses, swarm in forests up to all the outskirts, stretch into the country among fields and groves of trees; and along all the alleys flow variable streams, arrested and set in motion by an elaborate system of dykes. Under that hot sun in mid-winter, following little paths between the rows of palms, which ended in their tuft of feathers and their cluster of yellow dates so high above my head, hearing from that height the long, lingering, Moorish songs of the date-pickers, perched there with ropes about their waists, the mules waiting below with their panniers for the burdens, I seemed far from even Alicante, really deep in the tropics, and not (as I forced myself to reflect) a day's journey from Madrid.

It is after all with relief, as if I have shaken off some not quite explicable oppression, that I find myself back again at Alicante. How perfectly restful is this busy peace of the morning, in the blue harbour, where sea-gulls, white and black, fly among the ships; and in the bluer bay, where from moment to moment a great sail, passing çlose to land, blots out the sunshine which lies glittering on the placidly wrinkling water! As the boats pass, the men bending to their oars and stooping under the sail, I can see them taking silver fishes out of dark nets. Sails whiten on the horizon against a dull cloud, and darken against clouds shining with sunlight. The long plash of the tide coils in about the rocks

Cities and Sea-Coasts and Islands.

at my feet. They are loading the ships with a slow, rhythmical roll of machinery. Across the harbour a bell is tolling. All the rest is warm silence.

Spring, 1898.

A Spanish Music-Hall.

I AM *aficionado*, as a Spaniard would say, of music-halls. They amuse me, and I am always grateful to any one or anything that amuses me. The drama, if it is to be looked on as an art at all, is a serious art, to be taken seriously; the art of the music-hall is admittedly frivolous — the consecration of the frivolous. The more it approaches the legitimate drama the less characteristic, the less interesting it is. Thus what are called in England "sketches" are rarely tolerable; they may be endured. If I want a farce I will go elsewhere. I come to the music-hall for dancing, for singing, for the human harmonies of the acrobat. And I come for that exquisite sense of the frivolous, that air of Bohemian freedom, that relief from respectability which one gets here, and nowhere more surely than here. In a music-hall the audience is a part of the performance. The audience in a theatre, besides being in itself less amusing, is on its best behaviour; you do not so easily surprise its "humours." Here we have a tragic comedy in the box yonder, a farce in the third row of the stalls, a scene from a ballet in the promenade. The fascination of these private performances is irresistible; and they are so constantly changing, so full of surprises, so mysterious and so clear.

And then it is so amusing to contrast the Pavilion with the Trocadero, to compare the Eldorado with La Scala; to distinguish just the difference, on the stage and off, which one is certain to find at Collins's

145

Cities and Sea-Coasts and Islands.

and the Metropolitan, at La Cigale and the Divan Japonais. To study the individuality of a music-hall, as one studies a human individuality, that is by no means the least profitable, the least interesting of studies.

At the beginning of last May I spent a few days at Barcelona, and one night I went to the Alcazar Español, the most characteristic place I could find, extremely curious to see what a Spanish music-hall would be like. It was very near my hotel, in a side street turning out of the Rambla, and I had heard through the open window the sound of music and of voices. I got there early, a little before nine. The entrance was not imposing, but it was covered with placards which had their interest. I pushed open the swing-doors and found myself in a long vestibule, at the other end of which was a sort of counter, which did duty for a box-office. I paid, went down a step or two, and through another door. There was a bar at one end of the room, and a few small tables placed near two embrasures, through which one saw an inner room. This was the hall. At one end was a little stage; the curtain was down, and the musicians' chairs and desks were vacant. Except for the stage, and for a gallery which ran along one side and the other end, the room was just like an ordinary café. There were the usual seats, the usual marble-topped tables, the usual glasses, and, lounging sleepily in the corners, the usual waiters. Two or three people stood at the bar, a few more were drinking coffee

146

or *aguardiente* at the tables. Presently two women came in and began to arrange one another's dresses in the corner. Two of the performers, I thought, and rightly. Then a few more people came in, and a few more, and the place gradually filled. The audience was not a distinguished one. None of the women wore hats, and few of them assumed an air of too extreme superiority to the waiters. Two fantastic creatures at a table next to me seemed to find it pleasant as well as profitable to be served by a waiter who would sit down at the same table and pay open court to them. Women would appear and disappear at the door leading into the next room, the room with the bar. The red door by the side of the stage — the stage-door — began to open and shut. And now the musicians were assembling. The grey-haired leader of the orchestra, smoking a cigar, brought in the score. He sat down at his piano and handed round the sheets of music. The members of the orchestra brought newspapers with them. The man who played the clarionet was smoking a cigarette fixed in an interminable holder. He did his duty by his instrument in the overture that followed, but he never allowed the cigarette to go out. I thought the performance remarkable.

The band, for a music-hall of no higher pretensions, was extremely good. It had the genuine music-hall swing, and a sympathetic delicacy which I had not expected. The overture sounded very Spanish. It was a *potpourri* of some kind, with

147

Cities and Sea-Coasts and Islands.

much variety of airs, a satisfying local colour. After the overture the curtain rose on a *mise en scène* of astonishing meagreness. It was a *zarzuela* — a "sketch" — called *L'Ecrin du Shah de Perse*, in which the principal performer was Mlle. Anna Durmance, a lady who spoke excellent French on occasion, but who looked and acted as only a Spaniard could look and act. The Spaniards have very little talent for acting. They lack flexibility, they have not the instinctive sense of the situation, such as every Frenchman and every Frenchwoman possess by right of birth. The men move spasmodically, as if galvanised. The women place themselves — gracefully, of course — in certain positions, because they know that such positions are required. They use the appropriate gestures, their faces assume certain expressions; but it is all done with the air of one who has learnt a lesson. And the lesson has evidently been a difficult one. The *zarzuela* was amusing in its wildly farcical way — a farce of grotesque action, of incredible exaggeration. There was a great deal of excited movement, a series of rather disconnected episodes, a good deal of noise. Anna Durmance was best in a scene where she came on as a washerwoman. Spaniards, with whom the washerwoman's art is of public interest, an element of the picturesque, are very fond of personating washerwomen, and they do it particularly well. There were other moments when Mlle. Durmance was excellent; certain gestures, a typically Spanish

148

way of walking. But one was not sorry when, in the usual sudden way, all the performers rushed together upon the stage; there were some exclamations, some laughter, some joining of hands, and the curtain was down amid a thunder of applause.

The next performer was really a Frenchwoman. "Elle est affreuse," said a dark Southerner near me, whose "meridional vivacity" was unmistakably in evidence, "mais elle a été gracieuse." I could imagine she had once been very handsome. She was by no means "frightful" now, but one saw that she owed something to her "make-up." Her voice, as she sang some well-known French comic songs, in which my irrepressible neighbour joined from time to time, showed signs of having once been better. She was a great favourite with the audience, and in the pauses between the stanzas she would smile and nod to her friends here and there. I did not share in the enthusiasm, having heard the same songs much better given elsewhere. When, after an interval, she came on the stage again, dressed as a man, I was surprised to see how well she could look. She was to take charge of the Teatro Lilliputien, and she made her bow before disappearing behind the curtain. The Lilliputian Theatre has not, I think, reached England, though it has long been at home in Paris. It is a contrivance after the style of a Punch and Judy show, only, instead of marionettes who do all the action, there is a combination between the operator and his puppets. As in a certain sort of caricature,

Cities and Sea-Coasts and Islands.

one sees a large head supported by a tiny body, with finikin arms and legs, which move as they are worked from behind. The head is that of the performer, the rest belongs to the puppets; and it is indeed comic to see the perfect sympathy which exists between the head which sings, the puppet hands which gesticulate, and the puppet legs which dance. The *répertoire* of these miniature theatres seems to be limited. The songs I heard at the Alcazar Español at Barcelona were almost without exception the same that I had heard at the Montagnes Russes at Paris. There was the same red-haired Englishman who danced a hornpipe, the same "ténor qui monte le cou," the same caricature of the chorus of servant-girls in the *Cloches de Corneville* — "Voyez par ci, voyez par là." More thunders of applause — Spanish audiences are inconceivably enthusiastic — and the Frenchwoman was again bowing behind the footlights, drawing back rapidly to avoid the curtain which came down, as it had a way of doing, precipitately.

After this we had some more music, and the curtain rose for the *Baile español por las señoritas Espinosa*. This, despite its name, was not so typically Spanish as I had expected. The two girls wore ballet-skirts, which are never used in the characteristic Spanish dances. They had castanets, however, and there was something neither French nor English in the rhythm of their long, sweeping movements, their turn backward upon themselves, their sudden way of ending a figure by a stamp on

150

A Spanish Music-Hall.

the ground, followed by a pose of unexpected immobility. They gave us several dances. Between whiles one could see them, in the very visible and haphazard *coulisses* on the prompt side of the stage, chatting together, signalling to their friends in the audience, giving a last twitch to their tights, a final pat of adjustment to the saucer skirts.

As soon as this performance was over I saw four of the women at the other end of the room, whom I had already guessed to be some of the dancers, leave their places and make for the stage-door. The next entry on the programme was *Baile Sevillanas, por las parejas madre é hija, Isabel Santos, y las hermanas Mazantini.* Isabel Santos, the mother, was a vigorous, strongly-built, hard-featured, determined-looking woman of fifty. Her daughter was slight, graceful, delicately pink and white, very pretty and charming; her face was perfectly sweet and simple, with something of a remote and dreamy look in the eyes. One of the sisters Mazantini was fat, ugly, and unattractive; the other, a rather large woman, had an admirable figure and a gay and pleasant face. The curtain rose to a strange dance-measure. The four women took their places on the stage, facing one another by two and two. They raised their arms, the eight pairs of castanets clanged at once, and the dance began. Spanish dances have a certain resemblance with the dances of the East. One's idea of a dance, in England, is something in which all the movement is due to the legs. In Japan, in Egypt, the legs have very little to do with the dance. The exquisite rhythms of Japanese dancers are produced by the subtle gesture of hands, the manipulation of scarves, the delicate undulations of the body. In Arab dances, in the *danse du ventre*, the legs are more motionless still. They are only used to assist in producing the extraordinary movements of the stomach and the hips in which so much of the dance consists. It is a dance in which the body sets itself to its own rhythm. Spanish dancing, which no doubt derives its Eastern colour from the Moors, is almost equally a dance of the whole body, and its particular characteristic — the action of the hips — is due to a physical peculiarity of the Spaniards, whose spines have a special and unique curve of their own. The walk of Spanish women has a world-wide fame : one meets a Venus Callipyge at every corner; and it is to imitate what in them is real and beautiful that the women of other nations have introduced the hideous mimicry of the "bustle." The Baile Sevillanas, with all its differences, had a very definite resemblance to the Arab dances I had seen. It began with a gentle swaying movement in time to the regular clack-clack of castanets. Now the women faced one another, now they glided to and fro, changing places, as in a movement of the Lancers. The swaying movement of the hips became more pronounced; the body moved in a sort of circle upon itself. And then they would cross and re-cross, accentuating the rhythm with a stamp of the heels. Their arms waved and dipped, curving with the curves of the body. The dance grew more exciting, with a sort of lascivious suggestiveness, a morbid, perverse charm, as the women writhed to and fro, now languishingly, now furiously, together and apart. It ended with a frantic *trémoussement* of the hips, a stamp of the heels, and a last clang of the castanets as the arms grew rigid in the sudden immobility of the body. There were two encores and two more dances, much the same as the first, and then at last the curtain was allowed to descend, and the women went tranquilly back to the corner where they had been drinking coffee with their friends.

When the curtain rose again, after a long interval, the stage was empty but for a wooden chair placed just in the middle. The chair was waiting for Señor Pon, who was to give us a *concierto de guitarra*. Señor Pon, a business-like person, bustled on to the stage, seized the chair, and placed it nearer the footlights, sat down, looked around for his friends in the casual and familiar manner peculiar to the place, and began to tune his guitar. Then he plucked softly at the wires, and a suave, delicious melody floated across the clink of glasses. One wanted moonlight, a balcony, a woman leaning over the balcony, while the serenade rose out of the shadow. But indeed one saw all that. Then the melody ceased, and the business-like Pon was bowing to the audience. There was a torrent of applause, and he sat down again, and struck up an

153

Cities and Sea-Coasts and Islands.

imitative fantasia, in which one heard the bugles blowing the reveille, the march music of the troops, with clever realistic effects, and a really wonderful command of the instrument. The piece ended suddenly, the musician sprang up, bowed, and retreated with his chair, to avoid the irrepressible curtain. But the audience insisted on another encore, and when he had given it — a charming air played charmingly — they howled persistently, but unavailingly, for more.

Señor Pon was followed by Señorita Villaclara, a fair-complexioned woman, with dark, sleepy, wicked eyes, and black hair trailing over her forehead, with little curls near the ears. The leader of the orchestra began to play on the piano a brief, monotonous air, and the woman — looking out between her half-shut eyes — began the *Malagueña*. It was a strange, piercing, Moorish chant, sung in a high falsetto voice, in long, acute, trembling phrases — a wail rather than a song — with pauses, as if to gain breath, between. A few words seemed to be repeated over and over again, with tremulous, inarticulate cries that wavered in time to a regularly beating rhythm. The sound was like nothing I have ever heard. It pierced the brain, it tortured one with a sort of delicious spasm. The next song had more of a regular melody, though still in this extraordinary strained voice, and still with something of a lament in its monotony. I could not understand the words, but the woman's gestures left no doubt as to the character of the song. It was
154

assertively indecent, but with that curious kind of indecency — an almost religious solemnity in performer and audience — which the Spaniards share with the Eastern races. Another song followed, given with the same serious and collected indecency, and received with the same serious and collected attention. It had a refrain of "Alleluia!" and the woman, I know not why, borrowed a man's soft felt hat, turned down the brim, and put it on before beginning the song. When the applause was over she returned the hat, came back to the table at which she had been sitting, dismally enough, and yawned more desperately than ever.

The dance which came next was described on the programme as a *can-can*. It was really more like the *chahut* than the *can-can*. Four people took part, two men and two women. One of the men was as horrible a creature as I have ever seen — a huge, clean-shaved, close-cropped, ashen-hued sort of human toad; the other was preposterously tall and thin, all angles. Of the women, one was commonplace enough, with a seriousness worthy of Grille d'Egout, but the younger of the two, a piquant, amusing madcap, was as reckless as La Goulue. The band struck up a lively air from *Madame Angot*, and the *quadrille naturaliste* began. It was very like the *chahut* as one sees it at the Moulin Rouge, but there were differences, and the Spanish dance was certainly the merrier and the more like a quadrille, as certainly as it was a less elaborate and extraordinary performance. Skirts

155

whirled, legs shot into the air, there was a posturing, a pirouetting, and then each man seized his partner and led her round the stage at a gallop. Then the skirts rose and twirled again, the little shoes waved in the air, and the merry-faced woman laughed as she flung herself into the headlong movement of the dance. Not the least astonishing part of it was the series of hops by which the toad-like man defied every principle of equilibrium, now more than ever toad-like, as he squatted lumpishly on his heels. Dance followed dance, as tune changed to tune, and it was almost in a state of exhaustion that the quartet finally trailed off the stage.

There was still another dance to be given, and by the performers of the Baile Sevillanas. It was something between that and the *can-can*, with the high-kicking of the latter, and the swaying move-ment, accentuated by the heels of the former. In response to an encore, Isabel Santos, the sturdy old veteran, came forward alone, and it was indeed half comic, and soon wholly impressive, to see this incredibly agile middle-aged woman go through the wild movements of the dance. She did it with immense spirit, flinging her legs into the air with a quite youthful vivacity; she did it also with a profound artistic seriousness, which soon conquered one's inclination to see anything ridiculous or un-seemly in the performance. I am afraid the pretty daughter will never be such a dancer as the hard-featured mother. Isabel Santos the elder is, in her way, a great artist.

A Spanish Music-Hall.

After this — it was now past midnight — there was nothing specially new or interesting in the few numbers that a too liberal management wasted on the few drinkers who still sat about the hall. The Provençal near me had gone, in his turbulent way; the two women at the next table were gathering up their shawls; nearly all the glasses were empty, and no one clapped his hands for the waiter with the two kettles, the coffee and the milk. One by one the dancers left their corner and made for the door; and when, at last, Isabel Santos and her pretty daughter had said good-bye, I saw there was nothing to stay for, and I followed.

1892.

II.

London: A Book of
Aspects.

I.

THERE is in the aspect of London a certain magnificence: the magnificence of weight, solidity, energy, imperturbability, and an unconquered continuance. It is alive from border to border, not an inch of it is not alive. It exists, goes on, and has been going on for so many centuries. Here and there a stone or the line of a causeway fixes a date. If you look beyond it you look into fog. It sums up and includes England. Materially England is contained in it, and the soul of England has always inhabited it as a body. We have not had a great man who has never lived in London.

And London makes no display; it is there, as it has come, as fire and plagues have left it; but it has never had either a Haussmann or a Nero. It has none of the straight lines of Paris nor the tall lines of Vienna nor the emphatic German monotony. It has not the natural aids of Constantinople, with seas and continents about it, nor of Rome, with its seven hills, and its traces of all the history of the world. It was set in fertile soil, which has still left it the marvellous green grass of its parks, and on a river which has brought beauty along its whole course. Great architects have left a few unspoilt treasures: Westminster Abbey, the Banqueting Hall at Whitehall, an old church here and there. But for the most part the appeal of London is made by no beauty or effect in things themselves, but by the sense which it gives us of inevitable growth and impregnable strength, and

Cities and Sea-Coasts and Islands.

by the atmosphere which makes and unmakes this vast and solid city every morning and every evening with a natural magic peculiar to it.

English air, working upon London smoke, creates the real London. The real London is not a city of uniform brightness, like Paris, nor of savage gloom, like Prague; it is a picture continually changing, a continual sequence of pictures, and there is no knowing what mean street corner may not suddenly take on a glory not its own. The English mist is always at work like a subtle painter, and London is a vast canvas prepared for the mist to work on. The especial beauty of London is the Thames, and the Thames is so wonderful because the mist is always changing its shapes and colours, always making its light mysterious, and building palaces of cloud out of mere Parliament Houses with their jags and turrets. When the mist collaborates with night and rain, the masterpiece is created.

Most travellers come into London across the river, sometimes crossing it twice. The entrance, as you leave the country behind you, is ominous. If you come by night, and it is never wise to enter any city except by night, you are slowly swallowed up by a blank of blackness, pierced by holes and windows of dingy light; foul and misty eyes of light in the sky; narrow gulfs, in which lights blink; blocks and spikes of black against grey; masts, as it were, rising out of a sea of mist; then a whole street suddenly laid bare in bright light;

shoulders of dark buildings; and then black shiny rails, and then the river, a vast smudge, dismal and tragic; and, as one crosses it again, between the vast network of the bridge's bars, the impossible fairy peep-show of the Embankment.

All this one sees in passing, in hardly more than a series of flashes; but if you would see London steadily from the point where its aspect is finest, go on a night when there has been rain to the footpath which crosses Hungerford Bridge by the side of the railway-track. The river seems to have suddenly become a lake; under the black arches of Waterloo Bridge there are reflections of golden fire, multiplying arch beyond arch, in a lovely tangle. The Surrey side is dark, with tall vague buildings rising out of the mud on which a little water crawls: is it the water that moves or the shadows? A few empty barges or steamers lie in solid patches on the water near the bank; and a stationary sky-sign, hideous where it defaces the night, turns in the water to wavering bars of rosy orange. The buildings on the Embankment rise up, walls of soft greyness with squares of lighted windows, which make patterns across them. They tremble in the mist, their shapes flicker; it seems as if a breath would blow out their lights and leave them bodiless husks in the wind. From one of the tallest chimneys a reddish smoke floats and twists like a flag. Below, the Embankment curves towards Cleopatra's Needle: you see the curve of the wall, as the lamps light it, leaving the

163

obelisk in shadow, and falling faintly on the grey mud in the river. Just that corner has a mysterious air, as if secluded, in the heart of a pageant; I know not what makes it quite so tragic and melancholy. The aspect of the night, the aspect of London, pricked out in points of fire against an enveloping darkness, is as beautiful as any sunset or any mountain; I do not know any more beautiful aspect. And here, as always in London, it is the atmosphere that makes the picture, an atmosphere like Turner, revealing every form through the ecstasy of its colour.

It is not only on the river that London can make absolute beauty out of the material which lies so casually about in its streets. A London sunset, seen through vistas of narrow streets, has a colour of smoky rose which can be seen in no other city, and it weaves strange splendours, often enough, on its edges and gulfs of sky, not less marvellous than Venice can lift over the Giudecca, or Siena see stretched beyond its walls. At such a point as the Marble Arch you may see conflagrations of jewels, a sky of burning lavender, tossed abroad like a crumpled cloak, with broad bands of dull purple and smoky pink, slashed with bright gold and decked with grey streamers; you see it through a veil of moving mist, which darkens downwards to a solid block, coloured like lead, where the lighted road turns, meeting the sky.

And there are a few open spaces, which at all times and under all lights are satisfying to the

164

London.

eyes. Hyde Park Corner, for no reason in particular, gives one the first sensation of pleasure as one comes into London from Victoria Station. The glimpse of the two parks, with their big gates, the eager flow of traffic, not too tangled or laborious just there, the beginning of Piccadilly, the lack of stiffness in anything: is it these that help to make up the impression? Piccadilly Circus is always like a queer hive, and is at least never dead or formal. But it is Trafalgar Square which is the conscious heart or centre of London.

If the Thames is the soul of London, and if the parks are its eyes, surely Trafalgar Square may well be reckoned its heart. There is no hour of day or night when it is not admirable, but for my part I prefer the evening, just as it grows dusk, after a day of heavy rain. How often have I walked up and down, for mere pleasure, for a pleasure which quickened into actual excitement, on that broad, curved platform from which you can turn to look up at the National Gallery, like a frontispiece, and from which you can look down over the dark stone pavement, black and shining with rain, on which the curved fountains stand with their inky water, while two gas-lamps cast a feeble light on the granite base of the Nelson monument and on the vast sulky lions at the corners. The pedestal goes up straight into the sky, diminishing the roofs, which curve downwards to the white clock-face, alone visible on the clock-tower at Westminster. Whitehall flows like a river, on which

165

Cities and Sea-Coasts and Islands.

vague shapes of traffic float and are submerged.
The mist and the twilight hide the one harmonious
building in London, the Banqueting Hall. You
realise that it is there, and that beyond it are the
Abbey and the river, with the few demure squares
and narrow frugal streets still left standing in
Westminster.

It is only after trying to prefer the parks and
public gardens of most of the other capitals of
Europe that I have come to convince myself that
London can more than hold its own against them
all. We have no site comparable with the site
of the Pincio in Rome, none of the opalescent water
which encircles the gardens at Venice, no Sierras
to see from our Prado, not even a Berlin forest in
the midst of the city; and I for one have never
loved a London park as I have loved the Luxem-
bourg Gardens; but, if we will be frank with ourselves, and put sentiment or the prejudice of foreign
travel out of our heads, we shall have to admit
that in the natural properties of the park, in grass,
trees, and the magic of atmosphere, London is not
to be excelled.

And, above all, in freshness. After the London
parks all others seem dusty and dingy. It is the
English rain, and not the care of our park-keepers,
that brings this gloss out of the grass and gives
our public gardens their air of country freedom.
Near the Round Pond you might be anywhere
except in the middle of a city of smoke and noise,
and it is only by an unusually high roof or chimney,

somewhere against the sky, far off, that you can realise where you are. The Serpentine will never be vulgarised, though cockneys paddle on it in boats; the water in St. James's Park will always be kept wild and strange by the sea-gulls; and the toy-boats only give an infantile charm to the steel-blue water of the Round Pond. You can go astray in long avenues of trees, where, in autumn, there are always children playing among the leaves, building tombs and castles with them. In summer you can sit for a whole afternoon, undisturbed, on a chair on that green slope which goes down to the artificial end of the Serpentine, where the stone parapets are, over the water from the peacocks. It is only the parks that make summer in London almost bearable.

I have never been able to love Regent's Park, though I know it better than the others, and though it has lovely water-birds about its islands, and though it is on the way to the Zoological Gardens. Its flowers are the best in London, for colour, form, and tending. You hear the wild beasts, but no city noises. Those sounds of roaring, crying, and the voices of imprisoned birds are sometimes distressing, and are perhaps one of the reasons why one can never be quite happy or aloof from things in Regent's Park. The water there is meagre, and the boats too closely visible; the children are poorer and seem more preoccupied than the children in the western parks. And there is the perplexing inner circle, which is as

Cities and Sea-Coasts and Islands.

difficult to get in or out of as its lamentable name-sake underground. Coming where it does, the park is a breathing-place, an immense relief; but it is the streets around, and especially the Marylebone Road, that give it its value.

There remains what is more than a park, but in its way worth them all: Hampstead Heath. There are to be trains to bring poor people from the other end of London, philanthropic trains, but the heath will be spoilt, and it is almost the last thing left to spoil in London. Up to now, all the Saturday afternoons, the Sundays, the Bank Holidays, have hardly touched it. There are hiding-places, even on these evil days, and if one fails there is always another. And if one has the good fortune to live near it, and can come out in the middle of the night upon Judges' Walk, when the moonlight fills the hollow like a deep bowl, and silence is like that peace which passeth understanding, everything else in London will seem trivial, a mere individual thing, compared with it.

On the heath you are lifted over London, but you are in London. It is that double sense, that nearness and remoteness combined, the sight of St. Paul's from above the level of the dome, the houses about the pond in the Vale of Health, from which one gets so unparalleled a sensation. But the heath is to be loved for its own sake, for its peace, amplitude, high bright air and refreshment; for its mystery, wildness, formality; for its grassy pools and hillocks that flow and return like waves

168

of the sea; for its green grass and the white roads
chequering it; for its bracken, its mist and bloom
of trees. Every knoll and curve of it draws the
feet to feel their soft shapes; one cannot walk, but
must run and leap on Hampstead Heath.

II.

As you come back into London from the country, out of air into smoke, rattling level with the chimney-pots, and looking down into narrow gulfs swarming with men and machines, you are as if seized in a gigantic grip. First comes a splendid but dis-heartening sense of force, forcing you to admire it, then a desperate sense of helplessness. London seems a vast ant-heap, and you are one more ant dropped on the heap. You are stunned, and then you come to yourself, and your thought revolts against the material weight which is crushing you. What a huge futility it all seems, this human ant-heap, this crawling and hurrying and sweating and building and bearing burdens, and never rest-ing all day long and never bringing any labour to an end. After the fields and the sky London seems trivial, a thing artificially made, in which people work at senseless toils, for idle and imaginary ends. Labour in the fields is regular, sane, in-evitable as the labour of the earth with its roots. You are in your place in the world, between the grass and the clouds, really alive and living as na-turala life as the beasts. In London men work as if in darkness, scarcely seeing their own hands as they work, and not knowing the meaning of their labour. They wither and dwindle, forgetting or not knowing that it was ever a pleasant thing merely to be alive and in the air. They are all doing things for other people, making useless "improve-ments," always perfecting the achievement of

170

material results with newly made tools. They
are making things cheaper, more immediate in
effect, of the latest modern make. It is all a hurry,
a levelling downward, an automobilisation of the
mind.

And their pleasures are as their labours. In
the country you have but to walk or look out of
your window and you are in the midst of beautiful
and living things: a tree, a dimly jewelled frog,
a bird in flight. Every natural pleasure is about
you: you may walk, or ride, or skate, or swim, or
merely sit still and be at rest. But in London you
must invent pleasures and then toil after them.
The pleasures of London are more exhausting than
its toils. No stone-breaker on the roads works
so hard or martyrs his flesh so cruelly as the actress
or the woman of fashion. No one in London
does what he wants to do, or goes where he wants
to go. It is a suffering to go to any theatre, any
concert. There are even people who go to lectures.
And all this continual self-sacrifice is done for
"amusement." It is astonishing.

London was once habitable, in spite of itself.
The machines have killed it. The old, habitable
London exists no longer. Charles Lamb could
not live in this mechanical city, out of which everything old and human has been driven by wheels
and hammers and the fluids of noise and speed.
When will his affectionate phrase, "the sweet
security of streets," ever be used again of London?
No one will take a walk down Fleet Street any more,

Cities and Sea-Coasts and Islands.

no one will shed tears of joy in the "motley Strand,"
no one will be leisurable any more, or turn over
old books at a stall, or talk with friends at the street
corner.   Noise and evil smells have filled the streets
like tunnels in daylight; it is a pain to walk in the
midst of all these hurrying and clattering machines;
the multitude of humanity, that "bath" into
which Baudelaire loved to plunge, is scarcely dis-
cernible, it is secondary to the machines; it is only
in a machine that you can escape the machines.
London that was vast and smoky and loud,
now stinks and reverberates; to live in it is to
live in the hollow of a clanging bell, to breathe its
air is to breathe the foulness of modern progress.

London as it is now is the wreck and moral of
civilisation.   We are more civilised every day,
every day we can go more quickly and more uncomfortably wherever we want to go, we can have
whatever we want brought to us more quickly
and more expensively.   We live by touching
buttons and ringing bells, a new purely practical
magic sets us in communication with the ends of
the earth.   We can have abominable mockeries
of the arts of music and of speech whizzing in our
ears out of metal mouths.   We have outdone the
wildest prophetic buffooneries of Villiers de l'Isle
Adam, whose "celestial bill-sticking" may be
seen nightly defacing the majesty of the river;
here any gramophones can give us the equivalent
of his "chemical analysis of the last breath."   The
plausible and insidious telephone aids us and
172

intrudes upon us, taking away our liberty from us, and leaving every Englishman's house his castle no longer, but a kind of whispering gallery, open to the hum of every voice. There is hardly a street left in London where one can talk with open windows by day and sleep with open windows by night. We are tunnelled under until our houses rock, we are shot through holes in the earth if we want to cross London; even the last liberty of Hampstead Heath is about to be taken from us by railway. London has civilised itself into the likeness of a steam roundabout at a fair; it goes clattering and turning, to the sound of a jubilant hurdy-gurdy; round and round, always on the same track, but always faster; and the children astride its wooden horses think they are getting to the world's end.

It is the machines, more than anything else, that have done it. Men and women, as they passed each other in the street or on the road, saw and took cognisance of each other, human being of human being. The creatures that we see now in the machines are hardly to be called human beings, so are they disfigured out of all recognition, in order that they may go fast enough not to see anything themselves. Does any one any longer walk? If I walk I meet no one walking, and I cannot wonder at it, for what I meet is an uproar, and a whizz, and a leap past me, and a blinding cloud of dust, and a machine on which scarecrows perch is disappearing at the end of the road. The

Cities and Sea-Coasts and Islands.

verbs to loll, to lounge, to dawdle, to loiter, the verbs precious to Walt Whitman, precious to every lover of men and of himself, are losing their currency; they will be marked "o" for obsolete in the dictionaries of the future. All that poetry which Walt Whitman found in things merely because they were alive will fade out of existence like the Red Indian. It will live on for some time yet in the country where the railway has not yet smeared its poisonous trail over the soil; but in London there will soon be no need of men, there will be nothing but machines.

There was a time when it was enough merely to be alive, and to be in London. Every morning promised an adventure; something or some one might be waiting at the corner of the next street; it was difficult to stay indoors because there were so many people in the streets. I still think, after seeing most of the capitals of Europe, that there is no capital in Europe where so many beautiful women are to be seen as in London. Warsaw comes near, for rarity; not for number. The streets and the omnibuses were always alive with beauty or with something strange. In London anything may happen. "Adventures to the adventurous!" says somebody in *Contarini Fleming.* But who can look as high as the uneasy faces on a motor-omnibus, who can look under the hoods and goggles in a motor-car? The roads are too noisy now for any charm of expression to be seen on the pavements. The women are
174

shouting to each other, straining their ears to hear. They want to get their shopping done and to get into a motor-car or a motor-omnibus.

Could another Charles Lamb create a new London?

III.

How much of Lamb's London is left? "London itself a pantomime and a masquerade" is left, and "a mind that loves to find itself at home in crowds" is never without those streets and pavements to turn by its alchemy into pure gold. "Is any night-walk comparable," as he asks, and need not have waited for an answer, "to a walk from St. Paul's to Charing Cross, for lighting and paving, crowds going and coming without respite, the rattle of coaches and the cheerfulness of shops?" "St. Paul's Churchyard!" he cries, "the Strand! Exeter Change! Charing Cross, with the man *upon* the black horse! These are thy gods, O London!" One has to turn to the notes on the letters to find out that Exeter Change was "a great building, with bookstalls and miscellaneous stalls on the ground floor and a menagerie above." How delicious that sounds! But then "it was demolished in 1829." Temple Bar has gone, and the griffin, which would have seemed to Lamb as permanent as London Stone. Staple Inn would have been less of an anomaly to him in "noble Holborn" than it is to us, as it stands, with an aged helplessness, not far off from the useful horrors of Holborn Viaduct, a "modern improvement" which has swept away the old timbered houses that used to make an island in the middle of the street. Like all old London, that is not hidden away in a corner (as St. John's Gateway is, on its hill at the back of Smithfield, and St. Bartholomew's Church, which

176

hinders nobody's passing, and the Charterhouse, which has so far held its own), they have had to make way for the traffic, that traffic which is steadily pushing down the good things that are old and shouldering up the bad new things that will be temporary. We have still, and for historic and royal reasons will always have, Westminster Abbey: the Beautiful Temple, as Lamb called it, when he was religiously occupied in "shaming the sellers out of the Temple." A church that is not in the way of a new street, or does not intrude over the edge of a new widening, is, for the most part, safe. But we, who live now, have seen Christ's Hospital, that comely home and fosterer of genius, pulled down, stone by stone, its beautiful memory obliterated, because boys, they say, want country air. That was one of the breathing-places, the old quiet things, that helped to make the city habitable. Newgate has been pulled down, and with Newgate goes some of the strength and permanence of London. There was a horrible beauty in those impregnable grey stone walls, by the side of the city pavement. The traffic has fallen upon them like a sea, and they have melted away before it.

Lamb saw London changing, and to the end he said, "London streets and faces cheer me inexpressibly, though of the latter not one known one were remaining." But to his sister it seemed that he "found it melancholy," "the very streets," he says, "altering every day." Covent Garden, where he lived, has lasted; the house he lived in

Cities and Sea-Coasts and Islands.

still stands looking into Bow Street. And the
Temple, that lucky corner of the City which is
outside city jurisdiction, has been little spoiled
by time, or the worse improvements of restorers.
But I ask myself what Lamb would have said if he
had lived to see tram-lines sliming the bank of the
river, and the trees amputated to preserve the hats
of living creatures, in what way better or more
worthy of attention than those trees?

When I see London best is when I have been
abroad for a long time. Then, as I sit on the top
of an omnibus, coming in from the Marble Arch,
that long line of Oxford Street seems a surprising
and delightful thing, full of picturesque irregulari-
ties, and Piccadilly Circus seems incredibly alive
and central, and the Strand is glutted with a traffic
typically English. I am able to remember how
I used to turn out of the Temple and walk slowly
towards Charing Cross, elbowing my way medita-
tively, making up sonnets in my head while I
missed no attractive face on the pavement or on
the top of an omnibus, pleasantly conscious of the
shops yet undistracted by them, happy because I
was in the midst of people, and happier still because
they were all unknown to me. For years that was
my feeling about London, and now I am always
grateful to a foreign absence which can put me
back, if only for a day, into that comfortable frame
of mind. Baudelaire's phrase, "a bath of multitude," seemed to have been made for me, and I
suppose for five years or so, all the first part of

the time when I was living in the Temple, I never stayed indoors for the whole of a single evening. There were times when I went out as regularly as clockwork every night on the stroke of eleven. No sensation in London is so familiar to me as that emptiness of the Strand just before the people come out of the theatres, but an emptiness not final and absolute like that at ten o'clock; an emptiness, rather, in which there are the first stirrings of movement. The cabs shift slightly on the ranks; the cabmen take the nose-bags off the horses' heads and climb up on their perches. There is an expectancy all along the road: Italian waiters with tight greasy hair and white aprons stand less listlessly at the tavern doors; they half turn, ready to back into the doorway before a customer.

As you walk along, the stir increases, cabs crawl out of side streets and file slowly towards the theatres; the footmen cluster about the theatre-doors; here and there some one comes out hurriedly and walks down the street. And then, all of a sudden, as if at some unheard signal, the wide doorways are blocked with slowly struggling crowds, you see tall black hats of men and the many coloured hair of women, jammed together, and slightly swaying to and fro, as if rocked from under. Black figures break through the crowd, and detach themselves against the wheels of the hansoms, a flying and disclosing cloak swishes against the shafts and is engulfed in the dark hollow; horses start, stagger, hammer feverishly with their hoofs

179

Cities and Sea-Coasts and Islands.

and are off; the whole roadway is black with cabs and carriages, and the omnibuses seem suddenly diminished. The pavement is blocked, the crowd of the doorway now sways only less helplessly upon the pavement; you see the women's distracted and irritated eyes, their hands clutching at cloaks that will not come together, the absurd and anomalous glitter of diamonds and bare necks in the streets.

Westward the crowd is more scattered, has more space to disperse. The Circus is like a whirlpool, streams pour steadily outward from the centre, where the fountain stands for a symbol. The lights glitter outside theatres and music-halls and restaurants; lights coruscate, flash from the walls, dart from the vehicles; a dark tangle of roofs and horses knots itself together and swiftly separates at every moment; all the pavements are aswarm with people hurrying.

In half an hour all this outflow will have subsided, and then one distinguishes the slow and melancholy walk of women and men, as if on some kind of penitential duty, round and round the Circus and along Piccadilly as far as the Duke of Wellington's house and long Regent Street almost to the Circus. Few walk on the left side of Piccadilly or the right of Regent Street, though you hear foreign tongues a-chatter under the arcade. But the steady procession coils backward and forward, thickening and slackening as it rounds the Circus, where innocent people wait uncomfortably for omnibuses, standing close to the edge of the pavement. Men stand watchfully at all the corners, with their backs to the road; you hear piping voices, shrill laughter; you observe that all the women's eyes are turned sideways, never straight in front of them; and that they seem often to hesitate, as if they were not sure of the way, though they have walked in that procession night after night, and know every stone of the pavement and every moulding on the brass rims of the shop-windows. The same faces return, lessen, the people come out of the restaurants and the crowd thickens for ten minutes, then again lessens; and fewer and fewer trudge drearily along the almost deserted pavement. The staring lights are blotted suddenly from the walls; the streets seem to grow chill, uninhabited, unfriendly; the few hansoms roam up and down restlessly, seeking a last fare. And still a few dingy figures creep along by the inner edge of the pavement, stopping by the closed doors of the shops, sometimes speaking dully to one another; then trudging heavily along, and disappearing slowly through the side streets eastward.

The part of London I have always known best is the part that lies between the Temple and Piccadilly, and some of it no longer exists. When the Strand was widened, Holywell Street, one of the oldest and quaintest streets in London, was pulled down, Wych Street went too, and Clare Market, and many dingy and twisting lanes which could well be spared. But I deeply regret Holywell

Cities and Sea-Coasts and Islands.

Street, and when I tell strangers about it, it seems to me that they can never know London now. I suppose many people will soon forget that narrow lane with its overhanging wooden fronts, like the houses at Coventry; or they will remember it only for its surreptitious shop-windows, the glass always dusty, through which one dimly saw English translations of Zola among chemists' paraphernalia. The street had a bad reputation, and by night doors opened and shut unexpectedly up dark passages. Perhaps that vague dubiousness added a little to its charm, but by day the charm was a positive one: the book-shops! Perhaps I liked the quays at Paris even better: it was Paris, and there was the river, and Notre Dame, and it was the left bank. But nowhere else, in no other city, was there a corner so made for book-fanciers. Those dingy shops with their stalls open to the street, nearly all on the right, the respectable side as you walked west, how seldom did I keep my resolution to walk past them with unaverted eyes, how rarely did I resist their temptations. Half the books I possess were bought second-hand in Holywell Street, and what bargains I have made out of the fourpenny books! On the hottest days, there was shade there, and excuse for lounging. It was a paradise for the book-lover.

It never occurred to me that any street so old could seem worth pulling down; but the improvements came, and that and the less interesting streets near, where the Globe Theatre was (I thought it

no loss) had of course to go; and Dane's Inn went,
which was never a genuine "inn," but had some
of the pleasant genuine dreariness; and Clare
Market was obliterated, and I believe Drury Lane
is getting furbished up and losing its old savour
of squalor; and Aldwych is there, with its beautiful
name, but itself so big and obvious that I confess,
with my recollections of what was there before, I
can never find my way in it.

Striking westward, my course generally led
me through Leicester Square. The foreign quarter
of London radiates from Leicester Square, or winds
inward to that point as to a centre. Its foreign
aspect, the fact that it was the park of Soho, interested me. In Leicester Square, and in all the
tiny streets running into it, you are never in the
really normal London : it is an escape, a sort of
shamefaced and sordid and yet irresistible reminder
of Paris and Italy. The little restaurants all round
brought me local colour before I had seen Italy;
I still see with pleasure the straw-covered bottles
and the strings of maccaroni in the undusted windows. The foreign people you see are not desirable
people : what does that matter if you look on them
as on so many puppets on a string, and their shapes
and colours come as a relief to you after the uniform
puppets of English make ?

I have always been apt to look on the world as
a puppet-show, and all the men and women merely
players, whose wires we do not see working. There
is a passage in one of Keats' letters which expresses

Cities and Sea-Coasts and Islands.

just what I have always felt: "May there not,"
he says, "be superior beings, amused with any
graceful, though instinctive attitude my mind may
fall into, as I am entertained with the alertness of
the stoat or the anxiety of a deer?" Is there not,
in our aspect towards one another, something inevitably automatic? Do we see, in the larger part
of those fellow-creatures whom our eyes rest on
more than a smile, a gesture, a passing or a coming
forward? Are they more real to us than the actors
on a stage, the quivering phantoms of a cinemato-
graph? With their own private existence we have
nothing to do: do they not, so far as we are concerned, exist in part at least to be a spectacle to us,
to convey to us a sense of life, change, beauty,
variety, necessity? The spectacle of human life
is not only for the gods' eyes, but for ours; it is
ours in so far as we can apprehend it, and our
pleasure and satisfaction here are largely dependent
on the skill with which we have trained ourselves
to that instinctive, delighted apprehension. To
a few here and there we can come closer, we can
make them, by some illusion of the affections,
seem more real to us. But as for all the rest, let
us be content to admire, to wonder, to see the use
and beauty and curiosity of them, and intrude no
further into their destinies.

It was for their very obvious qualities of illusion
that I liked to watch the people in the foreign
quarter. They were like prisoners there, thriving
perhaps but discontented; none of them light-

hearted, as they would have been in their own country; grudgingly at home. And there was much piteous false show among them, soiled sordid ostentation, a little of what we see in the older songs of Yvette Guilbert.

London was for a long time my supreme sensation, and to roam in the streets, especially after the lamps were lighted, my chief pleasure. I had no motive in it, merely the desire to get out of doors, and to be among people, lights, to get out of myself. Myself has always been so absorbing to me that it was perhaps natural that, along with that habitual companionship, there should be at times the desire for escape. When I was living alone in the Temple that desire came over me almost every night, and made work, or thought without work, impossible. Later in the night I was often able to work with perfect quiet, but not unless I had been out in the streets first. The plunge through the Middle Temple gateway was like the swimmer's plunge into rough water: I got just that "cool shock" as I went outside into the brighter lights and the movement. I often had no idea where I was going, I often went nowhere. I walked, and there were people about me.

I lived in Fountain Court for ten years, and I thought then, and think still, that it is the most beautiful place in London. Dutch people have told me that the Temple is like a little Dutch town, and that as they enter from Fleet Street into Middle Temple Lane they can fancy themselves at the

Cities and Sea-Coasts and Islands.

Hague. Dutchmen are happy if they have much that can remind them of Middle Temple Lane. There is a moment when you are in Fleet Street; you have forced your way through the long Strand, along those narrow pavements, in a continual coming and going of hurried people, with the continual rumble of wheels in the road, the swaying heights of omnibuses beside you, distracting your eyes, the dust, clatter, confusion, heat, bewilderment of that thoroughfare; and suddenly you go under a low doorway, where large wooden doors and a smaller side-door stand open, and you are suddenly in quiet. The roar has dropped, as the roar of the sea drops if you go in at your door and shut it behind you. At night, when one had to knock, and so waited, and was admitted with a nice formality, it was sometimes almost startling. I have never felt any quiet in solitary places so much as the quiet of that contrast: Fleet Street and the Temple.

No wheels could come nearer to me in Fountain Court than Middle Temple Lane, but I liked to hear sometimes at night a faint clattering, only just audible, which I knew was the sound of a cab on the Embankment. The County Council, steadily ruining London with the persistence of an organic disease, is busy turning the Embankment into a gangway for electric trams; but when I knew it it was a quiet, almost secluded place, where people sauntered and leaned over to look into the water, and where, at night, the policemen

186

would walk with considerately averted head past the slumbering heaps of tired rags on the seats.

The gates on the Embankment shut early, but I often came home by the river and I could hardly tear myself away from looking over that grey harsh parapet. The Neva reminds me a little of the Thames, though it rushes more wildly, and at night is more like a sea, with swift lights crossing it. But I do not know the river of any great capital which has the fascination of our river. Whistler has created the Thames, for most people; but the Thames existed before Whistler, and will exist after the County Council. I remember hearing Claude Monet say, at the time when he came over to the Savoy Hotel, year by year, to paint Waterloo Bridge from its windows, that he could not understand why any English painter ever left London. I felt almost as if the river belonged to the Temple: its presence there, certainly, was part of its mysterious anomaly, a fragment of old London, walled and guarded in that corner of land between Fleet Street and the Thames.

It was the name, partly, that had drawn me to Fountain Court, and the odd coincidence that I had found myself, not long before, in what was once Blake's Fountain Court, and then Southampton Buildings, now only a date on a wall. I had the top flat in what is really the back of one of the old houses in Essex Street, taken into the Temple; it had a stone balcony from which I looked down on a wide open court, with a stone fountain in the

Cities and Sea-Coasts and Islands.

middle, broad rows of stone steps leading upward and downward, with a splendid effect of decoration; in one corner of the court was Middle Temple Hall, where a play of Shakespeare's was acted while Shakespeare was alive; all around were the backs of old buildings, and there were old trees, under which there was a bench in summer, and there was the glimpse of gardens going down to the Embankment. By day it was as legal and busy as any other part of the Temple, but the mental business of the law is not inelegantly expressed in those wigged and gowned figures who are generally to be seen crossing between the Law Courts and their chambers in the Temple. I felt, when I saw them, that I was the intruder, the modern note, and that they were in their place, and keeping up a tradition. But at night I had the place to myself.

The nights in Fountain Court were a continual delight to me. I lived then chiefly by night, and when I came in late I used often to sit on the bench under the trees, where no one else ever sat at those hours. I sat there, looking at the silent water in the basin of the fountain, and at the leaves overhead, and at the sky through the leaves; and that solitude was only broken by the careful policeman on guard, who would generally stroll up to be quite certain that it was the usual loiterer, who had a right to sit there. Sometimes he talked with me, and occasionally about books; and once he made a surprising and profound criticism, for on my asking him if he had read Tennyson he said no, but was he not rather a lady-like writer?

When Verlaine stayed with me he wrote a poem about Fountain Court, which began truthfully:

> *La Cour de la Fontaine est, dans le Temple,*
> *Un coin exquis de ce coin délicat*
> *Du Londres vieux.*

Dickens of course has written about the fountain, but there is only one man who could ever have given its due to that corner of the Temple, and he had other, less lovely corners to love. I say over everything Charles Lamb wrote about the Temple, and fancy it was meant for Fountain Court.

More than once, while I was living in the Temple, I was visited by a strange friend of mine, an amateur tramp, with whom I used to wander about London every night in the East End, and about the Docks, and in all the more squalid parts of the city. My friend was born a wanderer, and I do not know what remains for him in the world when he has tramped over its whole surface. I have known him for many years, and we have explored many cities together, and crossed more than one sea, and travelled along the highroads of more than one country. His tramping with me was not very serious, but when he is alone he goes as a tramp among tramps, taking no money with him, begging his way with beggars. A little, pale, thin young man, quietly restless, with determined eyes and tight lips, a face prepared for all disguises, yet with a strangely personal life looking out at you, ambiguously enough, from underneath, he is never quite at home under a roof or in the company of ordinary people, where he seems always like one caught and detained unwillingly. An American, who has studied in a German University, brought up, during all his early life, in Berlin, he has always had a fixed distaste for the interests of those about him, and an instinctive passion for whatever exists outside the border-line which shuts us in upon respectability. There is a good deal of affectation in the literary revolt against respectability, together with a child's desire to shock its elders, and snatch a lurid reputation from those whom it professes to despise. My friend has never had any of this affectation; life is not a masquerade to him, and his disguises are the most serious part of his life. The simple fact is, that respectability, the normal existence of normal people, does not interest him; he could not even tell you why, without searching consciously for reasons; he was born with the soul of a vagabond, into a family of gentle, exquisitely refined people: he was born so, that is all. Human curiosity, curiosity which in most of us is subordinate to some more definite purpose, exists in him for its own sake; it is his inner life, he has no other; his form of self-development, his form of culture. It seems to me that this man, who has seen so much of humanity, who has seen humanity so closely, where it has least temptation to be anything but itself, has really achieved culture

almost perfect of its kind, though the kind be of
his own invention. He is not an artist, who can
create; he is not a thinker or a dreamer or a man of
action; he is a student of men and women, and of
the outcasts among men and women, just those
persons who are least accessible, least cared for,
least understood, and therefore, to one like my
friend, most alluring. He is not conscious of it,
but I think there is a great pity at the heart of this
devouring curiosity. It is his love of the outcast
which makes him like to live with outcasts, not
as a visitor in their midst, but as one of themselves.

For here is the difference between this man
and the other adventurers who have gone abroad
among tramps and criminals, and other misunder-
stood or unfortunate people. Some have been
philanthropists and have gone with Bibles in their
hands; others have been journalists, and have gone
with note-books in their hands; all have gone as
visitors, as passing visitors, plunging into "the
bath of multitude," as one might go holiday-making
to the sea-side and plunge into the sea. But this
man, wherever he has gone, has gone with a complete abandonment to his surroundings; no tramp
has ever known that "Cigarette" was not really
a tramp; he has begged, worked, ridden outside
trains, slept in workhouses and gaols, not shirked
one of the hardships of his way; and all the time
he has been living his own life (whatever that
enigma may be!) more perfectly, I am sure, than

when he is dining every day at his mother's or his sister's table.

The desire of travelling on many roads, and the desire of seeing many foreign faces, are almost always found united in that half-unconscious instinct which makes a man a vagabond. But I have never met any one in whom the actual love of the road is so strong as it is in my friend. In America, where the tramps ride over and under the trains, in order that they may get on the other side of a thousand miles without spending a lifetime about it, he, too, has gone by rail, not as a passenger. And I remember a few years ago, when we had given one another rendezvous at St. Petersburg, that I found, when I got there, that he was already half-way across Siberia, on the new railway which they were in the act of making. Also I have been with him to Hamburg and Le Havre and Antwerp by sea: once on an Atlantic liner, loaded with foreign Jews, among whom he spent most of his time in the steerage. But for the most part he walks. Wherever he walks he makes friends; when we used to walk about London together he would stop to talk with every drunken old woman in Drury Lane, and get into the confidence of every sailor whom we came upon in the pot-houses about the docks. He is not fastidious, and will turn his hand, as the phrase is, to anything. And he goes through every sort of privation, endures dirt, accustoms himself to the society of every variety of his fellow-creatures without a murmur or regret.

London.

After all, comfort is a convention, and pleasure an individual thing, to every individual. "To travel is to die continually," wrote a half-crazy poet who spent most of the years of a short fantastic life in London. Well, that is a line which I have often found myself repeating as I shivered in railway-stations on the other side of Europe, or lay in a plunging berth as the foam chased the snow-flakes off the deck. One finds, no doubt, a particular pleasure in looking back on past discomforts, and I am convinced that a good deal of the attraction of travelling comes from an unconscious throwing forward of the mind to the time when the uncomfortable present shall have become a stirring memory of the past. But I am speaking now for those in whom a certain luxuriousness of temperament finds itself in sharp conflict with the desire of movement. To my friend, I think, this is hardly a conceivable state of mind. He is a Stoic, as the true adventurer should be. Rest, even as a change, does not appeal to him. He thinks acutely, but only about facts, about the facts before him; and so he does not need to create an atmosphere about himself which change might disturb. He is fond of his family, his friends; but he can do without them, like a man with a mission. He has no mission, only a great thirst; and this thirst for the humanity of every nation and for the roads of every country drives him onward as resistlessly as the drunkard's thirst for drink, or the idealist's thirst for an ideal.

Cities and Sea-Coasts and Islands.

And it seems to me that few men have realised, as this man has realised, that "not the fruit of experience, but experience itself, is the end." He has chosen his life for himself, and he has lived it, regardless of anything else in the world. He has desired strange, almost inaccessible things, and he has attained whatever he has desired. While other men have lamented their fate, wished their lives different, nursed vague ambitions, and dreamed fruitless dreams, he has quietly given up comfort and conventionality, not caring for them, and he has gone his own way without even stopping to think whether the way were difficult or desirable. Not long since, walking with a friend in the streets of New York, he said suddenly: "Do you know, I wonder what it is like to chase a man? I know what it is like to be chased, but to chase a man would be a new sensation." The other man laughed, and thought no more about it. A week later my friend came to him with an official document: he had been appointed a private detective. He was set on the track of a famous criminal (whom, as it happened, he had known as a tramp); he made his plans, worked them out successfully, and the criminal was caught. To have done was enough: he had had the sensation; he has done no more work as a detective. Is there not, in this curiosity in action, this game mastered and then cast aside, a wonderful promptness, sureness, a moral quality which is itself success in life?

To desire so much, and what is so human, to

make one's life out of the very fact of living it as
one chooses; to create a unique personal satisfaction
out of discontent and curiosity; to be so much
oneself in learning so much from other people:
is not this, in its way, an ideal, and has not my friend
achieved it? What I like in him so much is that
he is a vagabond without an object. He has
written one book, but writing has come to him as
an accident; and, in writing, his danger is to be
too literal for art, and not quite literal enough for
science. He is too completely absorbed in people
and things to be able ever to get aloof from them;
and to write well of what one has done and seen
one must be able to get aloof from oneself and from
others. If ever a man loved wandering for its
own sake it was George Borrow; but George
Borrow had a serious and whimsical brain always
at work, twisting the things that he saw into shapes
that pleased him more than the shapes of the things
in themselves. My friend is interested in what
he calls sociology, but the interest is almost as
accidental as his interest in literature or in phil-
anthropy. He has the soul and feet of the vagabond, the passion of the roads. He is restless under
any roof but the roof of stars. He cares passionately for men and women, not because they are
beautiful or good or clever, or because he can do
them good, or because they can be serviceable to
him, but because they are men and women. And
he cares for men and women where they are most
vividly themselves, where they have least need for

Cities and Sea-Coasts and Islands.

disguise; for poor people, and people on the roads, idle people, criminals sometimes, the people who are so much themselves that they are no longer a part of society. He wanders over the whole earth, but he does not care for the beauty or strangeness of what he sees, only for the people. Writing to me lately from Samarcand, he said: "I have seen the tomb of the prophet Daniel; I have seen the tomb of Tamerlane." But Tamerlane was nothing to him, the prophet Daniel was nothing to him. He mentioned them only because they would interest me. He was trying to puzzle out and piece together the psychology of the Persian beggar whom he had left at the corner of the way.

IV.

When my French friends come to London they say to me: where is your Montmartre, where is your Quartier Latin? We have no Montmartre (not even Chelsea is that), no Quartier Latin, because there is no instinct in the Englishman to be companionable in public. Occasions are lacking, it is true, for the café is responsible for a good part of the artistic Bohemianism of Paris, and we have no cafés. I prophesy in these pages that some day some one, probably an American who has come by way of Paris, will set back the plate-glass windows in many angles, which I could indicate to him, of the Strand, Piccadilly, and other streets, and will turn the whole wall into windows, and leave a space in front for a *terrasse*, in the Paris manner, and we shall have cafés like the cafés in Paris, and the *prestidigitateur* who has done this will soon have made a gigantic fortune. But meanwhile let us recognise that there is in London no companionship in public (in the open air or visible through windows) and that nothing in Cafés Royaux and Monicos and the like can have the sort of meaning for young men in London that the cafés have long had, and still have, in Paris. Attempts have been made, and I have shared in them, and for their time they had their entertainment; but I have not seen one that flourished.

I remember the desperate experiments of some to whom Paris, from a fashion, had become almost a necessity; and how Dowson took to cabmen's

197

Cities and Sea-Coasts and Islands.

shelters as a sort of supper-club. Different taverns were at different times haunted by young writers; some of them came for the drink and some for the society; and one bold attempt was made to get together a *cénacle* in quite the French manner in the upper room of a famous old inn. In London we cannot read our poems to one another, as they do in Paris; we cannot even talk about our own works, frankly, with a natural pride, a good-humoured equality. They can do that in Dublin, and in an upper room in Dublin I find it quite natural. But in London even those of us who are least Anglo-Saxon cannot do it. Is it more, I wonder, a loss to us or a gain?

This lack of easy meeting and talking is certainly one of the reasons why there have been in England many great writers but few schools. In Paris a young man of twenty starts a "school" as he starts a "revue"; and these hasty people are in France often found among the people who last. In modern England we have gained, more than we think perhaps, from the accidents of neighbourhood that set Wordsworth and Coleridge walking and talking together. As it was England, and one of them was Wordsworth, they met in Cumberland; in London we have had nothing like the time of Victor Hugo, when Baudelaire and Gautier and Gérard de Nerval and men of obscure and vagabond genius made Paris vital, a part of themselves, a form of creative literature. That is what London has in itself the genius, the men and the material,

198

to be; but of the men of our time only Henley and John Davidson have loved it or struck music out of it.

If we had only had a Walt Whitman for London! Whitman is one of the voices of the earth, and it is only in Whitman that the paving-stones really speak, with a voice as authentic as the voice of the hills. He knew no distinction between what is called the work of nature and what is the work of men. He left out nothing, and what still puzzles us is the blind, loving, embracing way in which he brings crude names and things into his vision, the name of a trade, a street, a territory, no matter what syllables it might carry along with it. He created a vital poetry of cities; it was only a part of what he did; but since Whitman there is no gainsaying it any longer.

When I came to London, I knew nothing of the great things that Whitman had done, or that it was possible to do them in such a way; but I had my own feeling for London, my own point of view there, and I found myself gradually trying to paint, or to set to music, to paint in music, perhaps, those sensations which London awakened in me. I was only trying to render what I saw before me, what I felt, and to make my art out of living material. "Books made out of books pass away" was a sentence I never forgot, and my application of it was direct and immediate.

I have always been curious of sensations, and above all of those which seemed to lead one into

Cities and Sea-Coasts and Islands.

"artificial paradises" not within everybody's reach. It took me some time to find out that every "artificial paradise" is within one's own soul, somewhere among one's own dreams, and that haschisch is a poor substitute for the imagination. The mystery of all the intoxicants fascinated me, and drink, which had no personal appeal to me, which indeed brought me no pleasures, found me endlessly observant of its powers, effects, and variations.

Many of my friends drank, and I was forced to become acquainted with the different forms which liquor could take, so that I could almost label them in their classes. Thus one, whom I will call A., drank copiously, continually, all drinks, for pleasure: he could carry so much so steadily that he sometimes passed his limit without knowing it: not that he minded passing the limit, but he liked to be conscious of it. B. drank to become unconscious, he passed his limit rapidly, and became first apologetic, then quarrelsome. His friend C., a man abstract in body and mind, who muttered in Greek when he was least conscious of himself, and sat with imperturbable gravity, drinking like an ascetic, until his head fell without warning on the table, seemed to compete with B. in how to finish soonest with a life which he had no desire to get rid of. I do not think he ever got any pleasure out of drinking: he would sit up over night with absinthe and cigarettes in order to be awake to attend early mass; but though his will was strong enough for that, the habit was stronger than his will, and he seemed like one condemned to that form of suicide without desire or choice in the matter. D. drank for pleasure, but he was scrupulous in what he drank, and would take menthe verte for its colour, absinthe because it lulled him with vague dreams, ether because it could be taken on strawberries. I remember his telling me exactly what it feels like to have delirium tremens, and he told it minutely, self-pityingly, but with a relish; not without a melancholy artistic pride in the sensations, their strangeness, and the fact that he should have been the victim.

There were others; there was even one who cured himself in some miraculous way, and could see his friends drink champagne at his expense, while he drank soda-water. All these I wondered at and fancied that I understood. I admit that I was the more interested in these men because they were living in the way I call artificial. I never thought any one the better for being a spendthrift of any part of his energies, but I certainly often found him more interesting than those who were not spendthrifts.

I also found a peculiar interest in another part of what is artificial, properly artificial, in London. A city is no part of nature, and one may choose among the many ways in which something peculiar to walls and roofs and artificial lighting, is carried on. All commerce and all industries have their share in taking us further from nature and further from our needs, as they create about us unnatural

Cities and Sea-Coasts and Islands.

conditions which are really what develop in us these new, extravagant, really needless needs. And the whole night-world of the stage is, in its way, a part of the very soul of cities. That lighted gulf, before which the footlights are the flaming stars between world and world, shows the city the passions and that beauty which the soul of man in cities is occupied in weeding out of its own fruitful and prepared soil.

That is, the theatres are there to do so, they have no reason for existence if they do not do so; but for the most part they do not do so. The English theatre with its unreal realism and its un-imaginative pretences towards poetry left me untouched and unconvinced. I found the beauty, the poetry, that I wanted only in two theatres that were not looked upon as theatres, the Alhambra and the Empire. The ballet seemed to me the subtlest of the visible arts, and dancing a more significant speech than words. I could almost have said seriously, as Verlaine once said in jest, coming away from the Alhambra: "J'aime Shakespeare, mais . . . j'aime mieux le ballet!" Why is it that one can see a ballet fifty times, always with the same sense of pleasure, while the most absorbing play becomes a little tedious after the third time of seeing? For one thing, because the difference between seeing a play and seeing a ballet is just the difference between reading a book and looking at a picture. One returns to a picture as one returns to nature, for a delight which, being purely of the senses, never tires, never distresses, never varies. To read a book even for the first time, requires a certain effort. The book must indeed be exceptional that can be read three or four times, and no book was ever written that could be read three or four times in succession. A ballet is simply a picture in movement. It is a picture where the imitation of nature is given by nature itself; where the figures of the composition are real, and yet, by a very paradox of travesty, have a delightful, deliberate air of unreality. It is a picture where the colours change, re-combine, before one's eyes; where the outlines melt into one another, emerge, and are again lost, in the kaleidoscopic movement of the dance. Here we need tease ourselves with no philosophies, need endeavour to read none of the riddles of existence; may indeed give thanks to be spared for one hour the imbecility of human speech. After the tedium of the theatre, where we are called on to interest ourselves in the improbable fortunes of uninteresting people, how welcome is the relief of a spectacle which professes to be no more than merely beautiful; which gives us, in accomplished dancing, the most beautiful human sight; which provides, in short, the one escape into fairyland which is permitted by that tyranny of the real which is the worst tyranny of modern life.

The most magical glimpse I ever caught of a ballet was from the road in front, from the other side of the road, one night when two doors were suddenly thrown open as I was passing. In the

moment's interval before the doors closed again, I
saw, in that odd, unexpected way, over the heads
of the audience, far off in a sort of blue mist, the
whole stage, its brilliant crowd drawn up in the
last pose, just as the curtain was beginning to go
down. It stamped itself in my brain, an impression
caught just at the perfect moment, by some rare
felicity of chance. But that is not an impression
that can be repeated. For the most part I like to
see my illusions clearly, recognising them as illusions, and so heightening their charm. I like
to see a ballet from the wings, a spectator, but in
the midst of the magic. To see a ballet from the
wings is to lose all sense of proportion, all knowledge
of the piece as a whole, but, in return, it is fruitful
in happy accidents, in momentary points of view,
in chance felicities of light and shade and movement. It is almost to be in the performance oneself,
and yet passive, with the leisure to look about one.
You see the reverse of the picture: the girls at the
back lounging against the set scenes, turning to
talk with some one at the side; you see how lazily
some of them are moving, and how mechanical and
irregular are the motions that flow into rhythm
when seen from the front. Now one is in the
centre of a joking crowd, hurrying from the dressing-
rooms to the stage; now the same crowd returns,
charging at full speed between the scenery, every
one trying to reach the dressing-room stairs first.
And there is the constant travelling of scenery,
from which one has a series of escapes, as it bears

down unexpectedly in some new direction. The ballet half seen in the centre of the stage, seen in sections, has, in the glimpses that can be caught of it, a contradictory appearance of mere nature and of absolute unreality. And beyond the footlights, on the other side of the orchestra, one can see the boxes near the stalls, the men standing by the bar, an angle cut sharply off from the stalls, with the light full on the faces, the intent eyes, the grey smoke curling up from the cigarettes: a Degas, in short.

And there is a charm, which I cannot think wholly imaginary or factitious, in that form of illusion which is known as make-up. To a plain face, it is true, make-up only intensifies plainness; for make-up does but give colour and piquancy to what is already in a face, it adds nothing new. But to a face already charming, how becoming all this is, what a new kind of exciting savour it gives to that real charm! It has, to the remnant of Puritan conscience or consciousness that is the heritage of us all, a certain sense of dangerous wickedness, the delight of forbidden fruit. The very phrase, painted women, has come to have an association of sin and to have put paint on her cheeks, though for the innocent necessities of her profession, gives to a woman a kind of symbolic corruption. At once she seems to typify the sorceries, and entanglements of what is most deliberately enticing in her sex:

Femina dulce malum, pariter favus atque venenum —

with all that is most subtle, least like nature, in her power to charm. Maquillage, to be attractive, must of course be unnecessary. As a disguise for age or misfortune, it has no interest. But, of all places, on the stage, and, of all people, on the cheeks of young people; there, it seems to me that make-up is intensely fascinating, and its recognition is of the essence of my delight in a stage performance. I do not for a moment want really to believe in what I see before me; to believe that those wigs are hair, that grease-paint a blush; any more than I want really to believe that the actor who has just crossed the stage in his everyday clothes has turned into an actual King when he puts on clothes that look like a King's clothes. I know that a delightful imposition is being practised upon me; that I am to see fairyland for a while; and to me all that glitters shall be gold.

The ballet in particular, but also the whole surprising life of the music-halls, took hold of me with the charm of what was least real among the pompous and distressing unrealities of a great city. And some form I suppose of that instinct which has created the gladiatorial shows and the bull-fight made me fascinated by the faultless and fatal art of the acrobat, who sets his life in the wager, and wins the wager by sheer skill, a triumph of fine shades. That love of fine shades took me angrily past the spoken vulgarities of most music-hall singing (how much more priceless do they make the silence of dancing!) to that one great art of fine shades, made up out of speech just lifted into song, which has been revealed to us by Yvette Guilbert.

I remember when I first heard her in Paris, and tried vainly at the time, to get the English managers to bring her over to London. She sang "Sainte Galette," and as I listened to the song I felt a cold shiver run down my back, that shiver which no dramatic art except that of Sarah Bernhardt had ever given me. It was not this that I was expecting to find in the thin woman with the long black gloves. I had heard that her songs were immoral, and that her manner was full of underhand intention. What I found was a moral so poignant, so human, that I could scarcely endure the pity of it, it made me feel that I was wicked, not that she was; I, to have looked at these dreadfully serious things lightly. Later on, in London, I heard her sing "La Soularde," that song in which, as Goncourt notes in his journal, "la diseuse de chansonnettes se révèle comme une grande, une très grande actrice tragique, vous mettant au cœur une constriction angoisseuse." It is about an old drunken woman, whom the children follow and laugh at in the streets. Yvette imitates her old waggling head, her tottering walk, her broken voice, her little sudden furies, her miserable resignation; she suggests all this, almost without moving, by the subtlest pantomime, the subtlest inflections of voice and face, and she thrills you with the grotesque pathos of the whole situation, with the intense humanity of it. I imagine such a situation

Cities and Sea-Coasts and Islands.

rendered by an English music-hall singer! Imagine the vulgarity, the inhumanity, of the sort of beery caricature that we should get, in place of this absolutely classic study in the darker and more sordid side of life. The art of Yvette Guilbert is always classic; it has restraint, form, dignity, in its wildest licence. Its secret is its expressiveness, and the secret of that expressiveness lies perhaps largely in its attention to detail. Others are content with making an effect, say twice, in the course of a song. Yvette Guilbert insists on getting the full meaning out of every line, but quietly, without emphasis, as if in passing; and, with her, to grasp a meaning is to gain an effect.

There was the one great artist of that world which, before I could apprehend it, had to be reflected back to me as in some bewildering mirror. It was out of mere curiosity that I had found my way into that world, into that mirror, but, once there, the thing became material for me. I tried to do in verse something of what Degas had done in painting. I was conscious of transgressing no law of art in taking that scarcely touched material for new uses. Here, at least, was a *décor* which appealed to me, and which seemed to me full of strangeness, beauty, and significance. I still think that there is a poetry in this world of illusion, not less genuine of its kind than that more easily apprehended poetry of a world, so little more real, that poets have mostly turned to. It is part of the poetry of cities, and it waits for us in London.

V.

A CITY is characterised by its lights, and it is to its lights, acting on its continual mist, that London owes much of the mystery of its beauty. On a winter afternoon every street in London becomes mysterious. You see even the shops through a veil, people are no longer distinguishable as persons, but are a nimble flock of shadows. Lights travel and dance through alleys that seem to end in darkness. Every row of gas lamps turns to a trail of fire; fiery stars shoot and flicker in the night. Night becomes palpable, and not only an absence of the light of day.

The most beautiful lighting of a city is the lighting of one street in Rome by low-swung globes of gas that hang like oranges down the Via Nazionale, midway between the houses. In London we light casually, capriciously, every one at his own will, and so there are blinding shafts at one step and a pit of darkness at the next, and it is an adventure to follow the lights in any direction, the lights are all significant and mean some place of entertainment or the ambition of some shopkeeper. They draw one by the mere curiosity to find out why they are there, what has set them signalling. And, as you walk beyond or aside from the shops, all these private illuminations are blotted out, and the dim, sufficing street-gas of the lamp-posts takes their place.

The canals, in London, have a mysterious quality, made up of sordid and beautiful elements, now a black trail, horrible, crawling secretly; now a sudden opening, as at Maida Vale, between dull houses, upon the sky. At twilight in winter the canal smokes and flares, a long line of water with its double row of lamps, dividing the land. From where Browning lived for so many years there is an aspect which might well have reminded him of Venice. The canal parts, and goes two ways, broadening to almost a lagoon, where trees droop over the water from a kind of island, with rocky houses perched on it. You see the curve of a bridge, formed by the shadow into a pure circle, and lighted by the reflection of a gas lamp in the water beyond; and the dim road opposite following the line of the canal, might be a calle; only the long hull of a barge lying there is not Venetian in shape, and, decidedly, the atmosphere is not Venetian. Verlaine, not knowing, I think, that Browning lived there, made a poem about the canal, which he dated "Paddington." It is one of his two "Streets," and it begins: "O la rivière dans la rue," and goes on to invoke "l'eau jaune comme une morte," with nothing to reflect but the fog. The barges crawl past with inexpressible slowness; coming out slowly after the horse and the rope from under the bridge, with a woman leaning motionless against the helm, and drifting on as if they were not moving at all.

On the river the lights are always at work building fairy-palaces; wherever there are trees they wink like stars through drifting cloud, and the trees become oddly alive, with a more restless life than their life by day. I have seen a plain churchyard with its straight grave-stones turn on a winter afternoon into a sea of white rocks, with vague rosy shore lights beyond. But it is the fog which lends itself to the supreme London decoration, collaborating with gaslight through countless transformations, from the white shroud to the yellow blanket, until every gas lamp is out, and you cannot see a torch a yard beyond your feet.

There is nothing in the world quite like a London fog, though the underground railway stations in the days of steam might have prepared us for it and Dante has described it in the "Inferno" when he speaks of the banks of a pit in hell, "crusted over with a mould from the vapour below, which cakes upon them, and battles with eye and nose." Foreigners praise it as the one thing in which London is unique. They come to London to experience it. It is as if one tried the experience of drowning or suffocating. It is a penalty worse than any Chinese penalty. It stifles the mind as well as choking the body. It comes on slowly and stealthily, picking its way, choosing its direction, leaving contemptuous gaps in its course; then it settles down like a blanket of solid smoke, which you can feel but not put from you. The streets turn putrescent, the gas lamps hang like rotting fruit, you are in a dark tunnel, in which the lights are going out, and beside you, unseen,

211

Cities and Sea-Coasts and Islands.

there is a roar and rumble, interrupted with sharp cries, a stopping of wheels and a beginning of the roar and rumble over again. You walk like a blind man, fumbling with his staff at the edge of the pavement. Familiar turnings, which you fancied you could follow blindfold, deceive you, and you are helpless if you go two yards out of your course. The grime blackens your face, your eyes smart, your throat is as if choked with dust. You breathe black foulness and it enters into you and contaminates you.

And yet, how strange, inexplicable, mysteriously impressive is this masque of shadows! It is the one wholly complete transformation of the visible world, the one darkness which is really visible, the one creation of at least the beauty of horror which has been made by dirt, smoke, and cities.

Yet the eternal smoke of London lies in wait for us, not only in the pestilence of chimneys, but rising violently out of the earth, in a rhetoric of its own. There are in London certain gaps or holes in the earth, which are like vent-holes, and out of these openings its inner ferment comes for a moment to the surface. One of them is at Chalk Farm Station. There is a gaunt cavernous doorway leading underground, and this doorway faces three roads from the edge of a bridge. The bridge crosses an abyss of steam, which rises out of depths like the depths of a boiling pot, only it is a witches' pot of noise and fire; and pillars and pyramids of smoke rise continually out of it, and there are

212

hoarse cries, screams, a clashing and rattling, the sound as of a movement which struggles and cannot escape, like the coiling of serpents twisting together in a pit. Their breath rises in clouds, and drifts voluminously over the gap of the abyss; catching at times a ghastly colour from the lamplight. Sometimes one of the snakes seems to rise and sway out of the tangle, a column of yellow blackness. Multitudes of red and yellow eyes speckle the vague and smoky darkness, out of which rise domes and roofs and chimneys; and a few astonished trees lean over the mouth of the pit, sucking up draughts of smoke for air.

VI.

Is there any city in which life and the conditions
of life can be more abject than in London, any city
in which the poor are more naturally unhappy
and less able to shake off or come through their
poverty into any natural relief? Those sordid
splendours of smoke and dirt which may be so fine
as aspects, mean something which we can only
express by the English word squalor; they mean
the dishumanising of innumerable people who
have no less right than ourselves to exist naturally.
I will take one road, which I know well, and which
every one who lives in London must know somewhat, for it is a main artery, Edgware Road, as a
parable of what I mean. Nowhere in London is
there more material for a comparative study in
living.

Edgware Road begins proudly in the West
End of London, sweeping off in an emphatic
curve from the railings of Hyde Park, beyond the
Marble Arch; it grows meaner before Chapel
Street, and from Chapel Street to the flower-shanty
by the canal, where Maida Vale goes down hill,
it seems to concentrate into itself all the sordidness
of London. Walking outward from Chapel Street,
on the right-hand side of the road, you plunge
instantly into a dense, parching, and enveloping
smell, made up of stale fish, rotting vegetables,
and the must of old clothes. The pavement is
never clean; bits of torn paper, fragments of
cabbage leaves, the rind of fruit, the stalks of
214

flowers, the litter swept away from the front of shops
and lingering on its way to the gutter, drift to and
fro under one's feet, moist with rain or greased
with mud. As one steps out of the way of a slimy
greyness on the ground, one brushes against a
coat on which the dirt has caked or a skirt which
it streaks damply. Women in shawls, with untidy
hair, turn down into the road from all the side
streets, and go in and out of the shops. They
carry baskets, bags, and parcels wrapped in newspapers; grease oozes through the paper, smearing
it with printer's ink as it melts. They push per-
ambulators in front of them, in which children with
smeared faces pitch and roll; they carry babies
under their shawls. Men with unshaven faces,
holding short clay pipes between their teeth, walk
shamblingly at their side; the men's clothes are
discoloured with time and weather, and hang
loosely about them, as if they had been bought
ready-made; they have dirty scarves knotted round
their necks, and they go along without speaking.
Men with thread-bare frock coats, ill-fitting and
carefully brushed, pass nervously, with white faces
and thin fingers. Heavy men with whips in their
hands, thin, clean-shaven men in short coats and
riding gaiters, lounge in front of the horse-dealer's
across the road, or outside dusty shops with bundles
of hay and sacks of bran in their doorways.

Here and there a gaudy sheet slung across a
window announces a fat woman on show, or a
collection of waxworks with the latest murder;

Cities and Sea-Coasts and Islands.

flags and streamers, daubed with ragged lettering, hang out from the upper windows. At intervals, along the pavement, there are girls offering big bunches of white and yellow flowers; up the side streets there are barrows of plants and ferns and flowers in pots; and the very odour of the flowers turns sickly, as the infection of the air sucks it up and mingles it with the breath and sweat of the people and the ancient reek of clothes that have grown old upon unwashed bodies.

Sometimes a pavement artist brings his pictures with him on a square canvas, and ties a string in front of them, propping them against the wall, and sits on the ground at one end, with his cap in his hand. At regular intervals a Punch and Judy comes to one of the side streets, just in from the road, a little melancholy white dog with a red ruff about its neck barks feebly as the puppets flap their noses in its face. On Sundays the Salvation Army holds meetings, with flags flying and loud brass instruments playing; the red caps and black sun-bonnets can be seen in the hollow midst of the crowd. Not far off, men dressed in surplices stand beside a harmonium, with prayer-books in their hands; a few people listen to them half-heartedly. There are generally one or two Italian women, with bright green birds in their cages, huddled in the corner of doorways and arches, waiting to tell fortunes. A blind beggar in a tall hat stands at the edge of the curbstone; he has a tray of matches and boot-laces to sell; he holds a stick in his hand, with which he paws nervously at an inch of pavement; his heel seeks the gutter, and feels its way up and down from gutter to pavement.

Somewhere along the road there is generally a little crowd; a horse has fallen, or a woman has lost a penny in the mud, or a policeman, note-book in hand, is talking to a cab-driver who has upset a bicycle. Two women are quarrelling; they tear at the handle of a perambulator in which two babies sit and smile cheerfully. Two men grapple with each other in the middle of the road, almost under the horses of the omnibus; the driver stops his horses, so as not to run them down. A coarse, red-faced woman of fifty drags an old woman by the arm; she is almost too old to walk, and she totters and spreads out her arms helplessly as the other pulls at her; her head turns on her shoulder, looking out blindly, the mouth falling open in a convulsive grimace, the whole face eaten away with some obscure suffering which she is almost past feeling. A barrel-organ plays violently; some youths stare at the picture of the fat, half-naked lady on the front of the instrument; one or two children hold out their skirts in both hands and begin to dance to the tune.

On Saturday night the Road is lined with stalls; naphtha flames burn over every stall, flaring away from the wind, and lighting up the faces that lean towards them from the crowd on the pavement. There are stalls with plants, cheap jewelry, paper

Cities and Sea-Coasts and Islands.

books, scarves and braces, sweets, bananas, ice-cream barrows, weighing-machines; long rows of rabbits hang by their trussed hind legs, and a boy skins them rapidly with a pen-knife for the buyers; raw lumps of meat redden and whiten as the light drifts over and away from them; the salesmen cry their wares. The shops blaze with light, displaying their cheap clothes and cheap furniture and clusters of cheap boots. Some of the women are doing their Saturday night's shopping, but for the most part it is a holiday night, and the people swarm in the streets, some in their working clothes, some in the finery which they will put on to-morrow for their Sunday afternoon walk in the Park; in their faces, their movements, there is that un-enjoying hilarity which the end of the week's work, the night, the week's wages, the sort of street fair at which one can buy things to eat and to put on, bring out in people who seem to live for the most part with preoccupied indifference.

As I walk to and fro in Edgware Road, I cannot help sometimes wondering why these people exist, why they take the trouble to go on existing. Watch their faces, and you will see in them a listlessness, a hard unconcern, a failure to be interested, which speaks equally in the roving eyes of the man who stands smoking at the curbstone with his hands in his pockets, and in the puckered cheeks of the woman doing her shopping, and in the noisy laugh of the youth leaning against the wall, and in the grey, narrow face of the child whose thin legs are

218

too tired to dance when the barrel-organ plays jigs. Whenever anything happens in the streets there is a crowd at once, and this crowd is made up of people who have no pleasures and no interests of their own to attend to, and to whom any variety is welcome in the tedium of their lives. In all these faces you will see no beauty, and you will see no beauty in the clothes they wear, or in their attitudes in rest or movement, or in their voices when they speak. They are human beings to whom nature has given no grace or charm, whom life has made vulgar, and for whom circumstances have left no escape from themselves. In the climate of England, in the atmosphere of London, on these pavements of Edgware Road, there is no way of getting any simple happiness out of natural things, and they have lost the capacity for accepting natural pleasures graciously, if such came to them. Crawling between heaven and earth thus miserably, they have never known what makes existence a practicable art or a tolerable spectacle, and they have infinitely less sense of the mere abstract human significance of life than the facchino who lies, a long blue streak in the sun, on the Zattere at Venice, or the girl who carries water from the well in an earthen pitcher, balancing it on her head, in any Spanish street.

Or, instead of turning to human beings, in some more favourable part of the world, go to the Zoological Gardens and look at the beasts there. The conditions of existence are, perhaps, slightly worse for the beasts; their cages are narrow, more securely

Cities and Sea-Coasts and Islands.

barred; human curiosity is brought to bear upon them with a more public offence. But observe, under all these conditions, the dignity of the beasts, their disdain, their indifference! When the fluttering beribboned, chattering human herd troops past them, pointing at them with shrill laughter, uneasy, preoccupied, one eye on the beasts and the other on the neighbour's face or frock, they sit there stolidly in their cages, not condescending to notice their unruly critics. When they move, they move with the grace of natural things, made rhythmical with beauty and strong for ravage and swift for flight. They pace to and fro, rubbing themselves against the bars, restlessly; but they seem all on fire with a life that tingles to the roots of their claws and to the tips of their tails, dilating their nostrils and quivering in little shudders down their smooth flanks. They have found an enemy craftier than they, they have been conquered and carried away captive, and they are full of smouldering rage. But with the loss of liberty they have lost nothing of themselves; the soul of their flesh is uncontaminated by humiliation. They pass a mournful existence nobly, each after his kind, in loneliness or in unwilling companionship; their eyes look past us without seeing us; we have no power over their concentration within the muscles of their vivid limbs or within the coils of their subtle bodies.

Humanity, at the best, has much to be ashamed of, physically, beside the supreme physical perfection of the panther or the snake. All of us look poor enough creatures as we come away from their cages. But think now of these men and women whom we have seen swarming in Edgware Road, of their vulgarity, their abjectness of attitude toward life, their ugliness, dirt, insolence, their loud laughter. All the animals except man have too much dignity to laugh; only man found out the way to escape the direct force of things by attaching a critical sense, or a sense of relief, to a sound which is neither a cackle nor a whinny, but which has something of those two inarticulate voices of nature. As I passed through the Saturday night crowd lately, between two opposing currents of evil smells, I overheard a man who was lurching along the pavement say in contemptuous comment: "Twelve o'clock! we may be all dead by twelve o'clock!" He seemed to sum up the philosophy of that crowd, its listlessness, its hard unconcern, its failure to be interested. Nothing matters, he seemed to say for them; let us drag out our time until the time is over, and the sooner it is over the better.

Life in great cities dishumanises humanity; it envelops the rich in multitudes of clogging, costly trifles, and cakes the poor about with ignoble dirt and the cares of unfruitful labour. Go into the country, where progress and machines and other gifts of the twentieth century have not wholly taken away the peasant's hand from the spade and plough, or to any fishing village on the coast, and you will see that poverty, even in England, can find some natural delights in natural things. You

Cities and Sea-Coasts and Islands.

will find, often enough, that very English quality of vulgarity in the peasant who lives inland; only the sea seems to cleanse vulgarity out of the English peasant, and to brace him into a really simple and refined dignity. And, after all, though the labourer who turns the soil is in unceasing contact with nature, he has not that sting of danger to waken him and cultivate his senses which is never absent for long from the life of the fisherman. People who cast their nets into the sea, on the hazard of that more uncertain harvest, have a gravity, a finished self-reliance, a kind of philosophy of their own. Their eyes and hands are trained to fineness and strength, they learn to know the winds and clouds, and they measure their wits against them, risking their lives on the surety of their calculations. The constant neighbourhood of death gives life a keener savour, they have no certainty of ever opening again the door which they close behind them as they go out to launch their boats under the stars. Tossing between a naked sea and a naked sky all night long, they have leisure for many dreams, and thoughts come into their heads which never trouble the people who live in streets. They have all the visible horizon for their own.

And the sea washes clean. In the steep Cornish village that I know best, I see, whenever I go out, bright flowers in front of white cottages, a cow's head laid quietly over a stone hedge, looking down on the road, the brown harvest in the fields that stretch away beyond the trees to the edge of the

222

cliff, and then, further on towards the sky, the blue glitter of the sea, shining under sunlight, with great hills and palaces of white clouds, rising up from the water as from a solid foundation. The sea is always at the road's end, and there is always a wind from the sea, coming singing up the long street from the harbour, and shouting across the fields and whistling in the lanes. Life itself seems to come freshly into one's blood, as if life were not only a going on with one's habits and occupations, but itself meant something, actually existed. Every one I meet on the road speaks to me as I pass; their faces and their voices are cheerful; they have no curiosity, but they are ready to welcome a stranger as if he were some one they knew already. Time seems to pass easily, in each day's space between sea and sky; the day has no tedium for them; and they need go no further than to the harbour or the farm for enough interest to fill out all the hours of the day. They have room to live, air to breathe; beauty is natural to everything about them. The dates in their churchyards tell you how long they have the patience to go on living.

1908.

III.
Sea-Coasts and Islands.

Dieppe, 1895.

I.

I WENT to Dieppe this summer with the intention of staying from Saturday to Monday. Two months afterwards I began to wonder, with a very mild kind of surprise, why I had not yet returned to London. And I was not the only one to fall under this inexplicable fascination. There is a fantastical quality in Dieppe air which somehow turns us all, at our moments, into amiable and enthusiastic lunatics. Relays of friends kept arriving, I as little as they knew why; and some of them, like myself, never went back. Others, forced to live mostly in London, and for the most part content to live there, went backwards and forwards every week. What is it, in this little French watering-place, that appeals so to the not quite conventional Englishman, brings him to it, holds him in it, brings him back to it so inevitably? Nothing and everything; an impalpable charm, the old-fashioned distinction of a little town which has still, in its faded lawns by the sea, in the line of white hotels beyond the lawns, something of that 1830 air which exhales for us from a picture of Bonington. And then Dieppe is so discreetly, and with such self-respect, hospitable to us English; so different from the vulgar friendliness of Boulogne, with its "English chop-houses" insulting one's taste at every step. Dieppe receives us with perfectly French manners, offers us politeness, and exacts it on our part, and pleases a sensitive and appreciative Englishman

227

Cities and Sea-Coasts and Islands.

because it is so charming in such a French way. And then life, if you will but abandon yourself to the natural current of things, passes in a dream. I do not quite know why, but one cannot take things seriously at Dieppe. Only just on the other side of that blue streak is England: England means London. At the other end of a short railway-line is Paris. But all that is merely so many words; the mind refuses to grasp it as a fact. One's duties, probably, call one to London or Paris, one's realisable pleasures; everything but the moment's vague immense, I say again, inexplicable, satisfaction, which broods and dawdles about Dieppe.

At Dieppe the sea is liberal, and affords you a long sweep from the cliffs on the left to the pier on the right. A few villas nestle under the cliffs; then comes the Casino, which takes its slice of the *plage* with excellent judgment. Built of peppermint-coloured brick, it sprawls its length insolently above the sea. It is quite nice, as casinos go; it is roomy, and has some amusing chandeliers hung up by ribbons; and the terrace is absolutely charming. If you are insular enough to wish it, you can sit and drink brandies and sodas all day; if you would do in France as the French do, you can sit nearer the parapet, with an awning stretched above your head, and look out drowsily over the sea, which is worth looking at here, opalescent, full of soft change. You will see around you beautiful, well-dressed women, princes, painters, poets, Cléo de Mérode. All around you, bright in the bright sun, there is a flow of soft dresses, mostly in sharp, clear colours, vivid yellows and blues and whites, the most wonderful blues, more dazzling than the sea. And there are delicious hats, floating over the hair like clouds; great floating sleeves, adding wings to the butterfly; all the fashions and felicities of a whole summer.

Ah! but the *plage*, on a sunny morning in mid-season, what a feast of colour, of movement, of the most various curiosities! The *plage* has its social laws, its social divisions, an etiquette almost as scrupulous as a drawing-room. All the space in front of the Casino is tacitly reserved for the people who subscribe to the Casino, and who are moving up and down the wooden staircase from the terrace to the beach all day long. Beyond that limit the *plage* is plebeian, and belongs to everybody. Women sit about there with shawls and babies and paper parcels. Outside the Casino there are fewer people, but one is more or less smart, and the barons and *beautés de plage* are alike here. In front of the double row of bathing-machines there is a line of little private boxes. Smart women sit on exhibition in every compartment, wearing their best hats and smiles, sometimes pretending to read or sew, as if one did anything but sit on exhibition, and flirt, and chatter, and look at the bathers! There is a constant promenade along the shifting and re-sounding pathway of boards laid over the great pebbles; chairs are grouped closely all along the *plage* between this promenade and the sea; there

229

Cities and Sea-Coasts and Islands.

is another little crowd on the *estacade*, from which the bathers are diving. The bright dresses glitter in the sunlight, like a flower garden; white *peignoirs*, bright and dark bathing costumes, the white and rose of bare and streaming flesh, passing to and fro, hurriedly, between the bathing-machines and the sea. The men, if they have good figures, look well; they have at least the chance of looking well. But the women! Rare, indeed, is the woman who can look pretty, in her toilette or herself, as she comes out of the sea, wraps herself in a sort of white nightgown, and staggers up the beach, the water running down her legs. Even at the more elegant moment when she drops her *peignoir* at the sea's edge, before stepping in, it is hard for her to look her best. Is it not with a finer taste, after all, that in some parts of England the women are not allowed to bathe with the men, are kept out of sight as much as possible? A sentimental sensualist should avoid the French seaside. He will be pained at seeing how ridiculous a beautiful woman may look when she is clothed in wet and dragging garments. The lines of the body are lost or deformed; there is none of the suggestion of ordinary costume, only a grotesque and shapeless image, all in pits and protuberances for which Nature should be ashamed to accept responsibility. Between nakedness and this compromise with clothes there is the whole world's length; and as for this state of being undressed and yet covered, in this makeshift, unmilliner-like way, it is too

barbarous, Mesdames, for the tolerance of any
gentleman of taste.

II.

The Casino has many charms. You can dance
there, listen to music, walk or sit on the terrace in
the sun, write your letters in the reading-room on
the very pictorial paper which is so carefully doled
out to you; but it is for none of these things that
the Casino exists, it is in none of these things that
there lies the unique fascination of the Casino, for
those to whom the Casino has a unique fascination.
The Casino, properly speaking, is only a gorgeous
stable for the little horses. All the rooms in the
Casino open into the room of the green tables;
all the alleys of the gardens lead there. In the
intervals of the concert, if you wish to stroll for a
few minutes on the terrace, you have to pass through
the room; you see the avid circle about the tables,
hear the swish of the horses, the monotonous
"Faites vos jeux, Messieurs. . . . Les jeux sont
faits. . . . Rien ne va plus," and then, after the
expectant pause, the number: "L'as, numéro
un." And in time, however strong, or however
idle, or however indifferent you are, you will be
drawn into that fascinated circle, you will be seized
by the irresistible impulse, you will begin to play.
The fascination of gambling, to the real amateur
of the thing, is stronger than any other passion.
Men forget that a beautiful woman is sitting opposite

231

Cities and Sea-Coasts and Islands.

to them; women do not so much as notice that a more beautiful toilette than their own has just come into the room. I have seen the most famous professional beauties of Paris sit at those green tables, and not a soul has looked at them except the croupiers and myself.

I said the impulse was irresistible. I have proved it on myself. Gambling in the abstract has no charms for me; I can go to the races without the slightest inclination to take the odds; it annoys me when little newspaper boys rush up to me as if expecting me to buy their papers because they are the first to shout "All the win-ner!" I lounged about the room of the *Petits Chevaux* for weeks without putting on more than two or three two-franc pieces, which I contentedly lost. I saw my friends winning and losing every afternoon and every evening; I saw them leaving the tables with their pockets bulging with five-franc pieces; I heard them discussing lucky numbers; I saw the strength of the passion which held them by the urgency and the futility of their remorse when they had lost; I heard them saying to me, "It will be your turn next," and I laughed, certain of myself. At last a woman, with a malicious confidence, tempted me. I put on a few francs to please her, and I found myself waiting with more interest for the turn of her head than for the gesture of the little horse who passed the winning post first. I knew by that that the demon of play had not bitten me; I felt absolutely safe.

Dieppe, 1895.

Well, of course, I succumbed, and the sensation I experienced was worth the price I paid for it. While I played nothing existed but the play; the money slipped through my fingers, I gathered it in, flung it forth, with an absorption so complete that my actions were almost mechanical. My brain seemed to act with instantaneous energy; no sooner had I willed than my fingers were placing the coins here, and not there, I knew not why, on the table. I followed no system, and I never hesitated. I then knew for the first time the strength of conviction for which there is not even the pretence of a foundation. While my money lasted, and I saw it flowing to me and from me so capriciously, I felt what I think must have been the intoxication of abandoning oneself to Fate, with an astonishing sense of superiority over ordinary mortals, from whom I was almost more absolutely removed than if I had been moving in a haschisch dream. And in the exaltation, the absorption of this dream, in which I was acting with such reckless and causeless certainty, there was no really disillusioning shock, either when I lost or when I won. My excitement was so great that I accepted these accidents as merely points in a progress. After a time I did not even play for the sake of winning. I played for the sake of playing.

After all, *Petits Chevaux* is the merest amateur gambling; the serious people who play baccarat next door, in the club, would laugh at it, and rightly, from the gambler's point of view. The interest of the thing is in its revelation of the universal humanity of the gambling instinct, which comes out so certainly and so unexpectedly in the people who gamble once in the year, for a few scores or a few hundreds of francs. And those green tables are so admirable in the view they afford of the little superstitions which exist somewhere in the background of all minds. This table is lucky to such a person, that column to another. The women swear by the croupiers, and will take any amount of trouble to get a seat by the side of the one they prefer. And the croupiers, little miserable engines of Fate, sit with folded hands and intent eyes, impassive, supercilious, like little Eastern gods, raking in the money without satisfaction, and tossing you your winnings with an air of disdain. Yet they, too, in spite of their air of supremacy, are entirely at the mercy of a moment's caprice. They may be dismissed if you win too much at their table; and here is the most imposing of all the croupiers offering himself and his wife, as servants, to a lady who played there.

III.

On certain afternoons there is a *Bal des Enfants* at the Casino. You cannot imagine anything more delicious. All around the room sit children, in their white dresses, their little, thin black and yellow legs set forth gravely. They are preoccupied with their fans, their sashes, their gloves; their hair is beautifully done all over their heads, and falls down their backs. The little boys, in velvet and navy suits, march to and fro, very solemnly, a little awkwardly, bow, and choose partners. The bigger girls (some of them are thirteen or fourteen) jump up, cross the room hurriedly, with the nervous movement of young girls walking, tossing their hair back from their shoulders; they form little groups, laugh and nod to the grown-up people who stand about the door; and every now and then pounce on a tiny sister, and pull about her dress until its set suits them. In the middle of the room stand two absurd persons; the blond Jew with the immense pink nose, the golden beard and moustaches, who acts as master of the ceremonies: he tries to assume a paternal air, his swollen eyes dart about nervously; and the middle-aged lady with the eyeglasses, who is more immediately concerned with the children's conduct. She is frankly anxious, fussy, and occupied. The orchestra is about to begin, and in the middle of the room a little helpless ring of very tiny children, infants, begins to walk gravely round and round; the tiny people hold one another's hands, wonderingly, and toddle along with their heads looking over their shoulders, all in opposite directions. The dance has begun: it is the Moska, with its funny rhythm, its double stamp of the heels. Some of the children dance charmingly, with a pretty exactness in the trip and turn of the toes, the fling of the leg. There are adorable frocks, marvellous faces. They turn, turn, stop short, stamp their heels, and turn again. The whole thing is so gay and simple and artificial, these little, got-up people who are playing at being their elders; it is so pretty altogether and so exciting, that I could watch it for hours. Nothing is more exciting than to see children masquerading. I am always disposed to take them, as they would be taken, very seriously, to think of them almost as of men and women. As if they were not so far more attractive than any possible men and women! I hate to think of all that floating hair being twisted up into coils and bundled together obscurely at the back of the head. I can see the elder sisters of these enchanting little absurdities standing beside me at the door. How uninteresting they are, how little they invite the wandering of even the vaguest emotion!

IV.

But all Dieppe is not to be seen at the Casino, and, perhaps, not the most intimate part of Dieppe. I had the good fortune to live in the very heart of the town, just outside the principal doorway of the Église Saint-Jacques. I have never in my life had a more genuine and, in its way, profound sensation than my daily and nightly view of that adorable old church, a somewhat flamboyant Gothic, certainly, which I grew to love and wonder at with an intimacy that was entirely new to me. To look out last thing at night, before getting into bed,

and see the grey stone flowering there before me,
rising up into the stars as if at home there, and so
full of solid shadow about its base, broadly planted
on the solid earth; to rise in the morning and look
out on the same grey mass, white in parts, and
warm in the early sunlight; there never was a
décor which pleased me so much, which put so many
dreams into my head. Every Gothic church is a
nest of dreams, and the least religiously minded
of men has his moments of devotion, of spiritual
exaltation before so delicate and so enduring a
work of men's hands in praise of God. Sight and
thought are lost in it; one feels its immensity as
one feels the immensity of the sea. And it was
as dear to me as the sea itself, this church of the
patron saint of fishermen, who leans upon his
staff, a sensual Jewish person with fleshy lips and
a smile which is somewhat sneering in the arch of
the doorway.

During the first part of my stay, the fineness,
the supremacy, the air of eternity of the church were
curiously accentuated by a little fair, horrid, an
oppression, a nightmare, which installed itself at
the church's very base, in every corner of the many-
cornered ground about it. All day long, into the
late evening, the wooden horses went swaying
round to the noise of two or three tunes; a transformation show of Joan of Arc, just below my
window, had a drum and a cornet at the door; a
peep-show had a piano, and shots were fired all day
long in the "Tir des Salons," next door to the

Cities and Sea-Coasts and Islands.

"Théâtre Moderne," which had a small band. Then, all around, clinging still closer to the skirts of the church, were caravans and tents, in which all these motley people lived and slept and did their cooking. They swarmed about it like a crowd of insects, throwing up their little mounds in the earth; and the church rose calmly, undisturbed, almost unconscious of the very existence of the swarm, as the Eternal Church rises out of the agitations and feverish coming-and-going of the world and the fashions of the world.

V.

Very characteristic of Dieppe, I thought, and certainly quite unlike anything you can see in England, is the aspect of the Place Nationale on a market-day, with its statue of Duquesne, so brilliant and vivid in his great, flapping hat, standing there in the middle; it reminded me somewhat of the Good-Friday fair at Venice, which is held round the Goldoni statue near the Rialto. But the colours, despite the strong sunlight, are far from Venetian. At the cathedral end of the square are the butchers; then come the vegetables, splashes of somewhat tawdry green, all over the ground, and up and down the stalls. The vegetables reach nearly as far as the statue; just this side of it begin the clothes and commodities, which give its fair-like air to the market. Stalls alternate with ground-plots, all alike covered with cheap trousers, flannel shirts, heavy boots and carpet shoes, braces, foulards, handkerchiefs, stays, bright ribbons, veils, balls of worsted, shoe-laces, and, above all, dress-pieces of every sort of common and trumpery pattern. The women stop, handle them, draw them out, and the saleswoman waits with a long pair of scissors in her hand to cut off a slice here, a slice there. One dainty little covered stall has nothing but white Norman caps, laid in rows and hung in rows, one after another. White-capped old peasant women stop in front of it, compare the frilling with their own, and try to make a bargain out of a sou. Not for off is an open and upturned umbrella full of babies' white caps and stomachers. A dazzling collection of tin spoons and gilt studs lies on the ground beside it, and the proprietors squat on their heels close by. After the clothes comes a little assemblage of baskets, brushes, and tin pails and saucepans, dazzlingly white in the sun. Then come the poultry, crates, and baskets of dead and living fowls and ducks and geese, with a few outside specimens; and then, as we reach the street, where the market flows all the way up and down, from the quay to the *Café des Tribunaux*, we have the fruit and flowers; the fruit all in pale yellows, with the vivid red of tomatoes: the flowers mainly white and red, with a row of small palms along the pavement. And as one follows the crowded alleys between the stalls one elbows against slow, staring country-people, the blither natives of the town, the indifferent visitors, and now and again a little

239

lounging line of sailors or fishermen in their sea-stained drab or brown.

The second-hand section of the market is strewn all around the cathedral, mainly about its front, and along the Rue de l'Oranger. Looking down from my window opposite the great doorway, the whole ground seems carpeted with old clothes, so old, so dirty, so discoloured, that one wonders equally how they could have got there, and how those who have brought them can possibly imagine that they will ever find purchasers. There are coats and trousers, petticoats and bodices, stockings, bed-covers, and even mattresses (once a whole four-poster was placed on the pavement, which it completely filled, just outside my door); everything that can be folded is folded neatly, with a great economy of space; and at intervals are collections of boots laid along side by side, eccentricities of rusty iron, which always look so amusing and so useless; old books, prints, frames, vases, tall hats, lamps, clocks under glass cases, crockery, and concertinas. There is a collection of earthenware, which is new; and there are some new teapots, ribbons, and tin pans. Beyond, where the Rue Ste. Catherine narrows back to the arcade at the side of the church, the market-carts are laid in rows, resting on their shafts. Few people pass. I have never actually seen anything bought, though I would not take upon myself to say that it never happens.

VI.

The most absolutely romantic spot in Dieppe,
a spot more absolutely romantic to its square inch
than anything I ever saw, is the little curiosity-shop
in the Rue de la Barre. You look in through a long
sort of covered alley, lined on both sides with old
tables, and mirrors, and bookshelves, and huge
wooden effigies of saints, and plaster casts, and
scraps of modern carpentry, and you see at the
farther end what looks like a garden of antiquities,
in which all the oddities of the earth seem to be
growing up out of trees and clinging on to vines,
tier above tier. You go in a little way, and you see,
first, an upper floor facing you, all the front covered
with glass, in which are laid out the most precious
items, the inlaid tables, the Empire clocks, the Louis
XV. chairs. You go in a little farther still, and
you find yourself in the garden of antiquities,
which is even more fantastic and impossible than
its first aspect had intimated. It fills the square
of a little court, round which curls a very old house
trailed over with vines and creepers ; a house all
windows and doors, one of the doors opening on
a spiral stone staircase like the staircase of a tower.
At the farther end there is a glass covering, like an
unfinished conservatory ; creepers stretch across
underneath the glass, and, in a huge mound, piled
quite up to the creepers so that they are covered
with its dust, I know not what astonishing *bric-à-brac*,
a mound which fills the whole centre of the court.

Cities and Sea-Coasts and Islands.

There are chairs and tables, beds, bundles, chests, pictures in frames, all sorts of iron things, and, very conspicuously, two battered wooden representations of the flames of hell (as I imagine), the red paint much worn from their artichoke-like shoots. All around the walls, wherever there is room for a nail between a window and a vine-branch, something is hung, plaster bas-reliefs and masks, Louis XVI. mirrors, lanterns, Japanese prints, arm-chairs without seats; frankly, an incredible rigmarole. I saw few desirable objects, but the charm of the whole place, its unaccountability, its absurd and delightful romanticism, made up in themselves a picture which hardly needed to be painted, it was so obviously a picture already.

VII.

One of the most characteristic corners of Dieppe lies in the unfashionable end of the town, the fisher quarter by the harbour, where the boats come in from Newhaven. Where the basin narrows to a close passage, just before you are past the pier, and in the open sea, there are two crucifixes, one on either side, guarding Dieppe. The boats lie all along the quay, their masts motionless above the water, and it is along the quay that the train from Paris comes crawling in its odd passage through the town. Arcades, reminding one of Padua, run along the townward side of the quay; they are stocked with cheap restaurants, and most of them

have tiny balconies on the first floor, just under the
roof of the arcades, and all of them have spread
tables in the passage-way itself: waiters and women
stroll up and down continually, touting for customers. From one of the little balconies you can
look across the fish-market, beyond the masts,
across the water, to the green hill opposite, with its
votive church on the summit. The picture is
framed in the oval of one of the arches, and it looks
curiously theatrical, and charmingly so, over the
heads of the fisher-people and townsfolk who
throng there. The crier passes, beating his drum;
sometimes, about dinner-time, a company of strolling
musicians, a harpist, his wife and daughter who
play violins (the little one with an air of professional
distinction) linger outside one of the *cafés*. Along
the quay, which stretches out towards the pier,
is a broken line of old, many-coloured houses;
there are endless little restaurants, hotels, and *cafés*,
meant mainly for the sailors, and two *cafés concerts*
of the seaside sort, with a piano (the pianist in one
of them has been an organist in Paris; drinks, of
course, and reproaches destiny), the usual platform,
and the usual enormous women, hoarse, strident,
and *décolletées*, who collect your pennies in a shell
after every song. There is a night *café*, too, on the
quay, which you can enter at any hour: you tap
on the glass door, a curtain is drawn back, and, if
you are not an *agent*, you will have no difficulty in
entering. An *agent*, when he makes his tour of
inspection, has sometimes to wait a little, while a

pack of drinkers is hurriedly bundled out at the back door. M. Jean's licence appears to be somewhat vague; the report that an *agent* is at the door causes a charming little thrill of excitement among his customers. Some of his customers, who are fishermen, I do not altogether like; their friendliness was a little boisterous; and, sometimes, when they lost their temper, M. Jean would knock them down, and roll them, quite roughly, out of the door. On the other side of the water, on the Pollet, as it is called, you find the real home of the fishermen, in those little battered houses, twisting around all sorts of odd corners, climbing up all sorts of odd heights, some of them with wooden beams along the front, all dirty with age, all open to the street, all with swarms of draggled, blue-eyed, gold-haired children playing around their doors. In a few corners one sees women making nets, once an industry, now fallen into some disuse. The whole place is thick with dust, faded with years, shrivelled with poverty; but Dowson loved it more than any part of Dieppe.

VIII.

The charm of Dieppe! No, I can never give the real sense of that charm to any one who has never experienced it; for myself, it is not even easy to realise all the elements which have gone to make up the happiness of these two summer months here. It always rests me, in body and

mind, to be near the sea; and then Dieppe is so
placid and indulgent, lets you have your way with
it, is full of relief for you, in old corners and cool
streets, warm and cool at once, if you take but
five steps from the Rue Aguado, modern and
fashionable along the sea-front, dazzling with sunlight, into any one of the little streets that branch
off from it townwards. And if the sun beats on
you again as you come out into the square about
Saint-Jacques you have but to go inside; better
still, if you seek the finer interior of Saint-Remy;
and, suddenly, you have the liquid coldness of stone
arches that have never felt the sun. And then the
sea, at night, from the jetty: the vast space of
water, fading mistily into the unseen limits of the
horizon, a boat, a sail, just distinguishable in its
midst, the lights along the shore, the glow of the
Casino, with all its windows golden, an infinite
softness in the air. I have spent all night wandering
about the beach, I have traced every change in sea
and sky from twilight to sunrise, inconceivable
delicacies of colour, rarities of tone. And what
dreams have floated up in the smoke of my cigarette,
mere smoke that would never reach the stars!
What memories I have evoked, what unforgotten
talks I have had, in the cool of the evening, on that
jetty! And the country round Dieppe, rarely as
I went into it, that, too, means something for me:
Puys, where I went with Beardsley to see Alexandre
Dumas, in the house in which his father died, the
house where so many of his own plays have been

written; Pourville, the road along the cliffs; Varengeville, with its deep, enchanting country lanes, its little sunken ways through the woods, its strange, stiff little pine-woods on the heights; the Manoir d'Ango, with its delicate approach through soft alleys of trees, and past a little shadowed pool, the palace degraded into a farm, but still with its memories of Francis I. and Diane de Poitiers, whose faces one sees, cheek by cheek, on a double medallion; Arques la Bataille, with its Italian landscape, so cunningly composed about the ruined castle on the hill. There is nothing in or near Dieppe which does not, in one way or another, appeal to me; nowhere that I do not feel at home. And the friends I have made, or found, or fancied at Dieppe, men and women of such varying charm and interest! The most amiable soul in all the world resides, I think, in the Anglo-maniac French painter in whose chalet I spent, so agreeably, so much of my time, in the studio where he paints the passing beauties as they fly. Was there not, too, the hospitable Norwegian painter, with the heart of a child in the body of a giant, who lived with his frank and friendly wife in the villa on the hill, where I spent so many good-tempered evenings? And the young English painter, Conder, who was my chief companion, a temperament of 1830, *né romantique*, in whose conversation I found the subtle superficialities of a profoundly sensitive individuality, it was an education in the fine shades to be with him. The other younger Englishman, an artist

of so different a kind, came into our little society
with a refreshing and troubling *bizarrerie;* all that
feverish brilliance, the boyish defiance of things,
the frail and intense vitality, how amusing and uncommon it was! And there were the two French
poets, again so different from one another; elegant
and enthusiastic youth, and the insistent reflective-
ness of a mind always reasoning. And then the
charming women one met as they flitted to and fro
between Dieppe and Paris and London and Monte
Carlo; the little French lady whose mother had
been one of the Court beauties of the Second
Empire; her *profile de mouton*, with the hysterical
piquancy of a mouth, perfect in repose, which would
never rest: heartless, exquisite, posing little person!
And there was Cléo de Mérode, with her slim,
natural, and yet artificial elegance, her little, straight
face, so virginal and yet so aware, under the
Madonna-like placidity of those smooth coils of
hair, drawn over the ears and curved along the
forehead; it is Cléo de Mérode, who, more than
any one else, sums up Dieppe for me. How many
other beautiful faces there were, people one never
knew, and yet, meeting them at every hour, at
dinner, on the terrace of the Casino, at the tables,
in the sea, one seemed to know them almost better
than one's friends, and to be known by them just
as well. Much of the charm of life exists for me
in the unspoken interest which forms a sort of
electric current between oneself and strangers. It
is a real emotion to me, satisfying, in a sense, for

the very reason that it leaves one unsatisfied. And of this kind of emotion Dieppe, in the season, is bewilderingly abundant. Is it, after all, surprising that I should have come to Dieppe with the intention of staying from Saturday to Monday, and that I should have stayed for two months?

Summer, 1895.

A Valley in Cornwall.

I.

Under the trees in the dell,
　Here by the side of the stream,
　Were it not pleasant to dream,
Were it not better to dwell?

Here is the blue of the sea,
　Here is the green of the land,
　Valley and meadow and sand,
Sea-bird and cricket and bee;

Cows in a field on the hill,
　Farmyards a-fluster with pigs,
　Blossoming birds on the twigs;
Cool, the old croon of the mill.

AT Helston the last Cornish railway ends, on a railed motor-track coming from Gwinear Road; and from Helston to Poltescoe it is a drive of ten miles, for the last part of the way along the edge of Goonhilly Downs. As we come into Poltescoe Valley the road becomes steeper, and we climb and descend through high green hedges, until, just after the bridge, we turn aside into a narrow lane, and, after passing a double cottage and a smithy, come around a slow curve to the thatched cottage standing inside a little garden. There are fields on the slope of a hill opposite, and, lower down, where the road turns around an edge of solid rock, there is a stream, going by an old mill, and, beyond it, a steep rocky hill, with clusters of trees, bracken, gorse, and rough green foliage, rising up against the sky, between the valley and the sea.

Cities and Sea-Coasts and Islands.

I have never lived in so peaceful a place, and the old miller who lives by himself at the mill — "like a single plover," he tells me — says that the people like the restfulness and do not willingly leave it. The washerwoman who has part of the double cottage along the lane says that she would go mad if she went to live in a town, and that the mere thought of it, sometimes, as she goes in and out of her door all day long, makes her feel uneasy. The miller says that the people do not notice the beauty of the place much, because they are used to it; but he himself told me that, so far as he can hear, it is the prettiest place in England.

The cottage has a few disadvantages. One is that I cannot stand quite upright in either of the lower rooms. When a labourer lived in it there was, of course, a stone floor, and the wooden floor which the new landlord has put in has brought the ceiling lower. Where the ceiling is plain I can stand upright; but there are cross-beams, and the doors are lower than the cross-beams, and I have to go about stooping, for fear of dashing my head against one or the other.

Then there is that very decorative and in some ways practical thing, a thatched roof. I have always wanted to sleep under a thatched roof, but the actual experience has chilled my enthusiasm. There is the delight of looking at it from the hill going up to Ruan Minor, like a corkscrew, on the other side of the valley; and there is the delight of sitting under the eaves and hearing the sudden soft rustle of wings as the birds fly in and out of their nests among the thatch. But when you find, on going to bed, a little red worm sitting on the pillow; when black spots of various shapes and sizes begin to move and crawl on the wall and ceiling; when the open window, which lets in all the scents and sounds of the country, lets in also whatever creeps and flies among the bushes — sleep under a thatched roof becomes a less desirable thing.

But for these slight drawbacks, which have their compensations as one sits at night, reading by lamp-light, in rooms so pleasantly and quaintly pro-portioned, and the painted butterflies and sombre moths come in at the window and dash themselves ecstatically at the light: well, I can ask no more of a cottage. And then, with the cottage, have we not the indispensable Mrs. Pascoe, and is not Mrs. Pascoe the contriver of all expedients and the journal and encylopædia of all local knowledge?

II.

All day I watch the sun and rain
That come and go and come again,
The doubtful twilights, and, at dawn
And sunset, curtains half withdrawn
From open windows of the sky.
The birds sing and the sea-gulls cry
All day in many tongues; the bees
Hum in and out under the trees
Where the capped foxglove on his stem
Shakes all his bells and nods to them.

Cities and Sea-Coasts and Islands.

All day under the rain and sun
The hours go over one by one,
Brimmed up with delicate events
Of moth-flights and the birth of scents
And evening deaths of butterflies.
And I, withdrawn into my eyes
From that strict tedious world within,
Each day with joyous haste begin
To live a new day through, and then
Sleep, and then live it through again.

What gives its chief charm to the country about Poltescoe Valley is its intimate mingling of two separate kinds of scenery — the wildest scenery of rocks, cliffs, and the sea, and the softest and most luxuriant scenery of an inland valley. And the two are not merely there side by side, but they interpenetrate one another in an indefinite series of surprises. Walking across meadows, one comes suddenly upon a ridge of rocks, like a reef in the sea, coming up out of the grass, and partly covered with greenery; sea-birds fly among rocks or stand in companies on the fields; one hears the sound of waves dashing on unseen cliffs as one saunters through a lane deep between hedges; a wheat-field stands out detached on a hill summit against the white sails of a ship at sea.

Among these valleys and on the wooded tops of the hills there are flowers around every cottage; flowers climb up the walls and about the door-posts, geraniums, nasturtiums, red and pink and veined roses; arum-lilies grow in the narrow strip of front garden; there are clusters of fuchsia and

252

A Valley in Cornwall.

veronica, there are hydrangeas and gladiolas and dahlias; and the hedges are full of honeysuckle, of foxgloves, of blue and yellow flowers. The air, as one passes, is laden with sweets; warm, aromatic winds blow softly across one's face; and the sleek and shining cattle graze in fields green to the sea's edge, and rest under the shadow of wide trees. At low tide the cows come down from the fields to Kennack Bay, and walk to and fro on the sand, pausing and looking at the sea, the rocks, and drinking from the streams of fresh water that run down the sand. Slow cart-horses, that walk freely about the lanes at all hours of the day and night, come down to the bay, and trudge to and fro, and lay their heads on one another's shoulders as they stand sleepily together.

After sunset, if you go up the road as far as Kuggar, and stand there between the fields and the sea, you will hear the drones humming by the way-side and throbbing about the flowers and gorse in the hedges, red cows graze in green fields, and you hear the deep, half-human sigh of some unseen beast behind the hedge, or a few late twitters among the branches. There is a moon in the pale sky growing from faint silver to a sickle golden as ripe corn; wide green valleys rising and dipping like sea waves, almost to the edge of the cliffs that go down dark into the sea; and, as far as the rim of the sky, the sea, grey-blue, motionless except where it curls into abrupt white waves and breaks into foam around the rocks or upon the beach. And as you stand there, seeing only faint sights and hearing only faint sounds, there is a delicate loneliness in things, not like a real feeling, not a weight, but an impression, vague and dim-coloured and wholly pleasant, like the sentiment, not of real things, but of a picture.

From Poltescoe the nearest way down to the sea is by Carleon Cove, but I only pass there on my way to the cliffs leading to Cadgwith; I never linger there. It is disfeatured and defeated, an ugly gash in the cliff-side. There is always something gloomy and uncomfortable in its cramped bed of pebbles, the great dark cliff, covered thinly with green turf, which rises to so steep a height above it, and the broken and deserted sheds, chimneys, and water-wheel, where the serpentine works had been. The water still runs along a wooden tray from the river to the great wheel, and sometimes, by accident, the rusty thing begins to turn, with a ghastly clanking, like a dead thing galvanised into some useless and unnatural semblance of life. The place is uncanny, like all solitary places which men have spoiled and then deserted.

Kennack Bay, where there is always a stretch of sand, and at low tide a long expanse of it, is like a broad and cheerful face, open to the light. You enter the bay by a latched gate, and then, at most seasons, cross a brook by stepping-stones. At each end of the sand there are clusters of rocks, beginning under the cliffs, and on one side going out a long way into the sea, looking at low tide like

254

the brown ridged backs of crocodiles that have swum to the surface of the water. On the other side the rocks nearest to the cliffs are seen, as you go near them, to be coloured as if the liquid colours of the sea, its many greens and its purple stains over hidden rocks, had been reflected and frozen in stone. When the tide is out, the farther rocks, left bare by the sea, are seen in strange outlines, sharp, broken, as if hewn into cavities and suffering from many rents and gashes. And there is one "cirque of fantastic rocks," half enclosing a little sea-pool, and flanked by a tall, broad, and twisted rock, which is like the sea cavern in Leonardo's *Virgin of the Rocks.* Animal content can go no farther than to lie, after bathing, on a natural pillow of hollowed rocks on the green edge of the cliff, and to look out through half-shut eyelids upon the wet sand of the beach, the dark semicircle of cliffs going round to the Lizard, and the softer semicircle of thin green meadows and wooded hollows inland; with the blue sky and the bluer sea, coloured like the Mediterranean, all around and all over one, glittering evenly in the sunlight. Little white waves break on the beach, with a low continuous sound of falling water; a bird's shadow darkens the sand, and if you lift your hat-brim you see the white sea-bird; sheep and cows bend over the grass together in fields; sleep hangs over land and sea with a delicate oppression.

Cities and Sea-Coasts and Islands.

III.

The woodpecker laughed as he sat on the bough,
  This morning,
   To give fair warning,
And the rain's in the valley now.

Look now and listen : I hear the noise
  Of the thunder,
   And deep down under
The sea's voice answers the voice.

All the leaves of the valley are glad,
  And the birds too,
   If they had words to,
Would tell of the joy they had.

Only you at the window, with rueful lips
  Half pouting,
   Stand dumb and doubting,
And drum with your finger-tips.

Cornish rain is a cheerful, persistent downpour, which comes down softly in a warm flood, washing the whole valley and the trees, and burnishing the grassy sides of the valley, and lying like a dark mist over the faded headlands and the grey sea. The stream that generally trickles over the pebbles by the old mill has swollen to a yellow river, and takes broad leaps from stone to stone. One can hear the whips of the rain steadily lashing the hedges and the trees. And, louder than the sound of wind and rain, is heard the sound of the river rushing, like the sound of the sea.

Going down to Kennack Bay, at high tide, after

A Valley in Cornwall.

a day of ceaseless rain, one sees a line of white foam around the whole coast, edging a sea which has turned to a strange leaden green, veiled with sea-mist, which comes driving across it in a wet vapour, which, as it floats up the valley, looks like a transparent gauze. One breathes water, one sees scarce anything but water, the solid mass of the sea and a racing vapour in the air; one hears nothing but water. The long level cliff going out to Pedn Boar has faded to a dim outline in a mist; white mists settle on the upper fields in the valley: the whole earth seems to melt away into a wreck and image of water.

Walking, after the rain, on the cliffs towards Cadgwith, the air is at once salt and sweet; the scent of the sea and of the earth mingles in it; and it is as if one drank a perfumed wine, in which there is a sharp and suave intoxication. Overhead the sea-gulls curve in wide circles; you see them at one moment black against the pale sky, then white against the dark cliffs, then matching the flakes of foam on the sea as they fly low over it. They poise in the air, and cry and laugh with their mocking half-human voices; and are always passing to and fro in some rhythm or on some business of their own.

Or, if one would taste a new sensation, neither of valley, cliff, nor sea, one has but to turn inland from Kennack and cross the downs. A path leads up between hedges full of honeysuckle, gorse, and tall white heather, among steep rocks covered almost

257

all over with green. Where the downs begin you
can see the sea, behind you, caught in an angle of
the land; and then the moorland, barer and barer,
until green turf stretches flat to a line of tall black
trees against the sky. A straight, flat, narrow
road goes across the downs, and as one walks along
it there is a sense of loneliness which is bare, severe,
but not desolate or unfriendly. The wind blows
across them from the sea, as from a living thing
not far off; and there is the freedom, the unspoilt
homeliness, of the earth left to itself.

IV.

To live and die under a roof
Drives the brood of thoughts aloof;
To walk by night under the sky
Lets the birds of thought fly;
Thoughts that may not fly abroad
Rot like lilies in the road;
But the thoughts that fly too far
May singe their wings against a star.

Outside the valley you may walk from sea to
sea by land. If you go north-west, you will come
to Coverack, along cliffs which grow barer and
barer as the trees dwindle and the road slopes down
to the seashore. If you go southward, you will
come to Cadgwith and the Lizard; and, again,
as you leave the region of Poltescoe Valley, you
will find the cliffs growing barer and barer, and will
come north-west to Kynance Cove, and thence to

A Valley in Cornwall.

Mullion, which lies almost level with Coverack, on the other side of Cornwall.

Coverack is a cluster of white houses built on the side of a headland which goes out delicately into the sea, curving round to the harbour, which the lowest houses seem to go down into. Low green land goes out across a breadth of water to form a bay; and you see the roads sloping precipitately over the downs to the pebbles on the edge of the blue water, and right above the roofs of the houses. On the other side of the headland there is another breadth of water; one feels the open sea.

At Cadgwith you see the sea from the beach as through the frame of a doorway narrowed to that measure; and the cramped and peevish beach is split in two by a rocky promontory, and gripped on either side by a tall cliff, which on one side is bare rock, and on the other a great swath of green, as if combed upward by the wind. Sea-gulls sit there, on the edge of the land, clustered like a bed of lilies; or swoop downward and fly to and fro over the beach, among the litter of boats and nets and lobster-pots, when the fishermen are cleaning the fish. Looking down from above, thick trees and the fold of sloping green meadows cut off all of the village but its brown thatched roofs and a glimpse of white-washed walls. It huddles there in the cleft of the valley where the valley slips feet foremost into the sea.

At Mullion Cove you are as if imprisoned, deep down, inside a narrow harbour, no more than two

Cities and Sea-Coasts and Islands.

boat-lengths wide at the entrance, where the sea chafes at the wall and at the rocks planted hugely without, great black heights which cut off half the sunlight as you pass into their shadow. Sea-gulls sit there in shoals, crying against the wind. There is a fierce seclusion in the place, disquieting, and with its own narrow and unfriendly charm.

Kynance Cove, with its mysterious regular daily appearance and disappearance, is like the work of a wizard, who has arranged its coming and going for magical purposes of his own, and has laid this carpet of pure sand about the bases of fantastic rocks and under the roof of sombre caverns, and has set the busy sea to wash and polish and scrub with sand and stones the smooth surface of the rocks and caverns, until they glow with a kind of flushed and fiery darkness, in which can be discerned colours of green and red and purple and grey, veining the substance of the rock as with the green of the sea and the purple of heather and as with pale jade and as with clots of blood. The cove is sunk deeply between green and stony cliffs, and the sea washes into it from all sides, hissing and shouting in crevices and passages which it has split and bored in the rock itself. It is a battle-ground of the sea, and a place of wild freshness, and a home of sea-birds. Man comes into it on sufferance, and at hours not of his choosing. He sets his wit against the craft of the tide, and wins no more than a humble edge or margin of permission.

I came first upon the Lizard across heathery

A Valley in Cornwall.

grass smelling of honey and sea-wind, on a day towards sunset when the sea lay steel blue to the immense circle of the horizon; fierce clouds rose there like barriers of solid smoke, and where the sun set unseen behind a cloudy darkness, throwing a broad sheet of shining light across the water, I could see a long line of land going out towards Land's End, hardly distinguishable from the spume and froth of rain-clouds darkening upon it. Unlimited water, harsh rock, steep precipices going down sheer into the sea; in the sea, fierce jags of rock, with birds clustered on them, and little circles of white foam around their bases; the strong air and stormy light seemed in keeping with this end of land where England goes farthest south into the sea.

V.

Leaves and grasses and the rill
That babbles by the water-mill;
Bramble, fern, and bulrushes,
Honeysuckle and honey-bees;
Summer rain and summer sun
By turns before the day is done;
Rainy laughter, twilight whir,
The nighthawk and the woodpecker;
These and such as these delights
Attend upon our days and nights,
With the honey-heavy air,
Thatched slumber, cream, and country fare.

In the valley, across fields in which rocks like the rocks on the seashore grow naturally, with ferns and bramble about them, buried deep among old trees, murmuring with rooks, there is a decayed manor-house, now a farm, called Erisey: an Erisey of Erisey is said to have danced before James I. The road leads over many Cornish stiles, and through farmyards where cows wait around the milking-stool, or hens scratch beside the barn door, or pigs hurry to a trough. The air is heavy with scents from the hedges and with the clean, homely odour of farms; there is nothing in this wooded place to remind one that the sea lies on the other side of a few fields. And yet I have always felt some obscure, inexplicable, uneasy sense or suggestion when I come near this old house set over against a little wood, in which Mélisande might have walked; the wood has a solemn entrance, through curved and pillared stone gateways; the grass is vivid green underfoot, and the tree trunks go up straight in a formal pattern. The old house at the door of the wood seems to slumber uneasily, as if secrets were hidden there, somewhere behind the thick ivy and the decayed stone. The villagers will not go that way after dark, because of a field that lies on the road there, which they call Deadman's Field.

Sunset comes delicately into the wood at Erisey, setting gold patches to dance on the dark trunks of the trees. But it is from the downs, or from the croft which lies between the cottage and the sea, that I like best to see the day end. From the downs, or from the road just above the cottage, the sky has often that amber light which Coleridge

A Valley in Cornwall.

notes in his poems; with infinite gradations of green, and a strange heaping of sullen and bodiless clouds against pure brightness. From the fields at Carleon, between the valley and the sea, night is seen touching the valley into a gentle and glowing harmony. The valley, a deep dell sunk into the midst of a circle of rocks covered with thin green foliage, is a nest and bower of soft trees, which rise cluster above cluster almost to the edge of the sky, where the rocky line of the fields ends it. Above, you see the bars of colour left over by the sunset; the moon hangs aloft between the valley and the sea; and as the valley withdraws into the rich darkness of the earth, the sea still glitters with grey light, to where white clouds come down out of the sky and rest upon it.

Tidings of the outer world come but rarely into the valley, except by way of the sky. Once a day the old postman comes down from Ruan Minor, and takes the letters back to the post-office. At times the sound of a siren, like the lowing of a brazen ox, comes paradoxically into the midst of the hot inland scents. At times a farm-boy following the cows, or a man sitting on the shafts of his cart, passes, whistling; and the tune will be a hymn tune, "Jesu, lover of my soul," or an air as old as "Rule Britannia," taken very slowly. If you hear the people talking to one another in the lane, you will notice that they speak and reply in phrases out of the Bible, as in a language of which they can catch every allusion. They never pass one another

Cities and Sea-Coasts and Islands.

without stopping to talk, and every one of them greets you with the time of the day as you pass.

All day long the tree before the door of the cottage is filled with music, and at night, when the moon is up, the sky before the windows is flooded with strange shapes and motions of light. I have never seen the moon's magic so nimbly or so continuously at work as upon that space of sky where the higher ridges of the croft ended. Kingdoms and seas of cloud passed before us under that calm radiance; they passed, leaving the sky clear for the stars; the polar star stood over the cottage, and the Great Bear flung out his paws at the moon.

> Gold and blue of a sunset sky,
>   Bees that buzz with a sleepy tune,
> A lowing cow and a cricket's cry,
>   Swallows flying across the moon.
>
> Swallows flying across the moon.
>   The trees darken, the fields grow white;
> Day is over, and night comes soon:
>   The wings are all gone into the night.

Summer, 1904.

At the Land's End.

THE temperament of Cornish landscape has many moods and will fit into no formula. To-day I have spent the most flawless day of any summer I can remember on the sands of Kennack Bay, at the edge of that valley in Cornwall which I have written about in these pages. Sea and sky were like opals, with something in them of the colour of absinthe; and there was a bloom like the bloom on grapes over all the outlines of cliff and moorland, the steep rocks glowing in the sunshine with a warm and rich and soft and coloured darkness. Every outline was distinct, yet all fell into a sort of harmony, which was at once voluptuous and reticent. The air was like incense and the sun like fire, and the whole atmosphere and aspect of things seemed to pass into a kind of happy ecstasy. Here all nature seemed good; yet, in that other part of Cornwall from which I have but just come, the region of the Land's End, I found myself among formidable and mysterious shapes, in a world of granite rocks that are fantastic by day, but by night become ominous and uncouth, like the halls of giants, with giants sitting in every doorway, erect and unbowed, watching against the piratical on-slaughts of the sea.

About the Land's End the land is bare, harsh, and scarred; here and there are fields of stunted grass, stony, and hedged with low hedges of bare stones, like the fields of Galway; and, for the rest, haggard downs of flowerless heather, sown with

Cities and Sea-Coasts and Islands.

grey rocks, and gashed with lean patches through which the naked soil shows black. The cliffs are of granite and go down sheer into the sea, naked, or thinly clad with lichen, grey, green, and occasionally orange; they are built up with great blocks and columns, or stacked together in tiers, fitted and clamped like cyclopean architecture; or climb rock by rock, leaning inwards, or lean outward, rock poised upon rock, as if a touch would dislodge them, poised and perpetual. They are heaped into altars, massed into thrones, carved by the sea into fantastic shapes of men and animals; they are like castles and like knights in armour; they are split and stained, like bulwarks of rusty iron, blackened with age and water; they are like the hulls of old battleships, not too old to be impregnable; and they have human names and the names of beasts. They nod and peer with human heads and wigs, open sharks' fangs out of the water, strut and poise with an uncouth mockery of motion, and are as if mysteriously and menacingly alive.

This is the land of giants: there is the Giant's Chair at Tol-Pedn, and the Giant's Pulpit at Boscawen, and the Giant's Foot at Tolcarne, and the Giant's Hand on Carn Brea. And there is a mediæval humour in Cornish legends which still plays freakishly with the devil and with the saints. Here, more than anywhere in Cornwall, I can understand the temper of Cornish legends, because here I can see the visible images of popular beliefs: the Satanic humour, the play of giants, the goblin

266

At the Land's End.

gambols of the spirits of the earth and of the sea. The scenery here is not sublime, nor is it exquisite, as in other parts of the county; but it has a gross earthly gaiety, as of Nature untamed and uncouth; a rough playmate, without pity or unkindness, wild, boisterous, and laughing. There is an eerie laughter along these coasts, which seem made not only for the wreckers who bloodied them, and for the witches whose rocky chairs are shown you, where they sat brewing tempests, but for the tormented and ridiculous roarings of Tregeagle and the elemental monsters.

In this remote, rocky, and barren land there is an essential solitude, which nothing, not the hotel, nor the coming and going of people in the middle of the day, can disturb. Whenever I get right out to the last point of rocks, where one looks straight down, as if between walls of granite, to the always white and chafing water, I feel at once alone and secure, like a bird in a cleft of the rock. There is the restfulness of space, the noise of sea-birds and the sea, and nothing else but silence. The sea-gulls cry and laugh night and day; night and day you hear the sea crying and laughing; sails and smoke pass on the sea, this side and that side of the Longships lighthouse, which stands, beautiful and friendly, on the reef in the water; and along the land, at morning and evening, nothing moves, all is waste, wide, and silent. Little brown donkeys start up among the rocks as you walk across the

Cities and Sea-Coasts and Islands.

cliffs at night; fat slugs lie in the way of your feet, black and burnished as coal; you see a vague movement, grey upon grey, and it is "the slow, soft toads," panting and leaping upon the stones.

In this solitude, away from the people of cities, one learns to be no longer alone. In the city one loses all sense of reality and of relationship. We are hedged in from the direct agency of the elements; we are hardly conscious of the seasons but for their discomforts; we are in the midst of manufactured things, and might forget that bread grew in the ground and that water existed except in pipes and cisterns. And the moment we leave the city we come to remember again that men and women are not alone in the world, but have countless living creatures about them, not pets nor beasts of burden, and with as much right to the earth and sunlight. First, there is the life of the fields and the farm-yards, a life attendant on ours, but familiar with us while we spare it. Then there is the unlimited life of birds, who, in these regions, have foothold in the sea as well as on land, and have two provinces, of water and of air, to be at home in. And, besides these, there is the tiny restless life of insects: the butterflies that live for the day, the bees with their polished mahogany backs and soft buzz that they call here "dummlederries," and that come out in the evening, the toads and slugs that come with the first dark, and the glow-worms that light their little lonely candle of pale gold at night. The

268

At the Land's End.

world suddenly becomes full of living beings, whose apparent happiness we are glad to be permitted to share.

In this air, in this region, an air of dreams, a region at once formidable and mysterious, every hour of the day has its own charm and character, which change visibly and in surprising ways. This morning was impenetrable with mist, and the lighthouse guns were firing until an hour after sunrise; greyness blotted out the whole sea. At last the brown reef of the lighthouse could be distinguished, but not the lighthouse; and then, suddenly, as one looked away and looked back again, there was a white, shining column, like a column of marble, glittering through the mist. As I started to walk along the cliffs towards the Logan Rock, I walked through wet vapours, soft, enveloping, and delicious. The mist faded and returned, showing one, in glimpses and under dripping veils, headland after headland, rivalling each other in boldness, in architecture of strangely shaped and strangely poised rocks, bare, splintered, crimped at the edges, cut into ladders, sheared into caverns, sundered by chasms, heaped crag upon crag with a romantic splendour. Now and then the path dropped to a little bay of white sand, and in the fishing-creek of Porthgwarra I met a little Italian boy with a concertina, who was quite alone, and spoke no English, and smiled with complete happiness, though shyly, as he told me that he did nothing, nothing. At

Cities and Sea-Coasts and Islands.

St. Levan I saw the little church, hidden in a hollow, with its beautiful and elaborate wood-carving, a whole monkish symbolism of bold fancy, and, in the churchyard, the single grave where the fragments of fifteen men, lost in the Khyber, had been buried, hands and feet and bones, and two heads, and one whole man, a Japanese; and, near the new grave, the old Levan Stone of splintered granite, with grass growing in the gap, of which the people say:

> When, with panniers astride
> A pack-horse can ride
> Through the Levan Stone,
> The world will be done.

The moorlands, in from the cliff, are all desolate, covered with short grass and heather, strewn with grey rocks, and cut into square patterns by stone hedges. About the Logan the shapes of the rocks become less grotesque, seem less strangely artificial; and the Logan point is like a house of rocks, chamber beyond chamber, with its corridors, doorways, and windows.

At mid-day I liked to go to Sennen Cove, because the sand there is whiter than any other sand, and the green slope above the sand more delicately green, and the water bluer and more glowing. At high tide the water comes in with a rejoicing exuberance, as if drawing into itself all the violence of the sun. It is exquisite, on a breathless July day about noon, to lie on the white sand without thought or memory, an animal in the sun, watching the painted sea, throbbing with heat, purple, grape-coloured, stained with the shadows of clouds and rocks; seeing the steamers pass as the clouds pass, with no more human significance; curious of nothing in the world but of the order and succession of the waves, their diligence, and when the next wave will obliterate the last wave-mark.

Twilight comes on most exquisitely, I think, over the cliffs towards Pardennick (the headland that Turner painted), looking down on Enys Dodman, the bare brown rock sheared off and pierced through by the sea, which is the loudest home of sea-gulls on the coast. There are rocky headlands to right and left, and that rock in the sea which they call the Armed Knight, but which to me seems like one of the Rhine castles, stands there, romantic and spectacular, not like any work of nature. Beyond, with the twilight-coloured sea around it, is the lighthouse, like a red star alighted on a pillar; far off, the golden light of the Wolf, and the two lights of Scilly. The sky, where the sun has gone down, is barred with dark lines and half-obscured outlines, like the outlines of trees seen in some shadowy mirror. Faint stains of gold and green and pink remain in the sky, still bright, and yet softened as if seen through water. Opposite, the moon has risen, and hangs in the sky, round and white; the sea darkens and shines, with strange glimmerings and dim banks of shadow, under the two lights from east and from west.

Cities and Sea-Coasts and Islands.

There is one boat on the sea: I see the two brown sails, and their shadows in the water. From the island of the sea-gulls there is a continual barking and chattering, as they walk to and fro, or stand and shout against the land. The rock darkens, and the white birds shine like white lilies growing out of brown earth. The castle in the sea turns black, and every peak and spire is sharply silhouetted upon the palely glittering water. Now it is like a magic castle, Klingsor's perhaps; or perhaps the last throne and ultimate stronghold of the night.

Here at the Land's End one is enveloped by water. The hotel, where I have been so well and so quietly served, so much alone when the brakes and motors do not come in to spoil some of the middle hours of the day, is built on the farthest habitable peak of land, and from my window I looked straight down into the sea, which I could see from horizon to horizon. Nothing was around me but naked land, nothing in front of me but a brief foothold of rocky cliff, and then the whole sea. For the first time in my life I could satiate my eyes with the sea.

In the country, between the grass and the sky, one may taste a measure of happiness, and the sight may be refreshed, rested, healed of many evils. But it is as if one ate good food without drinking. There is a thirst of sight which must wait unsatisfied until the eyes drink the sea.

Is it not because it is always moving, and because

At the Land's End.

one is not moving with it that the sea means so much more to one than any possible inland scenery? A tree, a meadow, though it grows and changes, grows and changes imperceptibly; I cannot see it in motion: it seems to be always there, irritatingly immobile. But the sea is always moving past me; it is like a friend who comes and goes and is faithful; its motion is all I have to give me some sense of permanency in a world where all things grow old and pass away, except the sea. Byron was right, though he spoke pompously: "Time writes no wrinkle on thine azure brow." Every part of the earth's body is growing old, and shows the signs and scars of age; only the sea is without that symptom of mortality, and remains a witness to the original youth of creation.

And the land too, here has in it something primeval. On this height one seems to stand among fragments of the making of the world; and, at so few hundred yards from the hotel, the tea-house, the picture post-cards, the brakes, and the motors, to be cut off from all these things by an impregnable barrier; alone, at the edge of the world, with the immovable rocks, and with the sea which is always moving and never removed.

Summer, 1905.

Cornish Sketches.

I. At Fowey.

As I entered Fowey, the little omnibus turned and twisted through streets so narrow that the people had sometimes to get into doorways to let it pass; it plunged downhill and climbed uphill, the driver blowing a whistle at certain points to clear the way; I caught, in passing, glimpses of an inch or two of water in the narrow space between two houses, and came out finally upon a high terrace from which I could look down on the harbour with its masts, the exquisite curve of Polruan across the harbour, the wedge of green land, dividing the two branches of the river, and outward, around the rocks, the sea itself. There was not a breath of wind; the sea lay as still as the harbour; the afternoon sun filled the air with dry heat; some yachts were coming in slowly, with white hulls and white sails, and a little boat with an orange sail passed close to the shore. I had felt, as the omnibus twisted in the narrow streets, as if I were entering Arles; but the hills and valleys were new to me; and there was something at once new and yet slightly familiar in this southern heat on a little town of old houses, spread out along the side of a hill which runs sharply in from the sea, where the river comes down to make a natural harbour. As I walked, afterwards, along the roads, at that height, looking down on the sea through trees and tall, bright flowers and green foliage, I could have fancied myself in Naples,

274

walking along the terrace-roads at Posilippo. And
the air was as mild as the air of Naples and the sea
as blue as the sea in the bay of Naples. It stretched
away, under the hot sunlight, waveless to the
horizon, scarcely lapping against the great cliffs,
covered with green to the sea's edge. Trees grew
in the clefts of the rock, they climbed up the hill,
covering it with luxuriant woods; deep country
lanes took one inland, and the butterflies fluttered
out of the bushes and over the edge of the cliff,
where they met the sea-gulls, coming in from sea
like great white butterflies. All day long the sea
lay motionless, and the yachts went in and out of
the harbour, and the steam-tugs brought in black,
four-masted ships with foreign sailors, and the
ferry-boat, rowed slowly by an old man, crawled
across from Fowey to Polruan and from Polruan
to Fowey. There was always, in those slow, sun-
warmed days, a sense of something quiet, unmoved,
in the place; and yet always a certain movement
on the water, a passing of ships, a passing and returning of boats, the flight of sea-gulls curving
from land to land.

To sit at an open window or in the garden under
an awning, and to look down on all this moving
quiet was enough entertainment for day or night.
I felt the same languid sense of physical comfort
that I have felt on the coast of Spain, with the same
disinclination to do anything, even to think, with
any intentness. The air was full of sleep; the
faint noise of the water flapping on the rocks, the

275

Cities and Sea-Coasts and Islands.

sound of voices, of oars, something in the dull brilliance of the water, like the surface of a mirror, reflecting all the heat of the sky, came up to one drowsily; the boats, with white or rusty sails, passed like great birds or moths afloat on the water. On the other side, over against me, Polruan lay back in the arms of the hill, with its feet in the water; and I was never tired of looking at Polruan. It seemed not so much to have been made, as to have grown there, like something natural to the rock, all its houses set as if instinctively, each in its own corner, with all the symmetry of accident. It nestled into the harbour; on the other side of the hill were the high cliffs and the sea.

At night, looking across at Polruan, I could see a long dark mass, deep black under the shadow of the moon, which sharpened the outline of its summit against the sky; here and there a light in some window, and beyond, to the right, the white glitter of the sea. The harbour was partly in shadow near the further shore, and the masts of the boats, each with its little yellow light, plunged into the water, almost motionless. The nearer part of the river was bright, like the sea, and glittered under the moon. An infinity of stars clustered together overhead. I could hear, if I listened, a very faint ripple against the rocks, and at intervals two fishing-boats, moored together, creaked heavily.

September 7, 1901.

Cornish Sketches.

II. The Cornish Sea: Boscastle.

You might pass Boscastle on the sea and not know that a harbour lay around a certain corner of rocks. This twisting way in from the sea gives something stealthy to the aspect of the place, as if a secret harbour had been prepared for smugglers. Few boats go in or out there now; rarely a pleasure-boat, more often a rowing-boat on its way to the lobster-pots. Green hills rise up steeply on both sides of the harbour, and a wooded valley follows the course of the little river flowing between them. The village is built around a single long, precipitous street, which winds uphill from the old bridge over the river, where you might stand looking seawards, and see nothing but two folding arms of rock that seem to overlap and make a barrier. Beyond the village the land still rises, and, looking across at it from the cliffs, it seems to nestle deep into the valley, a little white streak in the midst of green fields and green woods. From the higher part of the village you can catch glimpses of the sea across harvest fields or beyond Forrabury Church with its brown and white grave-stones.

Boscastle tantalises one, if one loves the sea for its own sake, by the height at which it sets one above the water. From these cliffs one sees, seeming to be close under one, the whole Atlantic; only it is three hundred feet below, perhaps, and there is not a beach or strip of sand on which to get level with it. Here and there are rocks on which it is

Cities and Sea-Coasts and Islands.

just possible to clamber down at low tide; there is a tiny cove or two, hard to reach at the best of times, and at high tide under water; but this side of Trebarwith, which is a couple of miles beyond Tintagel, only a single sandy bay. Even at Trebarwith the sand is covered at high tide, but when the water is out there is a long broad road of yellow sand, leading from the low rocks at one end of the bay to the caverns in the high rocks at the other end of the bay. On a hot almost still day, the waves, coming towards the shore in long thin lines white with foam, are blown into fine dust as they curve over. Seen from the sand, they can be watched at more stages of their movement than from the cliffs, where one gets only the final leap at the rocks.

At Boscastle the sea is almost always in movement, tossing restlessly, leaping at the rocks, whitening around them, flecked here and there with white, and the whole sea moves, as if the depths under it moved too. Even when there is not wind enough to ridge the water into separate waves, some energy seems to shoulder up through the surface and push for shore. When the wind urges it, it heaves into great billows, that rise up green and tilt over with a little burst of white, and roll one over another towards the shore, and as they come into a space of curdling foam, curdle, and turn to foam, and leap suddenly at the rocks, and hammer at them with a loud voluminous softness, and fall back like a blown cataract, every drop distinct in the sunlight.

278

Cornish Sketches.

It is as if a dome of whiteness sprang into the air and fell over with a crash of all its architecture of bubbles. Sometimes two columns of foam meet in the air, and pass through one another like a ghost through a ghost. Sometimes a great wave springs higher at the rocks, seems to take hold there, and then falls back, broken into spray, while the rock streams steadily; and then, after a pause, a thin white smoke-drift, incredibly thin and white, like the reflection of smoke in a glass, is blown far out from some corner or crevice in the rock that had sucked the water deep into it.

I am content to sit on the rocks, as near as I can to the water, and watch a few feet of sea for an hour together. There is enough entertainment in its recurrent and changing violence and stealthiness of approach, its unexhausted and unnumbered varieties of attack, the foam and disappointment of its foiled retreats. Form and colour change at every instant, and, if they return again, one is not conscious of the repetition. I suppose many waves are identical out of the infinite number of waves which break on any point of shore. But some happy accident of wind or tide or sunlight seems always to bring in its own variation.

At sunset the sea warms and lightens into strange colours. As the sun goes down in a ball of intense fire, the round seems to flatten itself out to a long, glowing bar, scorching the sea under it; a pale sunset leaves the sea chill, grey, uncoloured. The shadow of golden fire in the sky turns it to lavender;

Cities and Sea-Coasts and Islands.

a sunset of paler fire burnishes it into glittering steel, or it lies like a steel mirror misted by a breath. Every sunset here is a marvel, and the sea is a shining floor on which the marvel is built up. I remember a particular sunset after a day on which the rain had poured continuously; the sun sank slowly behind wet and shining clouds, through which it shone like a light in a crystal. These white clouds rose out of the sea, and their peaked and jagged upper edges gradually shone into bright gold as the sun sank lower behind them. Above, between them and the darker clouds still swollen with rain, a horizontal bar of gold glittered more faintly; and across the darker clouds a mist of rosy fire began to drift away, flushed softly like the feathers of a flaming wing; and this rosy mist floated onwards until it came to the edge of the furthest rain-clouds, and drooped over a space of pale green sky, clear, luminous, and transparent. The sea was the colour of lilac deepening into rose, and it lay like a field of heather washed by the rain, when the sun shines into every rain-drop.

There is a point at Trevalga where I like to look along the shore as it bends in an irregular curve, rising sharply out of the water in a series of torn and uneven crags, with, at some interval, the two high and steep rocks which rise up out of the sea some hundreds of yards away from the land, from which they had once been rent. The sea washes around the rocks and against the bases of the cliffs as far as the distant, smoother line of coast towards

Cornish Sketches.

Bude, where the Cornish wildness dies away, and it lies out towards the sky as far as the eye can follow it, an infinite space of unwearied water. Seen from a lower point, the cliffs are mountainous, and stand often against the sky like a mountain crowned by a castle. Tall cliffs covered to nearly the sea's edge by short grass and heather are indented by gullies, hollowed out of their very substance, and opening on the sea through a narrow and cornered entrance. The whole land seems to have been sheared into and sliced away at frequent intervals, and the colour of the rock varies in each, from slate to deep black. For the most part the rocks are made up of layers of slate, shale above shale, and they are cracking away and crumbling over continually; the sea picks at their bases, and hollows out caves and holes and niches; they stand straight up out of the sea, still impregnable, like great walls, black and jagged, and veined with yellow marble, and patched here and there with streaks of living green. They stand highest at Beeny High Cliff, a sheer wall of blackness, and St. Gennys, which rises less abruptly to a higher point. To the south-west one can see the wavering line of the coast as far as Trevose Head; to the north-east a less rugged line of cliffs curves into tiny bays, each with its handful of grey sand, as far as the point of Cambeak. Bracken growing intermingled with yellow gorse gives colour to a wild expanse of green moorland; the steep grey cliffs rise to the moorland out of a sea which should be seen, as I have seen it, not less

desolately grey, with a grey sky overhead. There
was a bitter wind blowing, which caught at one
furiously as one came to the edge of the cliff. As
the sun sank lower, it began to scorch the dark
clouds about it, shrivelling their edges ragged;
it went down into the sea rapidly, half hidden
behind the clouds; and the sea darkened to a sullen
colour, as of molten lead, that spread gradually
over its whole surface. A vivid and stormy darkness hung overhead, weighing heavily on land and
sea. Down below the sea roared with a loud and
continuous noise. There was something disquieting
in the air, in the aspect of things. Long after the
sun had gone down into the water a bright flame
licked up the lowest edge of sky, and ran there, as
I walked homewards, like travelling fire behind the
bushes and tree-trunks.

September 14, 1901.

III. THE CORNISH COAST.

I wonder if there is any form of the mere acceptance of happiness, more perfect, more explicit
than that which I have been enjoying until some
uneasy energy within drives me to shatter it by
analysis? I have been lying back on a high cliff
between Kennack Bay and Cadgwith, on a bed of
grass and heather, with my back against a rock
warmed by the sun; the sun's shadow, as it sets,
282

Cornish Sketches.

is slowly creeping over the grass at my feet; there is a slight breeze, which I can just feel on my cheek, but which is not nimble enough to stir the sea into more than a faint criss-cross of lines, which melt into one another before the eye has distinguished one from the other, and go on wavering, level to the horizon. Two white sails flicker near the shore; further out there are ships with white sails, a long dark steamer, and, almost on the horizon, a thin dark trail of smoke. Sea-gulls bark over my head and laugh in their throats, as they sail on level wings, the dark tips feeling their way in the sea of air like the rudders of white ships. The waves flash on the rocks below, with a gentle and sleepy sound, and I can hear nothing else except that rustle which the wind makes in the ferns and bracken as it passes over them.

If I lift my head and look to the right I see the southern point of the Lizard, with its white telegraph poles; if I look to the left I see the deep curve and long straight line of the cliffs ending far out at Black Head. Looking inland, I can see nothing but varying levels and varying shades of green, with darker trees in lines and clusters against the sky, beyond the fields and the downs. But if I lie still and do not raise or turn my head, I have enough for my pleasure in looking straight across the sea to the sky, letting sails or sea-gulls or clouds pass like illusions of movement in a world which has become stationary and which flows continually past me, as my eyes rest on the motionless diamond-like barrier of the sky and on the moving and changeless grey-blue pavement of the sea.

The sea, alone of natural things, obeys Aristotle's law in art, that for perfect pleasure there must be continual slight variety. It has the monotony of great art, and its continual slight variety. Everything else in nature wearies one by its stillness or its restlessness; by a limit which suggests constraint or by an open bareness which is but lawless and uncultured. But here the eye travels easily on to heaven; there is only that diamond barrier of sky between it and the end of the world. And the world itself seems no longer to have a limit; and, by these gentle degrees, infinity itself loses its horror. Only, as I lie here, I think none of these thoughts, which are but after-thoughts in the wake of sensation, and perhaps explain nothing; and in my acceptance of happiness I am hardly even conscious that to be thus, in body and mind, is to be perfectly happy.

If I could choose a place to build a cottage, where I could come and live when I wanted to be alone, a place for work and dreams, I would choose Kennack Bay, because there the land mingles more happily with the sea and the rocks with the sand, and the cliffs with the moorland than anywhere that I know in England. All along the coast here, from Kennack to the Lizard and from the Lizard to Mullion, there is little that has been spoilt by modern progress, little of the fretfulness, pretence, and vulgar crowding of so much of the English sea-coast. Fortunately Cornwall is a long way from London, half hidden in the sea, at the very end of the land, and the poisonous trail of the railway has not yet gone all over it. Here there is not a railway within ten miles. There is valley, moorland, and cliff; the smell of heather mingles with the sea-smell, and the cornfields go down green and golden to the sea. If one goes inland, roads wind up and down between deep hedges, and, as one comes to the top of a hill, in the moment before one goes down on the other side, there is a glimpse of the sea between the branches of trees, or coming blue and shining into a frame of meadow and cliffside. Following the whited stones of the coastguards, one can trace the whole coast-line, on narrow paths high above the sea and across the sand or pebbles of coves. And there is not a cliff where one cannot lie down and be alone, and smell salt and honey, and watch the flight of the sea-gulls, and listen to the sea, and be very idly happy.

Yet, to me, Kennack is the most restful and beautiful corner of the coast and the most enviable to live in. Not long ago there was a plot against its peace, and a gang of company-promoters had schemed to build a big hotel there, and the plans were made, and only the formality of buying the piece of land remained. What happened is what still happens in these parts, where Cornish gentlemen still own and still keep their incomparable share of Cornish land. The plot was scattered by a brief, irrevocable letter from Lord Falmouth's agent, and the company-promoters were left gasping at the modern anomaly of a landowner who would not part with his land for a profit.

And the people, too, in their measure, help the land owners to keep Cornwall for the Cornish. They do not encourage strangers; they are not at the beck and call of every one with a purse in his pocket; they reserve their opinions and their independence. There is a motor-car now running between Helston, where the railway ends, and the Lizard, where the land itself ends in the Atlantic. The people about here say that the motor-car is doing them more harm than good : it is destroying their roads, raising their rates, and disturbing their peace and quiet. They have no keen desire to make more money or to change the conditions under which their fathers have lived. In the hands of such landowners and of such tenants is not part at least of Cornwall still safe?

August 27, 1904.

IV. St. Levan.

On the way from the Land's End to the Logan Rock, just in from the cliff, after you have passed Tol-Pedn, and immediately before the road drops to Porthgwarra, there is a little valley, a big grassy nook, with one cottage, a rectory, and a church. This is the Parish Church of St. Levan, a fisherman saint of whom there are many legends; his path is
286

still seen by the track of greener grass that leads out to the rocks named after him, where he fished the traditional "chack-cheeld" chad. There is his stone, too, in the churchyard, one of those ominous stones which, in Cornwall, are thought to be the dials of Time itself, chroniclers of the hour of the Last Judgment. The Levan stone is a rock of granite, split in two, with grass and ferns growing in the gap between the two halves. The end of the world will come, says the rhyme, when the gap is wide enough for a pack-horse with panniers to pass through. "We do nothing to hasten it," the rector said to me reassuringly.

All that you can see of the church until you are quite close to it are the four pinnacles of its squat tower, like the legs and castors of an arm-chair turned upside down. It is hidden away in its hollow, out of the wind which is always coming and going on the wildest cliffs in Cornwall. Boulders piled with a sort of solid ricketiness on one another's shoulders (so old and grey and flighty!) climb the cliffside out of the sea, or stand propped and buttressed, holding on to the shelving edges of green land. Some are bare, some clothed with lichen as with a delicate green fur, and they lie about in fantastic attitudes, as if they had been flung together in the games of giants, and then forgotten for a few centuries. There is, in these clusters of vast rocks, that "delight in disorder" which Herrick knew in petty and lovely things; only here it is on the scale of giants. The pale colours

Cities and Sea-Coasts and Islands.

of the lichen soften what might otherwise be harshly jagged, rounding the edges and dressing the nakedness of the rocks. And the air, in which the scent of heather and gorse and thyme mingles with the salt smell of the sea, is tempered and made more exquisite by the drifting mists and vapours which come up out of the sea like a ghostly presence, and blot out headland after headland, as by a soft enchantment.

Inland there is barren moor, with here and there a scanty plot of herbage; and the moorland is all patterned out into squares and oblongs by the stone hedges which mark each man's property, little properties of gorse, grass, stones, and perhaps a patch of heather, meaningless as nought without a cipher, but held jealously from father to son. The skylarks have their nests in this rocky ground, and you hear them singing in the air their ecstatic hymns to light, while, below them, the sea-gulls drift to and fro between land and sea, crying their harsh and melancholy and complaining cry, the voice of restlessness, the voice of the restlessness of water.

It is in the midst of this eager and barren world, where only a few fishers live here and there in the creeks and coves, that the little church is hidden away in its green nook, like a relic of other ages. It is built in the Late Perpendicular style, and has fine heavy pillars, painted beams in the roof, an early font of some green granite, unknown in Cornwall. But it is chiefly for its carved woodwork

288

that the church is notable. The screen, carved thickly to the very beads of the mouldings, contains a whole homily in wood, a minute system of Catholic symbolism, in which the spiritual history of the world from the Creation to the Passion is imaged. There are the legged snakes of the first Eden, fiery flying serpents, symbols of the Trinity, the pelican, the Virgin's lily, the eagle of St. John; the sacred monogram is repeated continually, and there are the nail, the hammer, the spear, all the instruments of the Crucifixion; and there is an effigy of the Virgin, who is represented with a foolish round face, coiffed hair, necklace, and ruff, like a fine lady of the period. The carvings on the ends of the pews are less naïve, more skilful. There are the two fishes of St. Levan; the two cocks that crowed in answer to one another when St. Peter denied his Master; there is a palmer, with a cockle-shell on his hat; there are knights and ladies, fierce heathen, and there are two jesters. One of the jesters is supposed to typify Good, because he looks to the east smilingly, holding his cap and bells and ladle; while the other typifies Evil, because he turns his back on the altar, and holds askew a bishop's crozier with an ass's hoof for crook. All are carved patiently and livingly by carvers to whom the work was part of religion. "The soul of a man is in it," said the rector.

The learned and kindly rector told me, among many stories of his lonely parish, that there had been a rector once whose wits were none of the soundest, and, as they were liable to come and go with violence, he would be chained to his lectern when it was thought they were likely to leave him, so that he might read the Lessons without danger to his congregation. In Cornwall madness is no uncommon thing, and, like deformity, is looked on kindly. Most villages have their village idiot, or one of those large-skulled dwarfs who trudge painfully along the lanes with aged faces.

August 19, 1905.

V. The Colours of Cornwall.

The postman comes to me once a morning from Ruan Minor, and asks if I have any letters to be posted. If I go into the little shop of all sorts, which is the post office as well, half an hour before post time, I find him helping to sort the letters behind the grocery counter. Ruan Minor is a village without a .street. Most of the cottages are built by the roadside, some turn aside from the road, along lanes of their own, and are built crosswise or around corners, to suit the natural angles. Almost all are thatched, and have flower gardens in front and creepers up the wall. One cottage is built of corrugated iron, which is almost hidden by trails of purple clematis. There is only one shop besides the post office, though the shoemaker and the blacksmith and the carpenter have each a shanty. There is a church, and there are two

Cornish Sketches.

chapels; but there is not a public-house in the village.

The cottage where I am staying is down in the valley, and to get to it you must go down an incredibly steep and winding hill. I have once seen a horse and cart go up that hill; I have never seen one come down. If you stop half-way, where there is a cottage, and look across under the branches of the trees, you will see a triangular patch of blue sea, and, forming one side of the triangle, the high straight cliffs going out to Pedn Boar. Between you and the water there is a high rocky croft, and when you go down into the valley you will see nothing but steep walls of green on all sides, which seem at night to be built half-way to the stars, shutting out the sea and the winds, and sheltering the valley.

On the hill behind the cottage there is another village, Kuggar, or, as the people call it, Kigger. It is smaller than Ruan Minor, and has no post office, only a pillar-box, which is cleared once a day; no shop and no church. A steep road passes through it which leads down to Kennack Bay, winding between low hedges; on the further side there is another valley, with sloping corn-fields, scarred by waste rocky places which no plough can pass over, and green meadows where cattle graze; and then, beyond the first stretch of sand, yet another valley, like a hollow cut out of the solid earth, and now grown over with a soft multitude of trees and gorse and heather, which rise into rocks and drop to a stream flowing between reeds

291

Cities and Sea-Coasts and Islands.

on the edge of the sand. Beyond, in the eastern bay, there is another valley, and then the cliffs begin, and go on across rocky plains of heather to Coverack, where they turn bare, and so on to Pedn Boar and Black Head. The coast here, seen from Kennack, is at once violent and soft, at once wild and placid, with its broad outlines and delicacy of detail, the variety of its colour, form, and mingled rock and pasturage. Here things are constantly falling into pictures; nature here, though opulent, is by no means indiscriminate. And it is this touch of reticence, this fine composition, this natural finesse, that saves a country so picturesque from the reproach of an obvious picturesqueness: these soft gradations, this mastery of fine shades, nature's surprising tact in refraining from her favourite effects of emphasis.

If, instead of turning to the right as you go through Kuggar, you turn to the left and follow a flat road going inland, you will come out presently upon the downs. The road divides by the double cottage where the four dogs sit in their four barrels under the signpost; one way will take you across the downs to Mullion or the Lizard, and the other way will take you to Helston, or, if you turn aside from it, to a multitude of places with strange names, Constantine, Bosahan, or St. Anthony in Meneage. There is a walk from Gillan Creek, by the quaint little church of St. Anthony, along the edge of the cliff to Helford, which, in its mingling of sea and river and forest, its rocks and sandy coves and

Cornish Sketches.

luxuriant vegetation, is unlike anything I have seen in England. Leaving Dennis Head, from which you can see Falmouth across the curve of the sea, and following the broad Helford River by the rabbit-warrens, you go, by a public path, along the margin of the grounds of Bosahan, where woods carpeted with ferns come down to the sea's edge, and narrow paths lead up between clustering hydrangeas and exotic plants and grasses and tall bamboos, which grow there exuberantly, as if in their native soil.

I am never tired of walking and driving across the downs, though they are empty of shape, except where a barrow heaves them or a pool lies among reeds by the roadside. They are coloured with the white and purple of heather and with the yellow of gorse, and a wind from the sea passes over them and goes on to the sea. You can see the sea towards Cadgwith on one side of Cornwall and the Marconi posts at Mullion on the other side of Cornwall. And at night there are marvellous sunsets, filling the whole breadth of the sky and building up delicate patterns there, in colours like the colours of flowers transfigured by light.

It is for its colour, largely, that I love Cornwall, and wherever you walk, on moorland, croft, meadow, or cliffside, there is a continual soft insistence and alternation of colour. On the downs the heather grows sparely, and is less like a carpet of Eastern weaving than on the cliffs beyond Kennack, where one's feet tread upon colours and scents, and all the ground is in bloom. Grey rocks come up amongst

Cities and Sea-Coasts and Islands.

these soft coverings, and go down, tufted with the elastic green and faint yellow of samphire into the sea; and the rocks are spotted with lichen of violent gold, which is almost orange. Everywhere there is the sharp white of cottage walls and the gentle browns and greys of thatch; flowers of all colours swarm against the whitewash, and creepers catch at the eaves and nod in at the windows — red, white, purple, and yellow. White sea-gulls with their brown young ones fly out over the water in circles; cormorants sit like black weather-cocks, each on a solitary point of rock; inland, the crows cut black patterns on the sky; the grey sandpipers run over the grey sand. And there are the many colours of sand, sulphurous and salmon-coloured rocks, painted rocks, with all the intricate colourings of serpentine; and there is the sea, with its warm blue, when it seems almost human, and its chill green, when it seems fairy, and its white foam of delight, and the misery of its grey dwindling away into mist.

Autumn is beginning: the bracken is shrivelling brown, and the heather darkening, and the gorse drying to dust and flowering yellow, and the grasses withering, and the leaves of the trees yellowing and falling. The corn has all been carried, and stands, golden beside the pale hay, in great solemn ricks in the farmyards. All the green things of the earth begin to brighten a little before they fade.

October 8, 1904.

In a Northern Bay.

I HAVE only seen the bay when the sea has been gentle, at the most whitening a little against the yellow sand, into a sliding pattern like white lace. At sunrise, a steel mirror, coloured at sunset with more sombre lights, half deep shadow and half chilled into whiteness under moonlight, the sea lies there before one, filling one's eyes, as if there were nothing else in the world but changing and unchangeable water. Between the sea and the low bank on which the village has grouped itself, there is a narrow strip of sand, ending on one side in a curve of rocks and a sandy cliff, and on the other in a little rocky point running out into the sea, with its old church, its few, huddled cottages, the fishing-boats drawn up against it. Half-way along the naked ribs of a wreck clutch the sand, where a storm drove them deep into it. Cobles lie eagerly on the sand, with their delicately curved keels, waiting, like impatient horses, to race into the sea. Beyond the point lie miles of green moorland, along which you can follow the sea into other bays, which it does but drift into and drift out of, indifferent to the land, which has here no hold upon it, as it seems to stretch out ineffectual arms.

Between the house and the sea there is only a slope of grass and the narrow beach. The little world of the place passes to and fro under our eyes along the narrow beach; the fishing-boats and the yachts go out over the sea; nothing ever changes; there are always the same faces and the same sails.

295

Cities and Sea-Coasts and Islands.

Only the sea changes continually, like music, visible cadence after cadence. One seems to live with dulled senses, fantastically awake under a sort of exterior sleep, as if hypnotised by the sea. There is something terrible in so much peace. It is impossible that any one could be so sleepily happy as one ought to be here.

The sea is a mirror, not only to the clouds, the sun, the moon, and the stars, but to all one's dreams, to all one's speculations. The room of mirrors, in which the Lady of Shalott wove her fate, is but an image of the sea's irresistible imprisonment of oneself alone with oneself. Reflections enter from without, but only reflections, and these too are dimmed into the shadowy life of the mirror. The sea tells us that everything is changing and that nothing ever changes, that tides go out and return, that all existence is a rhythm; neither calm nor storm breaks the rhythm, only hastens or holds it back for a moment; all agitation being but a *tempo rubato*. Mountains give hope, woods a kind of mysterious friendliness with the earth, but the sea reminds us that we are helpless. In cities we can escape thought, we can deaden feeling, we can forget that yesterday mattered or that to-morrow will matter. But the sea has no compromises, no evasions, none of the triviality of meadows among which we can be petty without suffering rebuke. The sea is austere, implacable, indifferent; it has nothing to tell us; it is an eternal question. It comes seeming to offer us peace, a lullaby, sleep;

but it is the sleep of a narcotic, never quite releasing us from consciousness; and it is there always before us, like the narcotic, with the fascination of death itself.

Yet, as ecstasy is only possible to one who is conscious of the possibility of despair, so the sea, as it detaches us from the world and our safeguards and our happy forgetfulnesses, and sets us by ourselves, as momentary as the turn of a wave, and mattering hardly more to the universe, gives us, if we will take them, moments of almost elemental joy. The salt taste of the sea-wind, the soft enveloping touch of the water, the little voice whispering among the rocks, the wings of a sea-gull, rigid in the fierce abandonment of flight, the caress of the sand upon one's feet as one walks slowly at night under a great vault of darkness: these, surely, are some of the few flawless sensations which merely animal pleasure can give us. Happiness, no doubt, would be to put off our souls, as one puts off an uneasy garment, and enjoy these things as it would then be possible to enjoy them. Or do we, after all, feel them more keenly, since more consciously, for the moment, because they are not our inner life, but a release from our inner life?

September 22, 1900.

Winchelsea: An Aspect.

WE saw the pure lean harsh
Maid's body of the marsh,
Without one curve's caress
In the straight daintiness
Of its young frugal fine
Economy of line,
In faultless beauty lie
Naked under the sky.
Naked it lay and still,
Awaiting what new thrill
Of the ever-amorous light
In that austere delight?

That, at least, was the question I asked myself as I looked down from the highest garden in Winchelsea, that famous garden which has taken in part of the old town-gate, and seems to set you on a pinnacle and show you all the glory of the world. There was an expectancy throughout all the emptiness of the pale, delicate, and severe plain which lay there between the rock on which I stood and the sea. It was waiting for the sun to envelop, intoxicate, overwhelm it.

There is no other aspect quite like that aspect in England, and it was with difficulty that I realised myself to be in England. Across the marsh was Rye, piled up and embattled on its rock like Siena, with sharp red edges. The seashore might have been Rimini, only there were no Apennines going down fiercely into the sea. The meadows, white flat roads winding through them, the glimpses of water, of masts, of sails, of black rigging; the cows moving so formally through these meadows, in the

298

midst of these tokens of the sea; all formed themselves into a picture, and I felt that one could gaze
down on it always with the same surprise at its
being there. It was so improbable and so beautiful.

All Winchelsea is like a picture, and has other
suggestions of Italy, as one looks down a brief
street between old houses, as one does in the Alban
hill-towns, and sees another Campagna, more
wonderful than the Roman, because the sea com-
pletes it. From Frascati one only sees Rome.

Winchelsea is built in squares and at right
angles. It is formal and self-sufficient, neither
town nor village, guarding one of the loveliest of
ruins, but without the general quaint ancientness
of Rye; a comfortable place, with trees and fields
everywhere, with hardly any streets, hardly an
ugly building, hardly a shop. One climbs to it
as to a casket set on a hill; it seems to await the
visitor like a conscious peasant in costume; to live
in it would be like living in a museum. How much
longer will it remain unspoiled, when all the world
is so set on spoiling it?

Though one begins by thinking of Italy, there
are signs by which this un-English place may be
recognised as English. There are no guides, not
even children, and it is clean. It seems astonishing,
so foreign are these corners, that one can loiter in
them without reluctance. Even the old houses that
are dropping into decay crumble gently. Everywhere there is a discretion in things.

There are souls in places, and places draw to

Cities and Sea-Coasts and Islands.

them people made after their image. The person in whom I see Winchelsea may seem to have little in common with that windy height over the marsh and the glory of the world that is shown there. Yet that meekness and that outrageous beauty which are in the place would have their counterparts in the soul of the woman. She would live in a low red cottage in a side street, with no view out of any of the windows; and she would be shy and reticent, and no one would know why she lived there all alone, or why it was that she seemed to be at once so sad and so happy. They would see a small, neat woman with greyish hair, who passed in the street hurriedly, her lips moving as if she were repeating something to herself, her eyes always wide open, the humble and hungry eyes of the fanatic. The backward quiet, the silence, collectedness, and a certain thrill in the simplicity of the place would have passed into her, or seemed to find in her a reflection. She too will have had her ancient history, the romance that sometimes comes to those who are no longer young, and that, when it goes, takes everything out of life but memory. I said that Winchelsea is like a casket. She would have chosen it as a casket in which to keep her memory unspoiled. It has the likeness of all her recollections, as she sees them over again, never any greyer, but with the heat still in them, carefully hoarded. She has no associations with the place, but the place makes associations for her grief; it shuts her gently in with her grief, in an unbroken leisure,

300

Winchelsea.

where time seems to pause for her, in one of his rare intervals. It is in this hushed, aloof, eager, and remembering figure that I see the likeness of Winchelsea.

October 13, 1906.

The Islands of Aran.

For two hours and a half the fishing-boat had been running before the wind, as a greyhound runs, in long leaps; and when I set foot on shore at Ballyvaughan, and found myself in the little, neat hotel, and waited for tea in the room with the worn piano, the album of manuscript verses, and the many photographs of the young girl who had written them, first as she stands holding a violin, and then, after she has taken vows, in the white habit of the Dominican order, I seemed to have stepped out of some strange, half-magical, almost real dream, through which I had been consciously moving on the other side of that grey, disturbed sea, upon those grey and peaceful islands in the Atlantic. And all that evening, as we drove for hours along the Clare coast and inland into Galway, under a sunset of gold fire and white spray until we reached the battlemented towers of Tillyra Castle, I had the same curious sensation of having been dreaming; and I could but vaguely remember the dream, in which I was still, however, absorbed. We passed, I believe, a fine slope of grey mountains, a ruined abbey, many castle ruins; we talked of Parnell, of the county families, of mysticism, the analogy of that old Biblical distinction of body, soul, and spirit with the symbolical realities of the lamp, the wick, and the flame; and all the time I was obsessed by the vague, persistent remembrance of those vanishing islands, which wavered somewhere in the depths of my consciousness. When I awoke next morning

The Islands of Aran.

the dream had resolved itself into definite shape, and I remembered every detail of those last three days, during which I had been so far from civilisation, so much further out of the world than I had ever been before.

It was on the morning of Wednesday, August 5, 1896, that a party of four, of whom I alone was not an Irishman, got into Tom Joyce's hooker at Cashla Bay, on the coast of Galway, and set sail for the largest of the three islands of Aran, Inishmore by name, that is, Large Island. The hooker, a half-decked, cutter-rigged fishing-boat of seventeen tons, had come over for us from Aran, and we set out with a light breeze, which presently dropped and left us almost becalmed under a very hot sun for nearly an hour, where we were passed by a white butterfly that was making straight for the open sea. We were nearly four hours in crossing, and we had time to read all that needed reading of *Grania*, Miss Emily Lawless's novel, which is supposed to be the classic of the islands, and to study our maps and to catch one mackerel. But I found most to my mind this passage from Roderic O'Flaherty's *Chorographical Description of West or H-Iar Connaught*, which in its quaint, minute seventeenth-century prose told me more about what I was going to see than everything else that I read then or after on the subject of these islands. "The soile," he tells us, "is almost paved over with stones, soe as, in some places, nothing is to be seen but large stones with wide openings between

Cities and Sea-Coasts and Islands.

them, where cattle break their legs. Scarce any
other stones there but limestones, and marble fit
for tombstones, chymney mantle trees, and high
crosses. Among these stones is very sweet pasture,
so that beefe, veal, mutton are better and earlyer
in season here than elsewhere; and of late there
is plenty of cheese, and tillage mucking, and corn
is the same with the seaside tract. In some places
the plow goes. On the shores grows samphire
in plenty, ring-root or sea-holy, and sea-cabbage.
Here are Cornish choughs, with red legs and bills.
Here are ayries of hawkes, and birds which never
fly but over the sea, and, therefore, are used to be
eaten on fasting days: to catch which people goe
down, with ropes tyed about them, into the caves
of cliffs by night, and with a candle light kill abundance of them. Here are severall wells and pooles,
yet in extraordinary dry weather, people must turn
their cattell out of the islands, and the corn failes.
They have noe fuell but cow-dung dryed with the
sun, unless they bring turf in from the western
continent. They have *Cloghans*, a kind of building
of stones layd one upon another, which are brought
to a roof without any manner of mortar to cement
them, some of which cabins will hold forty men
on their floor; so antient that nobody knows how
long ago any of them was made. Scarcity of wood
and store of fit stones, without peradventure found
out the first invention." Reading of such things
as these, and of how St. Albeus, Bishop of *Imly*, had
said, "Great is that island, and it is the land of saints;
304

The Islands of Aran.

for no man knows how many saints are buried there,
but God alone"; and of an old saying: "Athenry
was, Galway is, Aran shall be the best of the three,"
we grew, after a while, impatient of delay. A
good breeze sprang up at last, and as I stood in the
bow, leaning against the mast, I felt the one quite
perfectly satisfying sensation of movement: to race
through steady water before a stiff sail, on which
the reefing cords are tapping in rhythm to those
nine notes of the sailors' chorus in *Tristan*, which
always ring in my ears when I am on the sea, for
they have in them all the exultation of all life that
moves upon the waters.

The butterfly, I hope, had reached land before
us; but only a few sea-birds came out to welcome
us as we drew near Inishmore, the Large Island,
which is nine miles long and a mile and a half broad.
I gazed at the long line of the island, growing more
distinct every moment; first, a grey outline, flat
at the sea's edge, and rising up beyond in irregular,
rocky hills, terrace above terrace; then, against
this grey outline, white houses began to detach
themselves, the sharp line of the pier cutting into
the curve of the harbour; and then, at last, the
figures of men and women moving across the land.
Nothing is more mysterious, more disquieting, than
one's first glimpse of an island, and all I had heard
of these islands, of their peace in the heart of the
storm, was not a little mysterious and disquieting.
I knew that they contained the oldest ruins and
that their life of the present was the most primitive

Cities and Sea-Coasts and Islands.

life of any part of Ireland; I knew that they were rarely visited by the tourist, almost never by any but the local tourist; that they were difficult to reach, sometimes more difficult to leave, for the uncertainty of weather in that uncertain region of the Atlantic had been known to detain some of the rare travellers there for days, was it not for weeks? Here one was absolutely at the mercy of the elements, which might at any moment become unfriendly, which, indeed, one seemed to have but apprehended in a pause of their eternal enmity. And we seemed also to be venturing among an unknown people, who, even if they spoke our own language, were further away from us, more foreign than people who spoke an unknown language and lived beyond other seas.

As we walked along the pier towards the three whitewashed cottages which form the Atlantic Hotel, at which we were to stay, a strange being sprang towards us, with a curiously beast-like stealthiness and animation; it was a crazy man, bare-footed and blear-eyed, who held out his hand and sang out at us in a high, chanting voice, and in what sounded rather a tone of command than of entreaty, "Give me a penny, sir! Give me a penny, sir!" We dropped something into his hat, and he went away over the rocks, laughing loudly to himself, and repeating some words that he had heard us say. We passed a few fishermen and some bare-footed children, who looked at us curiously, but without moving, and were met at the door of the middle cottage by a little, fat old woman with a round body and a round face, wearing a white cap tied over her ears. The Atlantic Hotel is a very primitive hotel; it had last been slept in by some priests from the mainland, who had come on their holiday with bicycles; and before that by a German philologist who was learning Irish. The kitchen, which is also the old landlady's bedroom, presents a medley of pots and pans and petticoats as you pass its open door and climb the little staircase, diverging oddly on either side after the first five or six steps, and leading on the right to a large dining-room, where the table lounges on an inadequate number of legs and the chairs bow over when you lean back on them. I have slept more luxuriously, but not more soundly, than in the little musty bedroom on the other side of the stairs, with its half-made bed, its bare and unswept floor, its tiny window, of which only the lower half could be opened, and this, when opened, had to be supported by a wooden catch from outside. Going to sleep in that little, uncomfortable room was a delight in itself; for the starry water outside, which one could see through that narrow slit of window, seemed to flow softly about one in waves of delicate sleep.

When we had had a hasty meal and had got a little used to our hotel, and had realised as well as we could where we were, at the lower end of the village of Kilronan, which stretches up the hill to the north-west on either side of the main road, we

Cities and Sea-Coasts and Islands.

set out in the opposite direction, finding many
guides by the way, who increased in number as we
went on through the smaller village of Kileaney
up to the south-eastern hill, on which are a holy
well, its thorn-tree hung with votive ribbons, and
the ruins of several churches, among them the church
of St. Enda, the patron saint of the island. At
first we were able to walk along a very tolerable
road, then we branched off upon a little strip of grey
sand, piled in mounds as high as if it had been
drifted snow, and from that, turning a little inland,
we came upon the road again, which began to get
stonier as we neared the village. Our principal
guide, an elderly man with long thick curls of
flaxen hair and a seaman's beard, shaved away from
the chin, talked fairly good English, with a strong
accent, and he told us of the poverty of the people,
the heavy rents they have to pay for soil on which
no grass grows, and the difficult living they make
out of their fishing, and their little tillage, and the
cattle which they take over in boats to the fairs at
Galway, throwing them into the sea when they get
near land, and leaving them to swim ashore. He
was dressed, as are almost all the peasants of Aran,
in clothes woven and made on the island — loose,
rough, woollen things, of drab, or dark blue, or grey,
sometimes charming in colour; he had a flannel
shirt, a kind of waistcoat with sleeves, very loose
and shapeless trousers worn without braces, an
old and discoloured slouch hat on his head, and on
his feet the usual *pampooties*, slippers of undressed
308

hide, drawn together and stitched into shape, with pointed toes, and a cord across the instep. The village to which we had come was a cluster of white-washed cabins, a little better built than those I had seen in Galway, with the brown thatch fastened down with ropes drawn cross-wise over the roof and tied to wooden pegs driven into the wall for protection against the storm blowing in from the Atlantic. They had the usual two doors, facing each other at front and back, the windier of the two being kept closed in rough weather, and the doors were divided in half by the usual hatch. As we passed, a dark head would appear at the upper half of the door, and a dull glow of red would rise out of the shadow. The women of Aran almost all dress in red, the petticoat very heavily woven, the crossed shawl or bodice of a thinner texture of wool. Those whom we met on the roads wore thicker shawls over their heads, and they would sometimes draw the shawls closer about them, as women in the East draw their veils closer about their faces. As they came out to their doors to see us pass, I noticed in their manner a certain mingling of curiosity and shyness, an interest which was never quite eager. Some of the men came out and quietly followed us as we were led along a twisting way between the cabins; and the children, boys and girls, in a varying band of from twenty to thirty, ran about our heels, stopping whenever we stopped, and staring at us with calm wonder. They were very inquisitive, but, unlike English

Cities and Sea-Coasts and Islands.

villagers in remote places, perfectly polite, and neither resented our coming among them nor jeered at us for being foreign to their fashions.

The people of Aran (they are about 3000 in all), as I then saw them for the first time, and as I saw them during the few days of my visit, seemed to me a simple, dignified, self-sufficient, sturdily primitive people, to whom Browning's phrase of "gentle islanders" might well be applied. They could be fierce on occasion, as I knew; for I remembered the story of their refusal to pay the county cess, and how, when the cess-collector had come over to take his dues by force, they had assembled on the seashore with sticks and stones, and would not allow him even to land. But they had, for the most part, mild faces, of the long Irish type, often regular in feature, but with loose and drooping mouths and discoloured teeth. Most had blue eyes, the men, oftener than the women, having fair hair. They held themselves erect, and walked nimbly, with a peculiar step due to the rocky ways they have generally to walk on; few of them, I noticed, had large hands or feet, and all, without exception, were thin, as indeed the Irish peasant almost invariably is. The women too, for the most part, were thin, and had the same long faces, often regular, with straight eyebrows and steady eyes, not readily changing expression; they hold themselves well, a little like men, whom, indeed, they somewhat resemble in figure. As I saw them, leaning motionless against their doors, walking

The Islands of Aran.

with their deliberateness of step along the roads, with eyes in which there was no wonder, none of the fever of the senses, placid animals on whom emotion has never worked in any vivid or passionate way, I seemed to see all the pathetic contentment of those narrow lives, in which day follows day with the monotony of wave lapping on wave. I observed one young girl of twelve or thirteen who had something of the ardency of beauty, and a few shy, impressive faces, their hair drawn back smoothly from the middle parting, appearing suddenly behind doors or over walls; almost all, even the very old women, had nobility of gesture and attitude, but in the more personal expression of faces there was for the most part but a certain quietude, seeming to reflect the grey hush, the bleak greyness of this land of endless stone and endless sea.

When we had got through the village and begun to climb the hill, we were still followed, and we were followed for all the rest of the way by about fifteen youngsters, all, except one, bare-footed, and two, though boys, wearing petticoats, as the Irish peasant children not unfrequently do, for economy, when they are young enough not to resent it. Our guide, the elderly man with the flaxen curls, led us first to the fort set up by the soldiers of Cromwell, who, coming over to keep down the Catholic rebels, ended by turning Catholic and marrying and settling among the native people; then to Teglach Enda, a ruined church of very early masonry, made of large blocks set together with

311

but little cement — the church of St. Enda, who came to Aran in about the year 480, and fifty-eight years later laid his bones in the cemetery which was to hold the graves of not less than a hundred and twenty saints. On our way inland to Teampull Benen, the remains of an early oratory, surrounded by cloghans or stone dwellings made of heaped stones which, centuries ago, had been the cells of monks, we came upon the large puffing-hole, a great gap in the earth, going down by steps of rock to the sea, which in stormy weather dashes foam to the height of its sixty feet, reminding me of the sounding hollows on the coast of Cornwall. The road here, as on almost the whole of the island, was through stone-walled fields of stone. Grass, or any soil, was but a rare interval between a broken and distracted outstretch of grey rock, lying in large flat slabs, in boulders of every size and shape, and in innumerable stones, wedged in the ground or lying loose upon it, round, pointed, rough, and polished; an unending greyness, cut into squares by the walls of carefully-heaped stones, which we climbed with great insecurity, for the stones were kept in place by no more than the more or less skilful accident of their adjustment, and would turn under our feet or over in our hands as we climbed them. Occasionally a little space of pasture had been cleared or a little artificial soil laid down, and a cow browsed on the short grass. Ferns, and occasionally maidenhair, grew in the fissures splintered between the rocks; and I saw mallow, stone-

312

crop, the pale blue wind-flower, the white campian, many nettles, ivy, and a few bushes. In this part of the island there were no trees, which were to be found chiefly on the north-western side, in a few small clusters about some of the better houses, and almost wholly of alder and willow. As we came to the sheer edge of the sea and saw the Atlantic, and knew that there was nothing but the Atlantic between this last shivering remnant of Europe and the far-off continent of America, it was with no feeling of surprise that we heard from the old man who led us that no later than two years ago an old woman of those parts had seen, somewhere on this side of the horizon, the blessed island of Tir-nan-Ogue, the island of immortal youth, which is held by the Irish peasants to lie somewhere in that mysterious region of the sea.

We loitered on the cliffs for some time, leaning over them, and looking into the magic mirror that glittered there like a crystal, and with all the soft depth of a crystal in it, hesitating on the veiled threshold of visions. Since I have seen Aran and Sligo, I have never wondered that the Irish peasant still sees fairies about his path, and that the boundaries of what we call the real, and of what is for us the unseen, are vague to him. The sea on those coasts is not like the sea as I know it on any other coast; it has in it more of the twilight. And the sky seems to come down more softly, with more stealthy step, more illusive wings, and the land to come forward with a more hesitating and gradual

313

Cities and Sea-Coasts and Islands.

approach; and land and sea and sky to mingle more absolutely than on any other coast. I have never realised less the slipping of sand through the hour-glass; I have never seemed to see with so remote an impartiality, as in the presence of brief and yet eternal things, the troubling and insignificant accidents of life. I have never believed less in the reality of the visible world, in the importance of all we are most serious about. One seems to wash off the dust of cities, the dust of beliefs, the dust of incredulities.

It was nearly seven o'clock when we got back to Kilronan, and after dinner we sat for a while talking and looking out through the little windows at the night. But I could not stay indoors in this new, marvellous place; and, persuading one of my friends to come with me, I walked up through Kilronan, which I found to be a far more solid and populous village than the one we had seen; and coming out on the high ground beyond the houses, we saw the end of a pale green sunset. Getting back to our hotel, we found the others still talking; but I could not stay indoors, and after a while went out by myself to the end of the pier in the darkness, and lay there looking into the water and into the fishing-boats lying close up against the land, where there were red lights moving, and the shadows of men, and the sound of deep-throated Irish.

I remember no dreams that night, but I was told that I had talked in my sleep, and I was willing to believe it. In the morning, not too early, we set

314

out on an outside car (that rocking and most comfortable vehicle, which I prefer to everything but a gondola) for the Seven Churches and Dun Aengus, along the only beaten road in the island. The weather, as we started, was grey and misty, threatening rain, and we could but just see the base-line of the Clare mountains across the grey and discoloured waters of the bay. At the Seven Churches we were joined by a peasant, who diligently showed us the ruined walls of Teampull Brecan, with its slab inscribed in Gaelic with the words, "Pray for the two canons"; the stone of the "VII. Romani"; St. Brecan's headstone, carved with Gaelic letters; the carved cross and the headstone of St. Brecan's bed. More peasants joined us, and some children, who fixed on us their usual placid and tolerant gaze, in which curiosity contended with an indolent air of contentment. In all these people I noticed the same discreet manners that had already pleased me; and once, as we were sitting on a tombstone in the interior of one of the churches, eating the sandwiches that we had brought for luncheon, a man, who had entered the doorway, drew back instantly, seeing us taking a meal.

The Seven Churches are rooted in long grass, spreading in billowy mounds, intertwisted here and there with brambles; but when we set out for the circular fort of Dun Onaght, which lies on the other side of the road, at no great distance up the hill, we were once more in the land of rocks; and it was through a boreen, or lane, entirely paved with

Cities and Sea-Coasts and Islands.

loose and rattling stones, that we made our way up the ascent. At the top of the hill we found ourselves outside such a building as I had never seen before: an ancient fort, 90 feet in diameter, and on the exterior 16 feet high, made of stones placed one upon another, without mortar, in the form of two walls, set together in layers, the inner wall lower than the outer, so as to form a species of gallery, to which stone steps led at intervals. No sooner had we got inside than the rain began to fall in torrents, and it was through a blinding downpour that we hurried back to the car, scarcely stopping to notice a Druid altar that stood not far out of our way. As we drove along, the rain ceased suddenly; the wet cloud that had been steaming over the faint and still sea, as if desolated with winter, vanished in sunshine, caught up into a glory; and the water, transfigured by so instant a magic, was at once changed from a grey wilderness of shivering mist into a warm and flashing and intense blueness, which gathered ardency of colour, until the whole bay burned with blue fire. The clouds had been swept behind us, and on the other side of the water, for the whole length of the horizon, the beautiful, softly curving Connemara mountains stood out against the sky as if lit by some interior illumination, blue and pearl-grey and grey-rose. Along the shore-line a trail of faint cloud drifted from kelp-fire to kelp-fire, like altar-smoke drifting into altar-smoke; and that mysterious mist floated into the lower hollows of the hills, softening their

316

The Islands of Aran.

outlines and colours with a vague and fluttering and luminous veil of brightness.

It was about four in the afternoon when we came to the village of Kilmurvey, upon the seashore, and, leaving our car, began to climb the hill leading to Dun Aengus. Passing two outer ramparts, now much broken, one of them seeming to end suddenly in the midst of a *chevaux de frise* of pillar-like stones thrust endways into the earth, we entered the central fort by a lintelled doorway, set in the side of a stone wall of the same Cyclopean architecture as Dun Onaght, 18 feet high on the outside, and with two adhering inner walls, each lower in height, 12 feet 9 inches in thickness. This fort is 150 feet north and south and 140 feet east and west, and on the east side the circular wall ends suddenly on the very edge of a cliff going down 300 feet to the sea. It is supposed that the circle was once complete, and that the wall and the solid ground itself, which is here of bare rock, were slowly eaten away by the gnawing of centuries of waves, which have been at their task since some hundreds of years before the birth of Christ, when we know not what king, ruling over the races called "the servile," entrenched himself on that impregnable height. The Atlantic lies endlessly out towards the sunrise, beating, on the south, upon the brown and towering rock of the cliffs of Moher, rising up nearly a sheer thousand feet. The whole grey and desolate island, flowering into barren stone, stretches out on the other side, where the circle of

317

Cities and Sea-Coasts and Islands.

the water washes from Galway Bay into the Atlantic. Looking out over all that emptiness of sea, one imagines the long-oared galleys of the ravaging kings who had lived there, some hundreds of years before the birth of Christ; and the emptiness of the fortress filled with long-haired warriors, coming back from the galleys with captured slaves, and cattle, and the spoil of citadels. We know from the Bardic writers that a civilisation, similar to that of the Homeric poems, lived on in Ireland almost to the time of the coming of St. Patrick; and it was something also of the sensation of Homer — the walls of Troy, the heroes, and that "face that launched a thousand ships" — which came to me as we stood upon these unconquerable walls, to which a generation of men had been as a moth's flight and a hundred years as a generation of men.

Coming back from Dun Aengus, one of our party insisted on walking; and we had not been long indoors when he came in with a singular person whom he had picked up on the way, a professional story-teller, who had for three weeks been teaching Irish to the German philologist who had preceded us on the island. He was half blind and of wild appearance; a small and hairy man, all gesture, and as if set on springs, who spoke somewhat broken English in a roar. He lamented that we could understand no Irish, but, even in English, he had many things to tell, most of which he gave as but "talk," making it very clear that we were not to suppose him to vouch for them. His own family,

318

he told us, was said to be descended from the roons, or seals, but that certainly was "talk"; and a witch had, only nine months back, been driven out of the island by the priest; and there were many who said they had seen fairies, but for his part he had never seen them. But with this he began to swear on the name of God and the saints, rising from his chair and lifting up his hands, that what he was going to tell us was the truth; and then he told how a man had once come into his house and admired his young child, who was lying there in his bed, and had not said "God bless you!" (without which to admire is to envy and to bring under the power of the fairies), and that night, and for many following nights, he had wakened and heard a sound of fighting, and one night had lit a candle, but to no avail, and another night had gathered up the blanket and tried to fling it over the head of whoever might be there, but had caught no one; only in the morning, going to a box in which fish were kept, he had found blood in the box; and at this he rose again, and again swore on the name of God and the saints that he was telling us only the truth, and true it was that the child had died; and as for the man who had ill-wished him, "I could point him out any day," he said fiercely. And then, with many other stories of the doings of fairies and priests (for he was very religious), and of the "Dane" who had come to the island to learn Irish ("and he knew all the languages, the Proosy, and the Roosy, and the Span, and the

Cities and Sea-Coasts and Islands.

Grig"), he told us how Satan, being led by pride to equal himself with God, looked into the glass in which God only should look, and when Satan looked into the glass, "Hell was made in a minute."

Next morning we were to leave early, and at nine o'clock we were rowed out to the hooker, which lifted sail in a good breeze, and upon a somewhat pitching sea, for the second island, Inishmaan, that is, the Middle Island, which is three miles long and a mile and a half broad. We came within easy distance of the shore, after about half an hour's quick sailing, and a curragh came out to us, rowed by two islanders; but, finding the sea very rough in Gregory Sound, we took them on board, and, towing the boat after us, went about to the Foul Sound on the southern side of the island, where the sea was much calmer. Here we got into the curragh, sitting motionless for fear a slight movement on the part of any of us should upset it. The curragh is simply the coracle of the ancient Britons, made of wooden laths covered with canvas, and tarred on the outside, bent into the shape of a round-bottomed boat with a raised and pointed prow, and so light that, when on shore, two men can carry it reversed on their heads, like an immense hat or umbrella. As the curragh touched the shore, some of the islanders who had assembled at the edge of the sea came into the water to meet us, and took hold of the boat, and lifted the prow of it upon land, and said, "You are welcome, you are welcome!" One of them came with us, a nimble

320

peasant of about forty, who led the way up the terraced side of the hill, on which there was a little grass, near the seashore, and then scarce anything but slabs and boulders of stone, to a little ruined oratory, almost filled with an alder tree, the only tree I saw on the island. All around it were grave-stones, half-defaced by the weather, but carved with curious armorial bearings, as it seemed, representing the sun and moon and stars about a cross formed of the Christian monogram. Among the graves were lying huge beams, that had been flung up the hillside from some wrecked vessel in one of the storms that beat upon the island. Going on a little farther we came to the ancient stone fort of Dun Moher, an inclosure slightly larger than Dun Onaght, but smaller than Dun Aengus; and coming down on the other side, by some stone steps, we made our way, along a very rocky boreen, towards the village that twisted upon a brown zigzag around the slope of the hill.

In the village we were joined by some more men and children; and a number of women, wearing the same red clothes that we had seen on the larger island, and looking at us with perhaps scarcely so shy a curiosity (for they were almost too unused to strangers to have adopted a manner of shyness), came out to their doors and looked up at us out of the darkness of many interiors, from where they sat on the ground knitting or carding wool. We passed the chapel, a very modern-looking building, made out of an ancient church, and turned in for

Cities and Sea-Coasts and Islands.

a moment to the cottage where the priest sleeps when he comes over from Inishmore on Saturday night to say early mass on Sunday morning before going on to Inisheer for the second mass. We saw his little white room, very quaint and neat; and the woman of the house, speaking only Irish, motioned us to sit down, and could hardly be prevented from laying out plates and glasses for us upon the table. As we got a little through the more populous part of the village, we saw ahead of us, down a broad lane, a very handsome girl, holding the end of a long ribbon, decorated with a green bough, across the road. Other girls and some older women were standing by, and, when we came up, the handsome girl, with the low forehead and the sombre blue eyes, cried out laughingly, in her scanty English, "Cash, cash!" We paid toll, as the custom is, and got her blessing; and went on our way, leaving the path, and climbing many stone walls, until we came to the great fort of Dun Conor on the hill, the largest of the ancient forts of Aran.

Dun Conor is 227 feet north and south and 115 feet east and west, with walls in three sections, 20 feet high on the outside and 18 feet 7 inches thick. We climbed to the top and walked around the wall, where the wind blowing in from the sea beat so hard upon us that we could scarcely keep our footing. From this height we could see all over the island lying out beneath us, grey, and broken into squares by the walled fields; the brown thatch of the village, the smoke coming up from the chimneys, here and there a red shawl or skirt, the grey sand by the sea and the grey sea all round. As we stood on the wall many peasants came slowly about us, climbing up on all sides, and some stood together just inside the entrance, and two or three girls sat down on the other side of the arena, knitting. Presently an old man, scarcely leaning on the stick which he carried in his hand, came towards us, and began slowly to climb the steps. "It is my father," said one of the men; "he is the oldest man on the island; he was born in 1812." The old man climbed slowly up to where we stood; a mild old man, with a pale face, carefully shaved, and a firm mouth, who spoke the best English that we had heard there. "If any gentleman has committed a crime," said the oldest man on the island, "we'll hide him. There was a man killed his father, and he came over here, and we hid him for two months, and he got away safe to America."

As we came down from the fort the old man came with us, and I and another, walking ahead, lingered for some time with the old man by a stone stile. "Have you ever seen the fairies?" said my friend, and a quaint smile flickered over the old man's face, and with many ohs! and grave gestures he told us that he had never seen them, but that he had heard them crying in the fort by night; and one night, as he was going along with his dog, just at the spot where we were then standing, the dog had suddenly rushed at something or some one,

Cities and Sea-Coasts and Islands.

and had rushed round and round him, but he could see nothing, though it was bright moonlight, and so light that he could have seen a rat; and he had followed across several fields, and again the dog had rushed at the thing, and had seemed to be beaten off, and had come back covered with sweat, and panting, but he could see nothing. And there was a man once, he knew the man, and could point him out, who had been out in his boat (and he motioned with his stick to a certain spot on the water), and a sea fairy had seized hold of his boat and tried to come into it; but he had gone quickly on shore, and the thing, which looked like a man, had turned back into the sea. And there had been a man once on the island who used to talk with the fairies; and you could hear him going along the roads by night swearing and talking with the fairies. "And have you ever heard," said my friend "of the seals, the roons, turning into men?" "And indeed," said the oldest man on the island, smiling, "I'm a roon, for I'm one of the family they say comes from the roons." "And have you ever heard," said my friend, "of men going back into the sea and turning roons again?" "I never heard that," said the oldest man on the island reflectively, seeming to ponder over the probability of the occurrence; "no," he repeated after a pause, "I never heard that."

We came back to the village by the road we had come, and passed again the handsome girl who had taken toll; she was sitting by the roadside knitting, and looked at us sidelong as we passed, with an almost imperceptible smile in her eyes. We wandered for some time a little vaguely, the amiability of the islanders leading them to bring us in search of various ruins which we imagined to exist, and which they did not like to tell us were not in existence. I found the people on this island even more charming, because a little simpler, more untouched by civilisation, than those on the larger island. They were of necessity a little lonelier, for if few people come to Inishmore, how many have ever spent a night on Inishmaan? Inishmore has its hotel, but there is no hotel on Inishmaan; there is indeed one public-house, but there is not even a policeman, so sober, so law-abiding are these islanders. It is true that I succeeded, with some difficulty, and under cover of some mystery, in securing, what I had long wished to taste, a bottle of poteen or illicit whisky. But the brewing of poteen is, after all, almost romantic in its way, with that queer, sophistical romance of the contraband. That was not the romance I associated with this most peaceful of islands as we walked along the sand on the seashore, passing the kelp-burners, who were collecting long brown trails of seaweed. More than anything I had ever seen, this seashore gave me the sensation of the mystery and the calm of all the islands one has ever dreamed of, all the fortunate islands that have ever been saved out of the disturbing sea; this delicate pearl-grey sand, the deeper grey of the stones, the more luminous

Cities and Sea-Coasts and Islands.

grey of the water, and so consoling an air as of immortal twilight and the peace of its dreams.

I had been in no haste to leave Inishmore, but I was still more loth to leave Inishmaan; and I think that it was with reluctance on the part of all of us that we made our way to the curragh which was waiting for us in the water. The islanders waved their caps, and called many good blessings after us as we were rowed back to the hooker, which again lifted sail and set out for the third and smallest island, Inisheer, that is, the South Island.

We set out confidently, but when we had got out of shelter of the shore, the hooker began to rise and fall with some violence; and by the time we had come within landing distance of Inisheer the waves were dashing upon us with so great an energy that it was impossible to drop anchor, and our skipper advised us not to try to get to land. A curragh set out from the shore, and came some way towards us, riding the waves. It might have been possible, I doubt not, to drop by good luck from the rolling side of the hooker into the pitching bottom of the curragh, and without capsizing the curragh; but the chances were against it. Tom Joyce, holding on to the ropes of the main-sail, and the most seaman-like of us, in the stern, shouted at each other above the sound of the wind. We were anxious to make for Ballyline, the port nearest to Listoonvarna, on the coast of Clare; but this Joyce declared to be impossible in such a sea, and with such a wind, and advised that we should make

The Islands of Aran.

for Ballyvaughan, round Black Head Point, where we should find a safe harbour. It was now about a quarter past one, and we set out for Ballyvaughan with the wind fair behind us. The hooker rode well, and the waves but rarely came over the windward side as she lay over towards her sail, taking leap after leap through the white-edged furrows of the grey water. For two hours and a half we skirted the Clare coast, which came to me, and disappeared from me, as the gunwale dipped or rose on the leeward side. The islands were blotted out behind us long before we had turned the sheer corner of Black Head, the ultimate edge of Ireland, and at last we came round the headland into quieter water, and so, after a short time, into a little harbour of Ballyvaughan, where we set foot on land again, and drove for hours along the Clare coast and inland into Galway, under that sunset of gold fire and white spray, back to Tillyra Castle, where I felt the ground once more solid under my feet.

Summer, 1896.

In Sligo.

Rosses Point is a village of pilots and fishing people, stretching out seawards in a long thin single line of thatched and whitewashed houses along the branch of the sea which goes from the little harbour of Sligo to broaden out into the bay beyond the edge of Dorren's or Coney Island, and the rocks of Dead Man's Point. It is a lazy village, where no one is very rich or very poor, but all are able, without too much exertion, to make just enough not to need to work any harder. The people are slow, sturdy, contented people, with a singular dislike of doing anything for money, except that they let rooms during the summer to the people of Sligo, who make it their watering-place, going in and out daily, when needful, on the little paddle-steamer which plies backward and forward between Sligo and the Point, or on the long car which takes in their messages and their marketing-baskets. Very few people from the outer world ever find their way here; and there are peasants living at the far end of the village who have never been so far as the village of Lower Rosses, on the other side of the green lands. They know more of the coast of Spain, the River Plate, and the Barbadoes than they know of the other side of their own mountains, for seafaring men go far. I have just been talking with a seaman, now a pilot here, who has told me of Venice and of the bull-fights he saw at Huelva, and of Antwerp, and the Riga, and Le Havre;

328

and of the coast of Cornwall, and Milford Haven, and the Firth of Forth; and of America and the West Indies. Yesterday I saw a bright green parrot on a child's hand; they have been telling me of "the black girl" who came here from some foreign ship and lived here, and knew better than any one else where to find the plovers' eggs; and I have seen the rim of a foreign ship, rising out of the sand at low tide, which was wrecked here seventy years ago, and is now turning green under the water.

Men and women, here at the Point, loiter about all day long; there are benches outside most of the cabins, and they sit there, or on the low, rough wall which skirts the road, or on the big stones at the edge of the water, or upon the green lands. Most of the women are bare-headed, none go barefoot, and only a few of the poorer children. And the children here are very proud. They will row you about all day for nothing, but they will not bring you a can of water from the well if you pay them for it. That is a point of view they have learnt from their parents, and it seems to me a simple and sufficing one. For these people have attained comfort, a certain dignity (that dignity which comes from concerning yourself only with what concerns you), and they have the privilege of living in a beautiful, harmonious place, without any of the distractions which harass poorer or less contented people in towns, and keep them from the one thing worth living for, the leisure to know oneself. This fine laziness of theirs in the open air, with the constant, subduing sense of the sea's peril, its hold upon their lives and fortunes, moulds them often into a self-sufficing manliness, a hardy womanhood; sometimes it makes them dreamers, and they see fairies and hear the fairy piper calling in the caves.

How, indeed, is it possible that they should not see more of the other world than most folk do, and catch dreams in their nets? For it is a place of dreams, a grey, gentle place, where the sand melts into the sea, the sea into the sky, and the mountains and the clouds drift one into the other. I have never seen so friendly a sea nor a sea so full of the ecstasy of sleep. On one of those luminous grey days, which are the true atmosphere of the place, it is like being in an eternal morning of twilight to wander over the undulating green lands, fringed at the shore by a soft rim of bent, a pale honey-coloured green, and along the delicate grey sands, from Dead Man's Point to the point of the Third Rosses. The sea comes in softly, rippling against the sand with a low plashing, which even on very warm days has a cool sound and a certain gentleness even on days of rough weather. The headland of Roughley O'Byrne runs on, a wavering line of faint green, from the dark and cloudy masses of the Lissadell woods into the hesitating line of the grey waters. On the other side of the bay Dorren's Island curves around, almost like part of the semi-circle of the mainland, its sickle-point leaning out towards the white lighthouse, which rises up out of the water like a phantom, or the stone image of a wave that has risen up out of the sea on a day of storm. Faint mountains glimmer out to sea, many-coloured mountains close in upon the land, shutting it off from the world of strange cities. And if you go a little in from the sea-edge, over the green lands, you will come to a great pool, where the waters are never troubled nor the reeds still; but there is always a sighing of wind in the reeds, as of a very gentle and melancholy peace.

Go on a little farther still, and you come to the fighting village of Magherow, where the men are red-bearded, fierce, great shouters, and not readier to row than to do battle with their oars. They come into Rosses Point, generally, at the regatta; and at that time the Point is at its liveliest, there is much whisky drunk, and many quarrels flame up. There is a great dance, too, most years, at the time of the regatta. It is known as the cake dance, and not so long ago a cake and a bottle of whisky were hung out of a window by green ribbons, the cake for the best woman dancer and the bottle of whisky for the best man dancer. Now there is no cake at all, and if there is much whisky, it is handed over the counter in big glasses, and not hung out of the window by green ribbons. The prize now is money, and so the people of the Point, with their fine, independent objection to doing anything for money, are less ready to show off their notable powers of dancing; and the women, who, besides, are getting to prefer the waltzes and quadrilles of the towns, will not take part in the dance at all.

The regatta this year was not too well managed, having passed out of the hands of the village pilots; and it was unwisely decided that the dance should be held the same evening, outside the door of a public-house where the crews of the losing boats had been drinking at the expense of the captains of the winning boats. It was very dark, and there was a great crowd, a great confusion. A somewhat battered door had been laid down for the dancing, and the press of people kept swaying in upon the narrow limits of the door, where only a few half-tipsy fellows pounded away, lurching into one another's arms. Everybody swayed, and yelled, and encouraged, and expostulated, and the melodion sounded fitfully; and presently the door was pulled from under the feet of the dancers and the police shouldered into the midst of what would soon have been a very pretty fight. The dance was postponed to Monday, when some of the boats were to race again.

On Monday, at about half-past six, I met eight small boys carrying a large door upon their shoulders. They were coming up through the village to the green lands, where they laid down the door on the grass. About an hour afterwards, as it began to get very dark, the people came slowly up from the village, and a wide ring was made by a rope carried around stakes set in the earth, and the people gathered about the ring, in the middle of which lay the door, lit on one side by a ship's lantern and on the other by the lamp of a bicycle. A chair was put for the judge, who was a pilot and a publican, and one of the few Gaelic speakers in the village, and a man of few words, and a man of weight; and another chair was put for the musician, who played on the melodion, an instrument which has long since replaced the fiddle as the national instrument of Ireland. A row of very small children lay along the grass inside the rope, the girls in one place, the boys in another. It was so dark that I could only vaguely distinguish, in a curve of very black shadow, the people opposite to me in the circle, and presently it began to rain a little and still we waited. At last a man came forward, and the musician began to play a lively tune on his melodion, keeping time with his feet, and there was a great cry of "Gallagher! Gallagher!" and much shouting and whistling. It was a shepherd from Lower Rosses, a thin and solemn young man, who began to dance with great vigour and regularity, tapping heavily on the rough boards with very rough and heavy boots. He danced several step-dances, and was much applauded. Then, after a pause, an old man from the Point, Redmond Bruen by name, a pilot, who had very cunningly won the duck-hunt at the regatta, stepped forward unevenly, and began to walk about on the door, shuffling his feet, bowing to right and left, and waving a stick that he held in his hand. "When he's sober, he's a great dancer," we were assured. He was not sober,

333

and at first did no more than shuffle. Then he stopped, seemed to recollect himself, and the reputation he had to keep up, and with more bowing to the public, began to sing, with variations, a song popular among the Irish peasants, "On the Rocky Road to Dublin." It is a dramatic song, and after every stanza he acted, in his dance, the fight on the road, the passage from Holyhead, and the other stirring incidents of the song. The old man swayed there in the vague light, between the two lanterns, a whimsical and pathetic figure, with his grey beard, his helpless gestures, and the random gaiety of his legs; he danced with a wonderful lightness, and one could but just hear his boots passing over the boards.

We applauded him with enthusiasm, and he came and sat on the grass inside the ring, near the children, who were gradually creeping closer in; and his place was taken by the serious Gallagher, who was quite sober, and who pounded away like clockwork, holding his body quite stiff, and rattling his boots with great agility. The old man watched him keenly, and presently got up and made for the door again. He began to dance, stopped, flung off his coat, and set off again with a certain elaboration, variety, and even delicacy in his dancing, which would have won him the prize, I think, if he had been sober enough to make the most of his qualities. He at least thoroughly appreciated his own skill. "That's a good reel," he would say when he halted for breath and emphasis.

334

In Sligo.

Meanwhile Gallagher was looking for a partner, and one or two young fellows took the boards, and did each a single dance, in pairs or singly. Then a young man who, like Bruen, was "a grand dancer when sober," but who was even less sober than Bruen, reeled across the grass, kicked over one of the lanterns, and began to dance opposite Gallagher. Then he pushed Gallagher off the board and danced by himself. He was in his shirt-sleeves and without hat or collar, and much of his dance was merely an unsteady walking. He stopped frequently, and appeared to think; and, after much thinking, it occurred to him that it was the music which would not keep time with his dancing. So he walked up to the musician, snatched the melodion away from him, and marched off with it, I suppose to find another player. He passed into the darkness; the melodion in his hands squealed out of the darkness. Then he came back dangling it, and was told to give it back again, which he did sulkily, with exactly the look and gesture of a naughty child who has been called to order. And then Gallagher came forward again, and, taking off his hat, said he would sing a song. He got through a verse or two, chanting gravely in a kind of sing-song, and then, coming to the line, "And *he* said *to* the landlord," paused, and said, "I am not able to do any more." There was a great laugh, and Gallagher returned to his dancing, in which he was presently joined by a new rival. Gallagher got the prize.

Cities and Sea-Coasts and Islands.

I was told that so poor a dance had not been seen before at Rosses Point, and the blame was laid on new ways, and the coming of the waltzes and quadrilles, and the folly of young people who think old things not good enough for them. And the old people shook their heads that night over the turf fires in their cabins.

Seven miles inland from Rosses Point the mountains open, and, entering a great hollow called the Windy Gap, you come upon a small lake with green fields around it and mountains full of woods and waterfalls rising up behind it. This is Glencar, and there is a cabin by the side of the lake where I spent a few enchanted days of rain and sunshine, wandering over the mountain-side and among the wild and delicate woods. Above the cabin there is a great mountain, and the woods climb from about the cabin to almost the summit of the mountain. Fir trees rise up like marching banners, line upon line; between them the foliage is softer, green moss grows on the tree-trunks and ferns out of the moss; quicken-berries flame on the heights above the streams; the many-coloured green of leaves is starred with bright orange, shadowed with spectral blue, clouded with the exquisite ashen pallor of decaying heather. Rocky steps lead from height to height along the edge of chasms veiled with leafy branches, and there is always a sound of many waters, falling in torrents down black stairways of rock, and rushing swiftly along narrow passages

336

between grass and ferns. Here and there a bridge
of fallen trunks, set roughly together, and covered
with the adventurous soil, which, in these parts,
bears fruit wherever it has an inch to cling to,
crosses a waterfall just above the actual descent.
Winding paths branch off in every direction, and
in the soft earth of these narrow and precipitous
ways one can see little hoof-prints, and occasionally
one meets a donkey going slowly uphill, with the
creels on its back, to fetch turf from the bog. And
always there is the sound of water, like the cool
singing voice of the rocks, above the sound of
rustling leaves, and birds piping, and the flapping
of great wings, which are the voices of the many-
instrumented orchestra of the woods. Here one
is in the heart of the mountains and in the heart of
the forest; and, wandering along a grassy path
at evening, one seems to be very close to something
very ancient and secret.

The mountains here are whole regions, and when
you have climbed to their summit through the
woods, you find yourself on a vast plain, and this
plain stretches so far that it seems to fill the horizon
and you cannot see anything on the other side of
it. Looking down into the valley, which seems
scooped out of the solid mountains, you can see,
on the other side of the Windy Gap, the thin line
of Rosses Point going out into the sea, and the sea
stretches out so far before it reaches the horizon
that you can catch a yellow glimmer of sunlight,
lying out beyond the horizon visible from the shore.

Cities and Sea-Coasts and Islands.

The fields, around and beyond the polished mirror of the lake, seem, in their patchwork of greens and browns, like a little map of the world. The mountain-top, which you have fancied from below to be such solid ground, proves, if you try to cross it, to be a great yielding bog, with intervals of rock or hard soil. To walk over it is to move in short jumps, with an occasional longer leap across a dried-up watercourse. I like the voluptuous softness of the bog, for one's feet sink luxuriously into even the pale golden mounds of moss which rise between the rusty heather and starveling grasses of the sheer morass. And it has the treachery which is always one of the allurements of voluptuous things. Nor is it the bog only which is treacherous on these mountains. The mist comes down on them very suddenly, and in that white darkness even the natives sometimes lose their way, and are drawn over the sheer edge of the mountain. My host has just come in to tell me that last night there was a great brewing of poteen on Ben Bulben, and that many of the drinkers wandered all night, losing their way in the mist, and that one of them, not having the drunkard's luck, fell over a rocky place, and is now lying dead on the mountain.

I had been thinking of such possibilities yesterday as I climbed, peak after peak, the mountains on the other side of the lake, Cope's Mountain, Lugnagall, Cashlagall, Cragnamoona. They are bare and treeless, crossed by a few donkey-tracks, and I sometimes deserted these looped and coiling

338

ways for the more hazardous directness of the dry watercourses which seam the mountains from head to foot. Once at the top, you look over almost the whole county, lying out in a green plain, ridged with hedges, clustered with woods, glittering with lakes; here and there a white cabin, a scattered village, and just below, in the hollow of the land and water, the little curving grey town of Sligo, with its few ships resting in harbour, and beyond them the long black line which is Rosses Point, and then the sea, warm with sunlight, and, as if islanded in the sea, the hills of Mayo. I have never seen anything resembling the view from these mountains; I have never seen anything, in its way, more beautiful. And when, last night, after a tossed and blood-red sunset, the white mist curdled about the heads of Ben Bulben and Knocknarea, and a faint, luminous mist filled the whole hollow of the valley, there seemed to be a mingling of all the worlds; and the world in which ships went out from the harbour of Sligo, and the poteen-makers wandered over the mountain, was not more real than the world of embodied dreams in which the fairies dance in their forts, or beat at the cabin doors, or chuckle among the reeds.

Summer, 1896.

From a Castle in Ireland.

In the mysterious castle, lost among trees that start up suddenly around it, out of a land of green meadows and grey stones, where I have been so delightfully living through the difficult month of August, London, and books, and one's daily habits seem scarcely appreciable; too far away on the other side of this mountainous land enclosing one within the circle of its own magic. It is a castle of dreams, where, in the morning, I climb the winding staircase in the tower, creep through the secret passage, and find myself in the vast deserted room above the chapel, which is my retiring-room for meditation; or, following the winding staircase, come out on the battlements, where I can look widely across Galway to the hills. In the evening my host plays Vittoria and Palestrina on the organ, in the half darkness of the hall, and I wander between the pillars of black marble, hearing the many voices rising into the dome: Vittoria, the many lamentable human voices, crying on the sins of the world, the vanity of pleasant sins; Palestrina, an exultation and a triumph, in which the many voices of white souls go up ardently into heaven. In the afternoon we drive through a strange land, which has the desolation of ancient and dwindling things; a grey land, into which human life comes rarely, and with a certain primitive savagery. As we drive seawards, the stone walls closing in the woods dwindle into low, roughly heaped hedges of unmortared stones, over which only an occasional

340

From a Castle in Ireland.

cluster of trees lifts itself; and the trees strain wildly in the air, writhing away from the side of the sea, where the winds from the Atlantic have blown upon them and transfixed them in an eternity of flight from an eternal flagellation. As far as one can see, as far as the blue, barren mountains which rise up against the horizon, there are these endless tracks of harsh meadow-land, marked into squares by the stone hedges, and themselves heaped with rocks and stones, lying about like some grey fungus growth. Not a sign of human life is to be seen; at long intervals we pass a cabin, white-washed, thatched roughly, with stopped-up windows and a half-closed door, from behind which a grey-haired old woman will gaze at you with her steady, melancholy eyes. A few peasants pass on the road, moving sombrely, without speaking; the men, for the most part, touch their hats, without change of expression; the women, drawing their shawls about their faces, merely look at you, with a slow, scrutinising air, more indifferent than curious. The women walk bare-footed and with the admirable grace and straightness of all who go with bare feet. I remember, in the curve of a rocky field, some little way in from the road, seeing a young woman wearing a blue bodice, a red petticoat, and a grey shawl, carrying a tin pail on her head, with that straight, flexible movement of the body, that slow and formal grace of Eastern women who have carried pitchers from the well. Occasionally a fierce old man on a horse, wearing the old costume,

that odd, precise kind of dress-coat, passes you
with a surly scowl; or a company of tinkers (the
Irish gipsies, one might call them) trail past, huddled
like crouching beasts on their little, rough, open
carts, driving a herd of donkeys before them. As
we get nearer the village by the sea, the cabins
become larger and more frequent; and just before
reaching it we pass a ruined castle, impregnably
built on a green mound, looking over the water to
the quay, where the thin black masts of a few vessels
rise motionless against the little whitewashed houses.
The road goes down a steep hill, and turns sharply,
in the midst of the grey village, with its thatched
and ragged roofs. The doors all stand open, the
upper windows are drawn half down, and from
some of them I see a dishevelled dark head, the
hair and eyes of a gipsy (one could well have fancied),
looking down on the road and the passers-by. As
the road rises again, we see the blue mountains
coming nearer to us, and the place where, one
knows, is Galway Bay, lying too low for any flash
of the waters. Now we are quite near the sea, and
in front of the house we are to visit (you will hear
all about it in M. Bourget's next *nouvelle*), a brown
mass of colour comes suddenly into the dull green
and grey of the fields, and one smells the seaweed
lying there in the pools.

I find all this bareness, greyness, monotony,
solitude at once primitive and fantastical, curiously
attractive, giving just the same kind of relief from
the fat, luxurious English landscape that these

From a Castle in Ireland.

gaunt, nervous, long-chinned peasants give from the red and rolling sleepiness of the English villager. And there is a quite national vivacity and variety of mood in the skies here, in the restless atmosphere, the humorous exaggerations of the sun and rain. To-day is a typical Irish day, soft, warm, grey, with intervals of rain and fine weather; I can see a sort of soft mist of rain, blown loosely about between the trees of the park, the clouds an almost luminous grey, the sun shining through them; at their darkest, scarcely darker than the Irish stone of which the castle is built. Driving, the other day, we passed a large pool among the rocks, in the midst of those meadows flowering with stones; the sky was black with the rain that was falling upon the hills, and the afternoon sun shone against the deep blackness of the sky and the shadowed blackness of the water. I have never seen such coloured darkness as this water; green passing into slate, slate into purple, purple into dead black. And it was all luminous, floating there in the harbour of the grass like a tideless sea. Then there is the infinite variety of the mountains, sloping in uneven lines around almost the whole horizon. They are as variable as the clouds, and, while you look at them, have changed from a purple darkness to a luminous and tender green, and then into a lifeless grey, and seem to float towards you and drift away from you like the clouds.

Among these solid and shifting things, in this castle which is at once so ancient a reality and so

343

Cities and Sea-Coasts and Islands.

essential a dream, I feel myself to be in some danger of loosening the tightness of my hold upon external things, of foregoing many delectable pleasures, of forgetting many things that I have passionately learnt in cities. If I lived here too long I should forget that I live in London and remember that I am a Cornishman.

Summer, 1896.

Dover Cliffs.

I.

Nature made Dover for her pleasure, and man
has remade Dover for his use. The cliffs have
been tunnelled within and fortified overhead; the
sea has been bound inside a vast harbour, and driven
back to make way for trucks and trolleys to carry
stones for its prison walls; the smoke of funnels
has superseded the gentle motions of sails; there
are forts and barracks and prisons, like great ware-
houses for human goods; everywhere there is
action, change, energy; there are foreign faces,
people coming and going from the ends of the
earth, to whom Dover is a stepping-stone; and it
is a gate, which can be opened to friends and closed
on enemies. A gate of England, one of the Cinque
Ports and the only one of them that has held its
own; it has always been a part of history; it is
our only port which has a natural magnificence
and a great tradition.

The sea at Dover, since the Admiralty has looped
it in with its stone barriers, can hardly be said to
have remained a quite wholly natural part of nature
any longer. It has been tamed, brought to serve
man meekly, and not at its own will. By day we
see the gap in its prison walls, and the ships going
in and out, to be caught or loosed. But by night
there is the aspect of a lake, and the gold and red
and green lights that go in a semicircle about it
seem like lights outlining a curving shore. The
execrable British pleasure-pier, with the "looped

Cities and Sea-Coasts and Islands.

and windowed nakedness" of its bulbed head thrust, impudently glittering, into the water, adds the last sign to the deeper signs of man's domination. Yet, by day or night, if you listen, you will hear the lisp of water on the pebbles, in a faint, powerless affirmation: you will know, in that faint sound, the sea's voice. But to see the sea, really itself, and to hear it speak out at its own pleasure, you must stand on the stone wall which binds it in from the west wind, or look down from the cliffs, on west or east. The cliffs share in its liberty; they have never consented to its bondage; they endure its buffetings with patience, as friendly losers do in a game. When the wind freshens and the water is whipped from green to white, and leaps at and over the great stone pier of the Admiralty in showers of white foam, the cliffs above it turn to the colour of thunder-clouds. Under a faint mist cliffs and sea suffer a new enchantment; a bloom comes out over them, seeming to melt them into a single intangible texture. And cliffs and sea, in sun or storm, are at one: the sea, the witch of destiny, at all her passes, and the cliffs, English women, white and tall and delicately shaped.

The loveliest of the cliffs is that one which should no longer be called Shakespeare's, for it has been desecrated by a foul black tunnel and the smoke of engines, and a railway-train, which has devastated the beach, goes through the tunnel to a bay beyond where a black chimney gapes at the mouth of a problematical coal-mine. This is one of the worst

346

things which man has done here in his struggle to subdue nature. A harbour may add less beauty than it takes from the sea; but it is a vast, kind, friendly thing in which the sea is not unwilling to co-operate. A harbour is that refuge in which ships that have come there from the ends of the world lie at rest: men have built it for them. But here, for the moment, man has beaten and defaced nature; beauty has been baffled, so far as man can do it. For the sea remains, and the cliff is still a white eminence, with a few pebbles at its feet and a thin green covering on its back. Broken beauty is remembered even after it has been utterly destroyed; and man and his works have their day and pass over. Here, too, nature will outlast him; and the sea waits, knowing that she will one day have her revenge on these sorry makings of his hands.

II.

It is the cliffs that make the best beauty of Dover. They are her crown, her support, her defence; they hold her in their arms as she sits, white and long, with her feet in the sea. They are beautiful, at all hours, with their white walls and the bare green and brown of their downs; they are like fortresses, calm, assured, steadfast, and ready to become impregnable. Everywhere towers, walls, the heavy, square castle, suggest ancient defences; and the friendliness of the cliffs to the town, which it holds against the sea, has a reticence of manner

Cities and Sea-Coasts and Islands.

towards strangers and foreign coasts. At night they rise mysteriously against the sky, with rows and patches of lights shining out of dull level walls, turned now into candelabra for candles of gold fire. The old, red, gabled, sordid harbour, seen dimly, its lights striking like red and yellow knives into the stagnant water, becomes a kind of fairy thing, which one vaguely remembers to have seen in foreign lands. Which? Venice has no such eager cliffs above her tamed water; and Venice, for a moment, has come into the memory, returning there, as she does at most sights of houses looking down into water. Is it Alicante? The palms on the sand are not here, nothing of what is African in that rare coast of Spain; but I remember a certain likeness in the hill with its castle rising more abruptly over a long, curved town whiter and stranger than Dover.

To see Dover as a whole, you must stand on the stone parapet above the landing-place, where the steamers slide in gently, hardly touching the quay with the wooden roofs over their propellers. You must turn your back on the sea, which is there really the sea, and not an enclosed bay, a harbour made for ships to come back into; and you must look across the black engine-smoke of the trains, to the white cliffs, which with evening turn to a dull grey, over the long curve of white-fronted houses, with their dark-green balconies and flat windows set at regular intervals; going on beyond them to the east, with many indentations, white, vast, and delicate, shutting in the sea with its high walls, and seeming to throw out long, thin piers to clutch and imprison it; on the west, Shakespeare's Cliff, and then smoke and the long mine-chimney, and the cliffs turn the corner and are beyond your sight. But, for the very heart of Dover, you must look under you, where dock after dock lies motionless, its long arms shut about its guests.

They are like most other harbour-docks, dingy, with low, irregular houses painted with signs and letterings; Hamburg-American Line, Hearts of Oak Dining-Rooms, Cope's Tobaccos. There are red roofs and gables and an old sordidness about everything at the edge of this pale-green stagnant water, which never moves except under some heavy hull, or under the feet of that white bird sitting disconsolately on the floating buoy. The inner and outer harbour has each its big ships, stacked side by side, funnels and masts together, against the same quay with the same little old gabled low red houses with the same modern signs. At night one sees beyond them only the lighted windows of flat house-fronts, showing nothing in the darkness but loop-holes, as if nothing were behind them. Masts, taut rope-ladders from mast to bulwark, furled sails laid by in the sides of the ship, the sharp lines of ropes stretched out in delicate patterns, it is these that give beauty, even before the night has come with its transformations, to this kind of sea-pool where vast many-tentacled animals crawl, clinging like limpets to the wet walls.

349

Cities and Sea-Coasts and Islands.

The ship's beauty was lost when sails went and masts went, and funnels and boilers took their place, as the modern machine has taken the place of every beautiful thing that went on the wind and was worked by human hands. The lovely shape was lost when great bulges came for useful purposes on either side of the carcase which they trampled into speed. Figments of scarcely serviceable masts remain, with a little of the spider's work of cords, waiting for sails which are never to fly up and run before wind. The wind is no longer, for those who go down to the sea in ships, more than an obstacle or a danger; it adds no swiftness to the course of sails flying before it, but may delay or incommode the steady indifferent progress of the steamer. Does not its name betray it? the thing that steams, a thing heated from within, a churner of waves. It is no longer a ship, which was a light, veering thing, like a bird, half tamed to a man's hand, escaping from him and unpunctually returning. Now, as I see a Channel steamer move slowly out backwards from the dock and turn slowly in the middle water of the harbour, I am reminded rather of the vast slowly stepping motion of elephants.

III.

Dover under all shades of mists is personal, up to a certain point beautiful. One night I saw from the window a thick white mist come almost suddenly out of the sea; the lights were blotted out, the mimic guns, the bells, the fog-horns, snoring in different keys, were heard all through the night. It was the intermittent battle going on between the stealthy white forces and the resistant brain of man. The fog lasted till early morning, when a blazing sun, like one of Blake's, came out and burned through the shivering vapours. On all the boats and planks lying on the pebbles of the beach one saw, still clinging there, as the sun lightened them, a white wetness which the fog had left on them like some sea-dew.

I write of it now as if it had been beautiful; but I got my own share of discomfort out of it, for I lay awake all night, unable to keep my mind from counting the horrible iteration of sounds, repeated with a monotony like that of some torture, between pit and pendulum. Every separate hoot, shriek, or boom struck into my ears with a steady violence, like blow after blow from a great fist; and what was most distressing in it was, not the sounds, but their succession and the necessity of counting them in my brain, waiting for them with all my nerves. The big sound, like the thud of a bomb, struck in with a measure of its own, at slower intervals than the hooters; and I waited with most anxiety for that shattering fall and rebound, whose place I could never quite calculate, between two or on the end of the second recurrent gasps. I covered my ears, but the sound, a little deadened, penetrated them in the same dismal rhythm; and

351

Cities and Sea-Coasts and Islands.

in my mind there was only a great emptiness, in which a vapour of suspense drifted to and fro.

But for those sounds I should have been perfectly happy in Dover. It is a place of winds, sea, and cliffs; it is alive, and the life in it varies with every tide, the beauty in it comes and goes with every change of hour or weather. The cramped beach seems to have lost all that Matthew Arnold found in it, except those

> edges drear
> And naked shingles of the world

which are still to be discerned there. And then, one day, a wind brings back some of its motion to the sea, and again, with Arnold:

> you hear the grating roar
> Of pebbles which the waves draw back, and fling,
> At their return, up the high strand,
> Begin, and cease, and then again,
> With tremulous cadence slow, and bring
> The eternal note of sadness in.

Sadness, however, is not the characteristic of the sea at Dover, nor of the white cliffs, battlemented and crowned with their castle, still alive. They change colour and aspect daily and nightly, with an uncertainty that is full of surprise and delight. And the place, the streets, the people, is there not some pleasant suggestion of France, not only in the Calais and Ostend boats, persevering travellers to and fro, but in the actual aspect of things? The streets are good to walk in, especially at night.

352

Dover Cliffs.

They are dimly lighted, and they have an old aspect, some of them are dark and narrow, and all wind to and fro, and some climb the hill or disappear under archways or come out unexpectedly upon the docks, or upon the sea-front. From the sea-front you see the crude line of window-lights in the barrack on the Western Cliff, and on the East Cliff nothing but a leash of lights, dropping down from the Castle like the tail of a comet. The people walk at nights, in the wandering friendly way of most sea-towns, up and down certain streets. On market-day, which is Saturday, they walk up and down past the noisy fish-sellers in the market-place, sometimes turning down Snargate Street. On Sunday night, after church-hours, all the young men and women walk up and down on the sea-front, or rather on the road and pavement which keep them back a little further from the sea. The lights are dim; over the sea they seem brighter as they come and go; as they will come and go all night; for Dover is never asleep. That gate of England is always open, and there are always warders awake at the gate.

1908.